This book unravels one of the most understudied and under-theorised aspect of humanitarian studies, namely the complexities of humanitarianism in the context of controlling – authoritarian – states. This poses many challenges where humanitarian organisations must adapt the theories defining their relationship with states and fine-tune their engagement strategies. This volume not only provides superior real-life analysis of state–aid relations, it also brings many pointers for humanitarians to improve how they negotiate humanitarian access with states.

Dorothea Hilhorst, *Professor of Humanitarian Studies*
at the International Institute for Social Studies of Erasmus
University in The Hague

Delivering vital aid to crisis-affected people often hinges on complex humanitarian negotiations within authoritarian environments. By combining concrete operational examples with political theory, Cunningham et al. offer a deeper understanding and sharper analytical lens for aid practitioners and scholars grappling with these issues.

Abby Stoddard, *PhD, author of* Necessary Risks: Professional
Humanitarianism and Violence against Aid Workers

T0271882

AUTHORITARIAN PRACTICES AND HUMANITARIAN NEGOTIATIONS

This book examines authoritarian practices in relation to humanitarian negotiations. Utilising a wide variety of perspectives and examining a range of contexts, the book considers how humanitarians assess and engage with authoritarian practices and negotiate access to populations in danger.

Chapters provide insights at the macro, meso, and micro levels through case studies on the international and domestic legal and political framing of humanitarian contexts (Xinjiang, Afghanistan, Venezuela, Russia, and Syria), as well as the actual practice of negotiating with authoritarian regimes (Ethiopia). A theoretical grounding is provided through chapters elaborating on the ethics and trust-building dimensions of humanitarian negotiations, and an overview chapter provides a theoretical framework through which to analyse humanitarian negotiations against the backdrop of different types of authoritarian practices.

This book provides a wide-ranging view which broadens the frame of reference when considering how humanitarians view and engage with authoritarian practices. The objective is to both put these contexts into conceptual order and provide a firm theoretical basis for understanding the politics of humanitarian negotiations in such difficult contexts. This book is useful for those studying international politics and humanitarian studies, as well as for practitioners seeking to better systematise their humanitarian negotiations.

Andrew J Cunningham has been in the aid business since the late 1980s and has spent 25 years with MSF. He has a PhD in War Studies from King's College London, and his research focuses on INGO–State relations. Andrew works as a researcher, strategic evaluator, and governance advisor for various humanitarian organisations. His last book with Routledge was *International Humanitarian NGOs and State Relations: Politics, Principles and Identity* (2018). Andrew is also a board member of the International Humanitarian Studies Association.

Routledge Humanitarian Studies Series

The Routledge Humanitarian Studies series in collaboration with the International Humanitarian Studies Association (IHSA) takes a comprehensive approach to the growing field of expertise that is humanitarian studies. This field is concerned with humanitarian crises caused by natural disaster, conflict or political instability and deals with the study of how humanitarian crises evolve, how they affect people and their institutions and societies, and the responses they trigger.

We invite book proposals that address, amongst other topics, questions of aid delivery, institutional aspects of service provision, the dynamics of rebel wars, state building after war, the international architecture of peacekeeping, the ways in which ordinary people continue to make a living throughout crises, and the effect of crises on gender relations.

This interdisciplinary series draws on and is relevant to a range of disciplines, including development studies, international relations, international law, anthropology, peace and conflict studies, public health and migration studies.

The Humanitarian Parent
Balancing Work and Family in the Aid Sector
Merit Hietanen

Young Children in Humanitarian and COVID-19 Crises
Innovations and Lessons from the Global South
Edited by Sweta Shah and Lucy Bassett

Authoritarian Practices and Humanitarian Negotiations
Edited by Andrew J Cunningham

For more information about this series, please visit: www.routledge.com/Routledge-Humanitarian-Studies/book-series/RHS

AUTHORITARIAN PRACTICES AND HUMANITARIAN NEGOTIATIONS

Edited by
Andrew J Cunningham

Routledge
Taylor & Francis Group

LONDON AND NEW YORK

Designed cover image: Fernando Garlin Politis
All images in commentaries: Fernando Garlin Politis

First published 2024
by Routledge
4 Park Square, Milton Park, Abingdon, Oxon OX14 4RN

and by Routledge
605 Third Avenue, New York, NY 10158

Routledge is an imprint of the Taylor & Francis Group, an informa business

British Library Cataloguing-in-Publication Data
A catalogue record for this book is available from the British Library

ISBN: 9781032327570 (hbk)
ISBN: 9781032326795 (pbk)
ISBN: 9781003316541 (ebk)

DOI: 10.4324/9781003316541

The Open Access version of chapter 1 was funded by Artsen zonder Grenzen.

The Open Access version of Chapter 6 and Commentary (end of Chapter 8) was supported by the European Research Council (ERC) Horizon 2020 programme [Grant number 884139].

The Open Access version of chapter 9 was funded by Research Council of Norway.

This volume is dedicated to all of the people living in danger in the midst of humanitarian crises and require appropriate assistance.

CONTENTS

CONTRIBUTORS

Claudia Astarita is a lecturer at Sciences Po Paris. She obtained her PhD in Asian Studies from Hong Kong University and her main research interests include China's political and economic development, Chinese and Indian Foreign policies, and East Asian regionalism and regional economic integration.

Mera Bakr is a consultant and junior researcher from the Kurdistan Region of Iraq (KRI). He has published several policy reports on security sector reform, immigration, and elections in the KRI. Currently, he is pursuing his master's degree in politics, economics, and philosophy at the University of Hamburg. Mera is a European and International Cooperation Scholarship holder of the German Konrad Adenauer Stiftung.

Maximilian Bertamini is a PhD student in international law at Ruhr University Bochum's interdisciplinary Institute for International Law of Peace and Armed Conflict (IFHV). Maximilian's research focus is on the history and theory of international law, with a particular interest in the concepts of sovereignty and property. As practical fields of application for his theoretical studies in international law, Maximilian examines both the law of outer space as well as humanitarian studies. He is the founder and operator of Scievon.com, a platform for finding and promoting digital academic events.

Peter Buth has been a humanitarian aid worker since 1994. His experience includes implementing and overseeing assistance programmes in various emergency and conflict settings for large international INGOs. His work now focuses on security and crisis management. He has four hens and goes to Newman's for a pint on Fridays.

Tom de Kok is a physician and aid worker and has long experience working for organisations such as MSF and the ICRC, leading to work managing operations in South Sudan, Darfur, the DRC, search and rescue in the Mediterranean, and prisons in Israel/Palestine, amongst other experiences. Tom's academic interest in negotiation was cultivated through a Peace Scholarship at Mills College, followed by a Peace Fellowship. He is presently reading practical ethics at Oxford. Tom practises medicine in rural and remote Canada and continues to hone his negotiating skills with his three-year-old daughter.

Dennis Dijkzeul is a Professor of conflict and organisation research at the Social Science School and the Institute for International Law of Peace and Armed Conflict at Ruhr University Bochum, Germany. Dennis was founding director of the Humanitarian Affairs Program at the School of International and Public Affairs of Columbia University. He has conducted research on humanitarian crises in the DRC, Uganda, South Sudan, and Afghanistan and has worked as a consultant for UN organisations and NGOs in Africa, Europe, Central Asia, and Latin America. His main research interests concern the management of international organisations and their interaction with local actors in crises.

Indira Govender is a medical doctor and specialist in public health medicine and epidemiology. Indira is based at the Africa Health Research Institute in rural KwaZulu-Natal, South Africa, where her research focuses on TB infection prevention and understanding TB transmission. Her advocacy interests are access to medicines, sexual and reproductive justice, and anti-racism. Prior to academic research, she worked for Médecins Sans Frontières in South Africa, Lesotho, South Sudan, and Sierra Leone.

Sean Healy is head of reflection and analysis for Médecins Sans Frontières' Operational Centre Amsterdam. At MSF, Sean coordinates and conducts research into global challenges facing humanitarians and provides strategic advice to the organisation. A particular focus has been on MSF's relationship with the societies it works in, including communities, local civil society actors, health authorities, and government officials. He was previously the Access Adviser, supporting negotiation efforts in Syria, Somalia, and Myanmar, amongst others. He has worked in a variety of other capacities in both field and headquarters since joining MSF in 2002.

Kristoffer Lidén is a Senior Researcher at the Peace Research Institute Oslo (PRIO) and a member of the Norwegian Centre for Humanitarian Studies (NCHS). Kristoffer holds a PhD in Philosophy and an MA in Peace and Conflict Studies. His research explores the ethics of international affairs, with a focus on the fields of peace-making, humanitarian action, security politics, and digital technology. He currently leads projects on ethics in peace negotiations and humanitarian negotiations, respectively, and coordinates the Law and Ethics research group at PRIO.

Rodrigo Mena is an Assistant Professor of Disasters and Humanitarian Studies at the Institute of Social Studies (ISS) of Erasmus University Rotterdam. Rod's research focuses on humanitarian responses and risk reduction to disasters and their interaction with other crises, such as violent conflict, climate change, and migration. Before his current position, he worked with local and international NGOs, the UN, ministries, and as consultant and researcher, particularly in disasters and conflict-affected places. Rodrigo also works on the ethical, safety, and security aspects of fieldwork research and is a board member of the International Humanitarian Studies Association and the Expertise Centre Humanitarian Communication.

S Mahdi Munadi is a lecturer on China's foreign policy at Sciences Po Paris and an IIE-SRF fellow focusing on the Central and South Asia region. Mahdi served as an Afghan diplomat in China and conducted research as a director at the Centre for Strategic Studies of the Afghanistan Ministry of Foreign Affairs and as a fellow at several institutions. He has published books and articles on Afghanistan, China's affairs, and terrorism.

Anaïde Nahikian is a Program Manager and a senior research and training consultant at the Harvard Humanitarian Initiative (HHI). Anaïde has dedicated her work to policy research, case studies, and professional development in humanitarian action through HHI and with operational agencies and think tanks including the World Bank Group, the International Committee of the Red Cross, Médecins Sans Frontières, Save the Children, the Norwegian Refugee Council, and the Geneva Centre for Security Sector Governance. She has led research, teaching, and training programmes across various regions worldwide, including the Middle East, East Africa, the Sahel, Southeast Asia, and Europe. Anaïde is currently a PhD candidate in sociology at the London School of Economics and Political Science.

Fernando Garlin Politis is a PhD candidate at the Université Paris Cité (CEPED, IRD, INSERM). Fernando's current thesis research is entitled: 'Humanitarian States? Ethnography of humanitarian policies and practices in Venezuela and Colombia'. His publications include 'Chacun sa fête: désaccords humanitaires et confrontations politiques' (FMSH editions) and 'Migrating Home, Going Home Abroad: Venezuelan Refugees' Detours Between Colombia and Venezuela During the Covid-19 Pandemic' (Noria Research).

Kristina Roepstorff is a senior researcher at the Peace Research Institute Oslo (PRIO). Kristina works on ethical dilemmas in humanitarian negotiations. She has been teaching on the European NOHA Master Programme in International Humanitarian Action since 2008 and is also associate faculty member at the School of Humanitarian Studies, Royal Roads University, Canada. As a trained intercultural mediator, trainer, and consultant, she seeks to bridge academic research and teaching with policy and practice. Kristina's research fields are humanitarian action, peacebuilding, and forced migration. Her research has been published as monographs, book chapters, journal articles, and policy papers.

Imri Schattner-Ornan is a humanitarian practitioner and lecturer. Initially trained in social anthropology in the UK and France, he later worked as project coordinator with humanitarian agencies such as the International Rescue Committee and Médecins Sans Frontières. As a humanitarian, Imri worked in Liberia, Ethiopia, Democratic Republic of the Congo, Central African Republic, and other countries. Since 2016, he has been teaching humanitarian and international development, and from 2020 Imri is a senior lecturer in humanitarian practice in the Liverpool School of Tropical Medicine (LSTM). Currently, he is the LSTM's humanitarian studies programme director and LSTM's lead for the LEAP programme.

Emmanuel Tronc is a senior humanitarian advisor at the Harvard Humanitarian Initiative. Emmanuel has worked in the humanitarian sector since 1996, specialising in conflict settings, emergency humanitarian response, and networking and dialogue with state and non-state actors. He worked with Médecins sans Frontières (MSF) as Head of Mission in several countries and developed and led humanitarian negotiation and diplomacy initiatives for its operations. Emmanuel also represented MSF among major stakeholders. He has designed and delivered over 80 professional training programmes on humanitarian negotiation and engagement practices with the Harvard Humanitarian Initiative and Conflict Dynamics International. Emmanuel holds advanced degrees in economics and political science.

Iana Vladimirova is an independent researcher from Cheboksary, Russia. She holds a bachelor of cultural studies (HSE, Moscow, 2018) and an MA in political science and international relations (MSSES, Moscow + University of Manchester, 2021). Iana has worked with human rights organisations as a volunteer translator and attendant for migrants and refugees in Moscow. Research interests include nationalism, ethnic minorities, refugees, political agency, and civic activism.

PREFACE

This edited volume documents a stop on a long journey. The proximate impetus for this collection was a double panel on the theme of the politics of negotiating with authoritarian regimes that I organised at the 2021 International Humanitarian Studies Association conference in Paris. Maximilian Bertamini, Claudia Astarita, Imri Schattner-Ornan, Kristoffer Lidén, and Kristina Roepstorff all participated in the panel and have translated their research into chapters for this book. The remaining chapters and commentaries have subsequently been added to the mix.

The ultimate cause for this collection is the fact that, working in the development and humanitarian sectors, one is confronted with how best to negotiate humanitarian access with states. The key is to find the right approach to solving this puzzle and a clever mix of academic research and humanitarian practice is essential. The discipline of history provides us with the tools to understand the background context and international relations by analysing the state system. The two disciplines pair well together, allowing for a more comprehensive view of the contentious relations between humanitarian actors, states, and history.

After working many years in the field negotiating access in various contexts with Médecins Sans Frontières where the relationship with states is often fraught, I moved to the humanitarian affairs department in Amsterdam where we wrestled more with this issue. With my colleague Clea Kahn, we co-edited a special issue of the journal Disasters entitled 'State sovereignty and humanitarian actors', where we explored various aspects of the relationship between states and humanitarian INGOs. My co-author of the first chapter in the volume, Sean Healy, co-wrote a chapter for this special issue. Following on from this experience, I completed a PhD on a similar topic, researching the relationship between MSF and the Government of Sri Lanka. This research resulted in a 2018 book, *International Humanitarian NGOs and State Relations: Politics, Principles and Identity*, with Routledge.

These initiatives show how my understanding of the state – INGO engagement theme has developed over time as different aspects have been homed in on and various research perspectives taken. There is no one way to look at such a complex question. Sovereignty tracks throughout, as does the need to negotiate access. But fine-tuned has been the concept of the nature of what constitutes 'difficult relations' and how we categorise them. This narrowed the theme down to a certain type of regime – authoritarian, widely considered to be the most problematic. But was this category the most appropriate?

When feedback came back from the proposal which launched this book project, guidance was provided to attend to the 'authoritarian practices turn' in the research literature. For after all, as humanitarians we negotiate against a set of practices facing us rather than with a regime type. This articulated an underlying concept that had gone unlabelled before. In the equation, the need for humanitarian negotiations remained constant, but the understanding of the actors on the other side of the table was insufficient. Sovereignty, regimes, government, state engagement – these all remain relevant, but how best to understand, categorise, and analyse these concepts in a coherent way? Practices have the advantage of focusing on the concrete barriers, actions, and concepts faced by INGOs. Practices also have the advantage, as described in the introduction, of broadening the set of states to be considered. This volume is therefore oriented around the relationship between authoritarian practices and humanitarian negotiations.

We live in an era where respect for and adherence to international norms of human rights, refugee law, and humanitarian law are decreasing. Warnings have been increasing that we are moving into a new era of authoritarianism or even fascism. Whether we are really faced with an authoritarian turn or not, it is easy to fear that we are. As I write this in London in 2023, the rhetoric of 'stop the boats' with its harsh critique of the asylum-seeking process and a denigrating portrayal of asylum seekers themselves is flung on the pages of the media by the current government in power.

This book draws upon the cutting-edge research on the topic of authoritarian practices and humanitarian negotiations. This is not a well-populated sub-field but growing in interest and active participants. The themes of sovereignty, regimes, practices, as well as the law and human rights, are all found in this volume. Some chapters hit the issue of humanitarian organisations and negotiations head-on; some are more oblique, as sometimes we learn the most about ourselves by studying others and how they respond to similar situations. But the field remains murky and we must explore, analyse, and elaborate widely to bring needed clarity. This is one stop on this path; there are many more to come.

I would like to give special acknowledgement to Fernando Garlin Politis for providing the cover art for this volume. Appreciation as well to the collegiality of all of the contributors to this volume. Special thanks go to the International Humanitarian Studies Association for facilitating the panel which was the impetus for this collection.

FIGURE 0.1   Tents by Fernando Garlin Politis

INTRODUCTION

Authoritarian practices and humanitarian negotiations

Andrew J Cunningham

Why explore the theme of authoritarian practices and humanitarian negotiations?

A key-word search for the term 'authoritarianism' returns a multitude of articles and books in the academic and popular press. There is a great mix of the past, the present, and prognoses for the future. Much ink has been spilled in outlining and framing the trajectory of a notoriously slippery concept, from the growth of fascism in Europe leading to World War II, through the Cold War, decolonialisation, and the rise of China (Hirono, 2013), and on to the current concern that there is a re-emergence of authoritarianism or even fascism in the 21st century (Gandesha, 2020b; Berberoglu, 2021). If one adds to the search dusty terms such as dictatorship (Dikotter, 2019), totalitarianism (Linz, 2000 [1975]; Arendt, 1951), autocracy (Gessen, 2020), or even despotism, and throws in allied concepts such as managed or illiberal democracy (Zakaria, 2004), the pile of reading becomes precarious. This edited volume focuses on one very particular problematic within the literature on authoritarianism: how international humanitarian non-government organisations (INGOs), as civil society actors, negotiate access in an environment of authoritarianism and conflict.

As with any political concept, there is a spectrum of interpretation and response upon which citizens, civil society actors, and scholars inhabit. Everyone must navigate the dynamic discursive environment in which they live. Citizens react to the government in power, mediated through their own memory and expectations, and civil society actors adapt to the space within which they negotiate at any given time. International non-governmental organisations implementing humanitarian activities are but one type of civil society

DOI: 10.4324/9781003316541-1

actor, and humanitarianism, it should be stressed, should not be confused with the international entities that sponsor emergency responses but at essence is constructed by citizens wishing to help others in need. The personal nature of humanitarian work is critical (see Schattner-Ornan in this volume). Beyond international humanitarian actors, there are a plethora of local and national organisations working in aid provision. International actors, however, face unique challenges, as by their nature, these are entities which emanate from outside a crisis but seek to work within it.

The proximate impetus for this book was a panel hosted at the International Humanitarian Studies Association conference in Paris in 2021 on the politics of negotiating with authoritarian regimes. Scholars have the advantage of a longer-term view and theoretical and conceptual frames to use in analysing political phenomena. Several chapters in this book are from this panel (Bertamini, Astarita, Schattner-Ornan, Lidén, and Roepstorff). Since the conference, the thematic has been sharpened to focus on authoritarian practices rather than regimes, emphasising the evolving nature of the study of humanitarian negotiations in relation to the changing political landscape globally (Nahikian and Tronc; Garlin Politis; Healy and Cunningham). Noted in the literature is a tension between categorising the nature of authoritarian regimes and focusing on the actual practice of authoritarianism. This book argues that INGOs seeking to negotiate operational access in a humanitarian crisis respond to the practices they encounter rather than type of regimes they perceive. What matters is what a government does rather than how it is labelled.

The ultimate impetus for this volume is the on-going concern within the humanitarian sector for how the relationship between states and INGOs develops and functions (Cunningham, 2018). As a humanitarian practitioner myself, I have been faced directly with the complications of conducting negotiations with a wide variety of governments. Those in the category of authoritarian, or what has been sometimes referred to as 'strong states', have often perplexed humanitarians (Kahn and Cunningham, 2013), especially in times of conflict (del Valle and Healy, 2013; Harvey, 2013) and when UN peacekeeping missions are present (Karlsrud and da Costa, 2013). As researchers, we are tasked with more objectively analysing these relationships in order to help guide practitioners in their work. This book will be of interest to researchers and students of authoritarianism and humanitarian studies, as well as aid practitioners.

A number of concepts must be defined to begin such a dialogue. This introduction will summarise the literature on authoritarian regimes and argue for the utility of using the concept of authoritarian practices when studying humanitarian negotiations. As this volume addresses the contemporary world, it is important to situate authoritarianism in the 21st century. The crux of this book, however, will be to examine the ways authoritarian practices impact humanitarian negotiations, and the chapters contributing to this goal will be reviewed.

Authoritarian regimes and practices

What is authoritarianism? It should be noted that the categorisation and analysis of differing types of strong governments and leaders and how they engage with their societies is not new. In the Western tradition, we can start with Plato's *Republic* and work through Machiavelli's *The Prince*, Hobbes' *Leviathan,* and Rousseau's *The Social Contract*, and onwards to the Nazi legal scholar Carl Schmitt's (2005 [1922]) *Political Theology*, Arendt's *The Origins of Totalitarianism*, Adorno, Frenkel-Brunswik, Levinson, and Sanford's (2019) *The Authoritarian Personality*, and Agamben's *State of Exception*, amongst many other works (2015).

Authoritarianism has also been influenced by the on-going process of decolonialisation (Bond, 2021) and highly influenced by the growth of neoliberalism (Brown, et al., 2018). The ups-and-downs of authoritarianism over time should be noted, as political developments do not progress in a linear fashion. Humanitarians are sometimes shortsighted when responding to a current crisis and need to be reminded that their era is but one of many, and even recent political cycles are often outside their vision. The political background to any crisis or regime is important to understand.

In the midst of the Cold War, Joan Linz defined authoritarian regimes as 'political systems with limited, not responsible political pluralism, without intensive nor extensive political mobilisation, and in which a leader or a small group exercise power within formally ill-defined limits but actually quite predictable ones' (Linz, 2000 [1975], 255). More recently, Erica Frantz has added to the definition the importance of placing loyalists in positions of power, often family members; the desire to control the media; the need to manipulate electoral rules to stay in power, often including the creation of new political parties; the passing of constitutional amendments to support the regime; the use of lawsuits, legislation, or referendums to sideline civil society; and the empowering of the security services to disempower government opposition (Frantz, 2018, 94–97 and 50–53). Alan Spector frames authoritarianism at three levels. At the micro level, a dictator's rule is idiosyncratic and based on personality characteristics. At the meso level, a regime may respond to any number of threats – terrorism, foreign influence, or domestic disturbances – with the restrictions of rights. Of most concern are the macro-level authoritarianisms 'that flow from fundamental structural political and economic changes in society', as they are the hardest to be reversed (Spector, 2021, 69).

A traditional way to study authoritarianism is to analyse, define, and categorise regime types and authoritarian regime typologies, either situating a regime on a democratic-authoritarian scale – continuous regimes; or examining how regimes differ from each other and placing them into certain categories, such as civilian, monarchical, or military, for example (Ezrow and Frantz, 2011). Either way, the objective is to examine regime types – how they gain, keep, and lose power; how they are constituted; who is in and out of the centre of power; and how regimes engage internationally. A glance at recent titles illustrates the point. Svolik (2012) examines *The Politics of Authoritarian Rule*, Geddes, Wright, and Frantz (2018) study *How Dictatorships Work*, Tansey (2016) researches *The International Politics of Authoritarian Rule*, and Escriba-Folch and Wright (2015) highlight *Foreign Pressure and the Politics of Autocratic Survival*.

Defining authoritarianism in terms of how power is maintained, developing regime typologies, and placing specific regimes within these typologies, is useful in helping to define the parameters of an analysis of authoritarianism. For academics working in comparative politics, international political science, or international relations, this work is certainly valuable. But does this make sense from a humanitarian organisation's standpoint? Are humanitarian INGOs concerned with the type of regime or more with what the regime does? Glasius (2018) takes an alternative perspective and examines authoritarian practice rather than regime types. For Glasius, authoritarian practice is 'a pattern of actions, embedded in an organised context, sabotaging accountability to people ('the forum') over whom a political actor exerts control, or their representatives, by disabling their access to information and/or disabling their voice' (527). From his fascist perspective, Carl Schmitt argued that 'every government is part of a continuum of dictatorship in its actual practices' (Johal, 2020, 104). Although Glasius focuses on domestic actors, international aid actors are also objects of governmental attention, much like domestic civil society actors. In relation to international aid actors, authoritarian practices attempt to disrupt accountability to humanitarian norms, limit access to populations assistance, and constrain humanitarian action and advocacy. This focus on practice is therefore a good starting point for analysing how INGOs negotiate access in authoritarian environments.

The concept of authoritarian practice is epistemologically curious. Is there a set of observable and verifiable actions to be analysed and labelled as authoritarian? Or is the concept constructed by each participant and observer based on their own expectations, worldviews, and cultural orientations? Those working for INGOs, for example, have their own way of looking at the world and see trends from a unique referential perspective – as individuals (citizens), as representatives of organisations, and as civil society actors embedded in an overlapping set of political, social, and moral communities. This book attempts a middle way between documenting how certain practices negatively affect humanitarian negotiations on the ground and the articulation of a theoretical framework of understanding. We must be more rigorous in how we understand authoritarian practices, but this should not lead to such levels of abstraction that research is not useful to those struggling to work in the real world. Humanitarianism, after all, is about humans helping other humans in need and is not an academic endeavour.

It should be noted that authoritarian practice is distinct from illiberal practice, which is 'a pattern of actions, embedded in an organised context, infringing on the autonomy and dignity of the person' (Glasius, 2018, 530). In this way, 'authoritarian practices primarily constitute a threat to democratic processes, while illiberal practices are primarily a human rights problem' (517). Although illiberal practices do not normally directly target international aid actors (as institutions), these practices are directed at the populations with whom aid actors work and contribute to the creation of a humanitarian crisis. The pattern of action states direct at international aid actors should be differentiated from the practices governments target at their own people and civil society actors. Both authoritarian and illiberal practices operate at various levels: local, national, and global. In humanitarian contexts, the dynamic of crisis adds to the form and robustness of these practices. Aid actors, therefore, are often concerned with illiberal practices not on their own behalf but on behalf of the populations they are attempting to assist, and this concern may limit the space for humanitarian negotiations. There is a dynamic interplay between authoritarian and illiberal practices that must be unpacked when considering how international aid actors negotiate humanitarian access. However, although illiberal practices may inform humanitarian negotiations, the primary focus in this volume remains on authoritarian practices.

Over time there are innovations in authoritarian practices (Curato and Fossmati, 2020). First, the practice-oriented approach places dynamism in the foreground when analysing authoritarian politics. Second, the concept of authoritarian practices emphasises the fluidity of governance arrangements, such that authoritarian practices can unfold outside authoritarian regimes. Finally, investigating authoritarian practices prompts us to consider new political trajectories that regimes take as these practices get institutionalised or normalised through informal means. Thus, things change over time, especially with practices, much more than regime type. Schmitt also 'evoke[d] the notion of a situational rather than universal law, whether to change or suspend laws according to the crisis at hand' (Johal, 2020, 103).

The key elements to be considered in discussing authoritarian practices are therefore: time (innovations), practices (burden of constraints), and negotiation (response type); added to these are basic frameworks such as ethics and law. Practices and negotiations will always be implemented against a legal and regulatory order, on the part of governments as well as organisations themselves and their institutional donors. Humanitarian principles often form the normative basis of aid, although there are other ethical frameworks as well, such as medical ethics. Humanitarian organisations work within a web of ethical and regulatory obligations: institutional donors, public supporters, public relations, and personally felt norms of behaviour (see Lidén and Roepstorff in this volume).

Authoritarianism in the 21st century

All of this begs the question: has there actually been an 'authoritarian turn' over the last couple of decades? Whether popular, academic, or polemical, a trend in recent literature has been to speak about an authoritarian turn in the 21st century. Gandesha (2020a) states it plainly: 'there can be little doubt today that, after a long period of dormancy, authoritarianism and, at times, downright fascistic elements have returned to public life with a vengeance', throughout Europe, in the UK and the US (Gandesha, 2020a, 120), as well as in Turkey (Atasoy, 2021), India – 'Saffron fascism' (Kumbamu, 2021), and Brazil (Petras and Veltmeyer, 2021), amongst many other examples.

Besides the traditional ways of looking at authoritarianism as described above, the recent turn is seen to involve increasingly assertive foreign policies, nationalist practices, intolerance for immigrants and minorities, limitations on freedom of speech and the free press, and hostility towards the liberal world order and international organisations (Hussain and Ahmad, 2020, 68). Democracy itself is seen to be in danger, negatively affecting civil liberties (Freedom House, 2009). In this view, a 'redefined and heavily distorted version of the concept [of democracy] is communicated to domestic audiences through state-dominated media'. To the point of aid budgets, 'these regimes are using soft-power methods to advance their interests internationally, particularly through billions of dollars in no-strings attached development aid' (ibid., 4).

One range of explanations for a rise in authoritarianism revolves around the response to neoliberalism. Neoliberalism can be defined as 'a set of economic policies promoting unrestricted actions, flows, and accumulation of capital by means of low tariffs and taxes, reregulation of industries, privatisation of formerly public good and services, stripped-out welfare states, and the breakup of organized labor' (Berberoglu, 2021, 11). In this view, cold war authoritarian regimes aimed to protect corporate interest or block the Soviets (Spector, 2021, 70). Post-Cold War there was a hope for a reconfiguration of the world order, yet the neoliberal order was resilient. The current rise of neoliberalism and the social reactions against it have been manipulated by the very forces that created the dissatisfaction in the first place. The US has especially been an important instigator of unequal wealth creation through propagation of open markets and perpetrator of violence through use of military power (Rhodes, 2021, 15). The role of discourse in defining an anti-democracy narrative has been discussed (ibid., 27).

The sub-title of a recent edited volume on the global rise of authoritarianism in the 21st century, *Crisis of Neoliberal Globalization and the Nationalist Response* (Berberoglu, 2021), is telling. There is a pervasive fear of populism: 'The immediate danger of right-wing populism is that has an affinity for and may already be in the process of creating authoritarian capitalism, which retains neoliberal policies yet dumps liberal democracy' (Bonanno, 2021, 23). Neoliberalism can be summarised as 'the ideology of global capitalism' (Berberoglu, 2021, 2). Reaction by those left behind in an age of increasing inequality has led to a populist reaction propagated by 'pseudo-nationalist forces that have mobilized people under the banner of ultra-nationalism and xenophobia to prevent the rise of a socialist or communist movement against global capitalism' (ibid., 4). Liberal democracy is said to be in 'crisis' or even in a 'state of siege' (Brown, et al., 2081, vi). In this view, 'social movements and political leaders have succeeded in activating reactionary populism, nativism, racism, and xenophobia', and 'rhetorics and policies of exclusion and marginalisation' abound. This trend lacks ideological coherence: at the same time as the state is the neoliberal enemy, statism and nationalism are on the rise, and they are anti-political political projects (ibid., 2). When nations become focused on the economy above all else and are atomised into family units seeking protection from others, 'universality, equality, and openness are jettisoned, and the nation becomes legitimately illiberal towards those designated as aversive insiders or invading outsiders' (Brown et al., 2018, 22). Governments do not actively help people but rather reinforce their social grievances and blame others. Post-truth, nihilistic 'branding' of whatever feeds into 'resentment, impulse, or outrage' occurs (ibid., 27). A social contract which implies being kind and helpful to others breaks down (ibid., 28). Identity politics is strengthened; society is told what to be against rather than what it should be for (Rhodes, 2021, 27). Referenda such as Brexit and a whole crop of neo-authoritarian leaders and politicians in the West, such as Viktor Orban in Hungary, Marine Le Pen in France, Nigel Farage in the UK, Geert Wilders in the Netherlands, or Donald Trump in the US, have all caused concern in the liberal elites of Europe and the US. All of this has effects on civil society when being 'woke', a stand-in term for social justice, is used as a curse in the populist media.

Within this discursive environment, humanitarian INGOs have increasingly been concerned about such themes as securitisation, politicisation, and shrinking humanitarian space (Cunningham, 2018) and the decreasing respect for international legal norms of humanitarian action, the laws of war, and refugee regimes (UN SC, 2013). Western INGOs within their own societies or as transnational actors working within other political and social environments must adapt and reorient to the changing realities. International NGOs work in an increasingly perilous environment even in their home societies. Humanitarian aid is not a politically neutral phenomenon nor as morally unambiguous as aid workers may perceive it to be. Humanitarian action is often directed as the very scapegoats that are being vilified.

It is not for this book to prove the existence of an authoritarian turn but, taking it as a given, to provide reflections and analysis on the lived experiences of humanitarian organisations and the structures they work in the world of the early 21st century. In response to this predominant political environment of a time and place, INGOs will begin the process of negotiating access. The next section will orient humanitarian negotiations with the larger political environment. The dedicated chapter in this volume (Nahikian and Tronc) will go into details about the practice of humanitarian negotiations.

Humanitarian negotiations

International humanitarian actors working outside their own countries are external actors attempting to work within the internal political, economic, and social environment of a specific country or region in which a humanitarian crisis occurs. To effectively provide assistance to people affected by a humanitarian crisis, these external actors must negotiate access with all relevant civic, military, and governmental actors, be they state or non-state authorities. Even considering the existence of international legal norms surrounding humanitarian action, organisations cannot simply show up and start working (Hours, 2008). States, or more precisely, the governments that represent them at any given time, have their own set of perspectives, worldviews, and preconditions concerning aid provision, particularly if implemented by international actors.

States also work within international banking and financial management systems, where funds and budgets can be frozen and sanctions put into place, negatively affecting the ability of international actors to work. Humanitarian aid then becomes the victim of war through other means – in this case, global finance. Afghanistan (see Munadi and Mena in this volume), Iran, and Russia are examples. Another 'war by other means' is high politics, such as international treaties and agreements around access and the level of the United Nations. High politics, as well as high finance, impact how INGOs operate on the ground, such as in Syria (see Bertamini in this volume) or Venezuela (see Garlin Politis in this volume).

Governments are almost always actors in the humanitarian crisis and are not neutral arbitrators of aid distribution. A humanitarian crisis occurs within an arena (Hilhorst and Jansen 2010). A political crisis and the humanitarian environment are therefore intimately associated with the political actors involved with its cause, development, and response, and as part of this political environment, humanitarian organisations become political actors themselves. Not only ideologies, interests, and territories are contested in this political arena, but also the space within which humanitarian actors attempt to work.

This humanitarian space is not only symbolic but also geographical – INGOs must work in specific physical locations within a conflict zone. As such, humanitarian INGOs are external actors attempting to work internally (Cunningham, 2018). In some cases, humanitarian access will be nearly impossible, either because of outright restrictions or the depth of compromise needed to be made by international actors to enter. China's Xinjiang (discussed by Astarita in this volume), North Korea, Eritrea, and Turkmenistan are good examples. Sudan and Ethiopia (examined by Schattner-Ornan in this volume) are notorious cases of difficult negotiations.

Against this backdrop, the state-INGO relationship is often examined through the lenses of instrumentalism, security, and sovereignty. Instrumentalisation of aid agencies by states, whether by host states, aid funding donor states, or any other relevant state involved in the conflict, occurs when agencies are used by states to contribute to meeting their foreign policy goals. In this conceptualisation, aid actors are considered part of a hearts and minds strategy and allied members of a state-led team sharing similar values, or even 'force-multipliers'.[1] States can justify limiting access to humanitarian organisations as a way to protect its sovereignty which is under threat by foreign agents. In the context of a conflict, protecting sovereignty is a priority, and INGOs are a threat, particularly if they are thought to be instrumentalised by external political actors. A related theme is where security is the justification for limiting access. On the surface, a state is concerned with ensuing INGO security, but hidden agendas are feared by INGOs – limitations to access based on security are often thought to be simply control of their activities.

The relationship between states and humanitarian INGOs can also be framed as a dichotomy between principles and politics mediated through discussions about identity (Cunningham, 2018; Fast, 2014). In this characterisation, humanitarian organisations either admit to the existence of the political space within which they work but attempt to remain outside this political environment – the 'humanitarian exceptionalism view' – or INGOs actively embrace a political role. In the former situation, humanitarian actors argue their exceptionalism based on humanitarian principles – humanity, impartiality, neutrality, and independence. On the latter view, the use of principles and protective humanitarian emblems is at best delusional and at worst contributes to the prolongation of the conflicts themselves by ignoring the positive political potential of humanitarian action.

A state must protect the interests of its population, and faced with an identified danger, it will attempt to manage the threat to achieve a state of security. Security threats are at times serious enough to be framed as existential in nature, and in such cases, states will justify instituting emergency measures beyond the rules that would otherwise be in place – security management essentially becomes a matter of survival (Knudsen, 2001). In such a context, a state can be considered a 'securitising agent' – an actor which identifies another actor as a serious security threat which must be quickly and effectively managed (Buzan et al., 1998). A threat is often another political or military actor, but as will be argued, civil society actors can also be characterised as serious threats.

Instrumentalisation, politicisation, and securitisation are all symptoms of a difficult state-INGO relationship and will often be found in contexts where regimes, of whatever category, implement what can be considered authoritarian practices (see Healy and Cunningham in this volume). But practices should not be examined in isolation but need to be framed by the intent and objectives of negotiations on the part of the state. There is not a direct correlation between these contexts of difficult negotiation and the types of regimes where authoritarian practices are common, but there is certainly an overlap. This is often seen more easily through an analysis of state discourse related to humanitarian action (Cunningham, 2018). By analysing a government's discourse around aid and aid actors, a clearer view can be obtained on their practices. Many humanitarian INGOs take a pragmatic view of negotiating access, and the question of why things are the way they are is less important than figuring out how to manage the constraints to action. This is not the perspective of this book, which will rather analyse the actual locus of contact between INGOs and governments through the conceptual lens of authoritarian practices as introduced above. After Kinne, a poliheuristic theory approach will be argued, which asserts that state leaders assign primary importance to their political survival; however, the meaning of 'the political' varies dramatically from country to country. Furthermore, the types of actors who hold leaders politically accountable also vary between countries (Kinne, 2005). Humanitarian action is in fact an arena of actors (Hilhorst and Jansen, 2010).

The structure of the book

Within the humanitarian sector, the process of negotiation has always been integral to aid provision, but the nature of negotiations changes over time and place. There has never been a golden age of access. This book presents case studies at various levels of negotiation and offers theoretical considerations, and proposes methodologies. Diverse levels are described—from the highest, macro level of diplomacy – the UN Security Council negotiations around aid to Syria, through meso-level examinations of China, Afghanistan, Russia, and Venezuela, to the micro-field-level experience of negotiating work in a project (Ethiopia). Framing the question of humanitarian negotiations will be a key focus. Ethical dilemmas are a special topic, as negotiating within an environment of authoritarian practices brings its own challenges and informs responses, as does the response to illiberal actions by states. Humanitarian principles are useful but other ethical frameworks are available and innovations needed.

Chapter descriptions

Each chapter is paired with a commentary by either a practitioner or an academic, with the aim to provide an alternative, or even challenging, view on the chapter findings. Research is not static but is the impetus for a dialogue. This book's structure has been designed to begin this debate.

Chapter 1, by Sean Healy and Andrew J Cunningham, describes the 'friction of practice' through reflections on the Médecins Sans Frontières experience with 'authoritarian regimes'. The chapter relates the MSF experience with states through a historical review and presentation of initial results from state engagement research in Bangladesh and the Kurdish Region of Iraq. In summary, there are no 'strong' or 'weak' states, but practises that all states engage in that are not confined to regime types which are themselves considered 'authoritarian'. As commentary Tom de Kok and Andrew Cunningham reflect on the question: What is discourse analysis?

Chapter 2, by Anaïde Nahikian and Emmanuel Tronc, with acknowledgement to Julian Watkinson for his contributions, discusses humanitarian negotiations and the challenges and compromise in negotiating access in hard-to-reach areas. Recent decades have seen increasing recognition of humanitarian negotiation as a field of both theoretical inquiry and operational practice to better comprehend how humanitarians negotiate. During negotiations in authoritarian contexts, humanitarians may struggle with inherent tensions of upholding humanitarian principles in the face of political interests, the competing needs for confidentiality and coordination between different organisations, and the challenges of adequately assessing interlocutors in a fluid environment where control of territory frequently shifts. Against this backdrop, this chapter discusses the working definition of humanitarian negotiation, the broader political context of humanitarian negotiations, and aims to offer the reader reflections on engaging with authoritarian regimes from research and practice. In contrast to the organisational theory presented in the chapter, a commentary by Indira Govender follows, which presents a real-world anecdote entitled 'security reasons'.

Chapter 3, by Maximilian Bertamini, discusses the Syrian context through an exposition on the vocabulary of negotiations. The chapter seeks to understand the relationship between sovereignty and authoritarian arguments in the United Nations Security Council. The chapter analyses the extent to which sovereignty-based arguments can be qualified as authoritarian and argues that some of the ways in which sovereignty is invoked can be considered authoritarian. It aims to sensitise international negotiators to the problem of incompatible understandings of sovereignty and points out the opportunities and costs of addressing them openly, highlighting the way in which non-authoritarian positions can be 'authoritarianised' through the context in which they are invoked. A critique of the chapter's themes is then provided by Dennis Dijkzeul.

Chapter 4, by Claudia Astarita, changes focus to the Xinjiang context and its implications for the rights debate in China and discusses the role for NGOs and humanitarian negotiations in such an environment. The chapter aims at providing a better understanding of both the origins and the impact of the China Communist Party (CCP) in Xinjiang in order to precise the state of the art of this massive 'transformation through education' campaign, as well as to decode the narrative that has been associated with it at the national level. This chapter re-enacts the way in which academics, media, and foreign actors have adjusted their understanding and their narrative about Xinjiang since 2014 to disclose if any of their actions had a real impact on the concerned region and the on-going humanitarian crisis. Finally, the last section of the chapter delves into the world of humanitarian actions and practitioners to offer recommendations to advance the level of consciousness, the debate on rights, and on humanitarian negotiations and interventions in either Xinjiang or China. A commentary based on personal experience working in China is provided by S. Mahdi Munadi.

Chapter 5, by Imri Schattner-Ornan, shifts continents to describe the realities of daily negotiations with state agencies in the field by reflecting on an experience of working in refugee camps in Western Ethiopia. This personal reflection is organised around key objects or moments in the daily management of a health project by an international humanitarian NGO. The chapter looks at how documents such as the MoU and the camp entrance permit are used by a national agency to control a foreign NGO and how an environment of opaque rules and unknown regulations aims to reduce the humanitarian agency to a service provider. The chapter examines the way NGO staff try to appeal restrictions placed by the authorities and how these appeals evoke assumptions of personal official power of discretion, though the veracity of these assumptions is never fully known. Practice is examined through the lenses of exception and its relation to sovereignty and examines the broader relationship between the humanitarian agency and the state's authority via the consideration of a 'strategic relationship' and the different visions of collaboration. A commentary on the concept of independence by Peter Buth follows the chapter.

Chapter 6, by S. Mahdi Munadi and Rod Mena, presents reflections on the dilemmas of working in Afghanistan under a renewed Taliban regime. This chapter examines the complexity of humanitarian negotiations in authoritarian settings using the case study of Afghanistan after the Taliban takeover in August 2021. Humanitarian negotiations in Afghanistan involve a range of actors, including humanitarian organisations, the Taliban as the de facto regime resting on top of the previous government institutions, and local communities that occur at different levels – macro, meso, and micro across different social and cultural dimensions. It draws on a comprehensive literature review and informal conversations with humanitarian actors working in the country and with people who have received assistance in Afghanistan. The authors ultimately provide a reflective piece on the tough negotiations and renegotiations in Afghanistan with the Taliban, who are without political recognition yet control the country and where its discriminatory policies against women and minorities have created enormous challenges. A brief critique on Afghanistan is presented by Mera Bakr.

Chapter 7, by Iana Vladimirova, locates us in Russia, where Roma structural discrimination is discussed by examining institutions involved and measures (not) taken. In 1996, Russian legislation provided ethnic minorities with a unique institutional structure: National-Cultural Autonomy (NCA). Due to their NCA status, activists found themselves in the public space and entered the political field as agents within the political structure, although at present activities of Roma organisations are mainly reduced to the organisation of ethnocultural events that practically do not raise the relevant issues regarding the vulnerable position of structurally discriminated against Roma. Focusing on the institutional limitations for political agency of Roma public associations and their leaders, the chapter examines who is currently responsible for solving the problems of Roma population in Russia and how effective the communication is between such actors. Particular attention is given to the aspects of international cooperation and shifts in Russia's foreign and domestic policies. The chapter is followed by a commentary by Andrew J Cunningham on different types of organisations and their different types of responses to crises.

Chapter 8, by Fernando Garlin Politis, transports us to Latin America where the humanitarian apparatus of silence, authoritarian denial, and the aid assemblage in Venezuela are examined. The case of Venezuela is distinguished by the perpetuation of its multiple crises and the political polarisation around humanitarian aid. The government's official denial to recognise the crises in the country has not prevented the deployment of two 'humanitarian apparatuses': on the one hand, the 'humanitarian public action' organised in a civic-military alliance and represented by the structures of the communal councils, and, on the other hand, the interventions of international humanitarian aid agencies. This chapter explains how articulating both apparatuses is only possible in this context precisely because of the silence, introducing the notion of aid assemblage to propose a broader reflection of power distribution by reframing repertoires of action that overflow the country's current scope of humanitarian governance mutism. A commentary by Rodrigo Mena follows, locating the chapter's themes between instrumentalisation, depoliticisation, and legitimation.

The final chapter before the conclusion, by Kristoffer Lidén and Kristina Roepstorff, examines ethical dilemmas in humanitarian negotiations with authoritarian regimes and proposes a conceptual framework of 'mopping up, keeping down, and propping up'. This chapter examines the ethical problems that humanitarian agencies face when working under authoritarian rule and negotiating with authoritarian regimes. These problems entail ethical dilemmas, presenting humanitarian agencies with a difficult choice between a principled concern of avoiding complicity and failing to assist people in dire need. These 'authoritarian dilemmas' can be categorised into three general types: (1) mopping up after the humanitarian problems caused by regimes; (2) keeping down marginalised groups and political opposition by distributing aid in line with partial dictates from the authorities; and (3) propping up the authorities by aligning with their general political interests and strategies (beyond mopping up or keeping down) and thereby undermining the prospects for political change. Assessing ethical justifications when confronted with these dilemmas from four relevant ethical positions, namely deontological and consequentialist professional ethics and pluralist and solidarist political ethics, this chapter demonstrates how these ethical positions may lead to different prescriptions in particular settings, arguing against an oversimplified understanding of moral dilemmas and complicity in scholarly and public discourse on humanitarian ethics.

The conclusion by Andrew J Cunningham focuses on the theory and praxis of constructing the relationship between authoritarian practices and humanitarian negotiations and brings together the various strands of the book into a coherent whole and identifies the gaps in understanding and based on this will propose a research agenda.

Next steps

This book is a starting point for exploring the theme of authoritarian practices and humanitarian negotiations, yet much remains to be done. As the literature on the authoritarian turn of the 21st century and the accompanying work on authoritarian practices and humanitarian negotiations develop, the space at their confluence must be further integrated. These themes impact each other like tectonic plates. As the political environment changes so must INGOs. This book has outlined some concepts at the macro, meso, and micro levels, but there is much more analysis to be done at each level of analysis. It behoves humanitarian organisations to be better attuned to the political environment within which they work.

It should be noted that this edited volume has failed to include voices closer to the humanitarian crises themselves and lacks case studies from the Global North. The lived experiences of practitioners and academics who live, work, and are embedded in the contexts of humanitarian crisis and authoritarian practices are for the most part missing in this volume dominated by northern academics and practitioners. This must be rectified in further research. Practices can and should be seen from a variety of political perspectives.

Note

1 In 2001 the US Secretary of State, Colin Powell, referred to INGOs as 'force multipliers'. The remark is still current in discussions about state-INGO aid relations. See, for example: Williams, M. and Briggs, C. (2019). The last straw for independent Australian aid? *The Strategist.* Australian Strategic Policy Institute.

References

Adorno, T., Frenkel-Brenswik, E., Levinson, D. J., and Sanford, R. N. (2019). *The Authoritarian Personality.* London: Verso Books.

Agamben, G. (2005). *State of Exception.* Chicago, IL: University of Chicago Press.

Arendt, H. (2017 [1951]). *The Origins of Totalitarianism.* London: Penguin Books.

Atasoy, Y. (2021). Neoliberalism and the Rise of Authoritarianism in Turkey under the AKP. In: Berberoglu, B. (ed.). *The Global Rise of Authoritarianism in the 21st Century: Crisis of Neoliberal Globalization and the Nationalist Response.* New York, NY: Routledge.

Berberoglu, B. (ed.) (2021). *The Global Rise of Authoritarianism in the 21st Century: Crisis of Neoliberal Globalization and the Nationalist Response.* New York, NY: Routledge.

Bonanno, A. (2021). The Crisis of Neoliberalism, Populist Reaction, and the Rise of Authoritarian Capitalism. In: Berberoglu, B. (ed.). *The Global Rise of Authoritarianism in the 21st Century: Crisis of Neoliberal Globalization and the Nationalist Response.* New York, NY: Routledge.

Bond, P. (2021). Neoliberalism, Authoritarianism, and Popular Resistence in Africa. In: Berberoglu, B. (ed.). *The Global Rise of Authoritarianism in the 21st Century: Crisis of Neoliberal Globalization and the Nationalist Response.* New York, NY: Routledge.

Brown, W., Gordon, P. E., and Pensky, M. (2018). *Authoritarianism: Three Inquires in Critical Theory.* Chicago: University of Chicago Press.

Buzan, B., et al. (1998). *Security: A New Framework for Analysis.* London: Lynne Rienner.

Cunningham, A. J. (2018). *International Humanitarian NGOs and State Relations: Politics, Principles and Identity.* London: Routledge.

Curato, N. and Fossmati, D. (2020). Authoritarian Innovations: Crafting Support for a Less Democratic Southeast Asia. *Democratization* 27(6), 1006–1020.

Del Valle, H. and Healy, S. (2013). Humanitarian Agencies and Authoritarian States: A Symbiotic Relationship. *Disasters* 37(supplement 2), S188–S201.

Dikotter, F. (2019). *Dictators: The Cult of Personality in the Twentieth Century.* London: Bloomsbury.

Escriba-Folch, A. and Wright, J. (2015). *Foreign Pressure and the Politics of Autocratic Survival.* Oxford: Oxford University Press.

Fast, L. (2014). *Aid in Danger: The Perils and Promise of Humanitarianism.* Philadelphia: University of Pennsylvania Press.

Frantz, E. (2018). *Authoritarianism.* Oxford: Oxford University Press.

Freedom House. (2009). *Undermining Democracy: 21st Century Authoritarians.*

Gandesha, S. (2020a). 'A Composite of King Kong and a Suburban Barber': Adorno's 'Freudian Theory and the Pattern of Fascist Propaganda'. In: Gandesha, S. (ed.).

Spectres of Fascism: Historical, Theoretical and International Perspectives. London: Pluto Press.

Gandesha, S. (ed.) (2020b). *Spectres of Fascism: Historical, Theoretical and International Perspectives.* London: Pluto Press.

Geddes, B., Wright, J., and Frantz, E. (2018). *How Dictatorships Work.* Cambridge: Cambridge University Press.

Gessen, M. (2020). *Surviving Autocracy.* New York: Riverhead Books.

Glasius, M. (2018). What Authoritarianism Is ... and Is Not: A Practical Perspective. *International Affairs* 94(3), 515–533.

Harvey, P. (2013). International Humanitarian Actors and Governments in Areas of Conflict: Challenges, Obligations, and Opportunities. *Disasters* 37(supplement 2), S151–S170.

Hilhorst, D. and Jansen, B. J. (2010). Humanitarian Space as Arena: A perspective on the everyday politics of aid. *Development and Change* 41(6), 1117–1139.

Hirono, M. (2013). Three Legacies of Humanitarianism in China. *Disasters* 37(supplement 2), S202–S220.

Hours, B. (2008). NGOs and the Victim industry. *Le Monde Diplomatique – English Edition*, 14 November.

Hussain, S. and Ahmad, A. (2020). The Rise of Authoritarianism in the 21st Century and the World Order. *Journal of Contemporary Studies* IX(1 Summer), 64–85.

Johal, A. (2020). The Post-democratic Horizon: Friend and Enemy in the Age of New Authoritarianism. In: Gandesha, S. (ed.). *Spectres of Fascism: Historical, Theoretical and International Perspectives.* London: Pluto Press.

Kahn, C. and Cunningham, A. (2013). Introduction to the Issue of State Sovereignty and Humanitarian Action. *Disasters* 37(supplement 2), S139–S150.

Karlsrud, J. and da Costa, D.F. (2013). Invitation Withdrawn: Humanitarian Action, United Nations Peacekeeping, and State Sovereignty in Chad. *Disasters* 37(supplement 2), S171–S187.

Kinne, B. J. (2005). Decision making in Autocratic Regimes: A Poliheuristic Perspective. *International Studies Perspectives* 6, 114–128.

Knudsen, O. F. (2001). Post-Copenhagen Security Studies: Desecuritizing Securitization. *Security Dialogue* 32(3), 355–368.

Kumbamu, A. (2021). Saffron Fascism: The Conflux of Hindutva Ultra-nationalism, Neoliberal Extractivism, and the Rise of Authoritarian Populism in Modi's India. In: Berberoglu, B. (ed.). *The Global Rise of Authoritarianism in the 21st Century: Crisis of Neoliberal Globalization and the Nationalist Response.* New York, NY: Routledge.

Linz, J. J. (2000 [1975]). *Totalitarian and Authoritarian Regimes.* Boulder, CO: Lynne Rienner Publishers.

Petras, J. and Veltmeyer, H. (2021). The Latin American Politics of Neoliberal Authoritarianism. In: Berberoglu, B. (ed.). *The Global Rise of Authoritarianism in the 21st Century: Crisis of Neoliberal Globalization and the Nationalist Response.* New York, NY: Routledge.

Rhodes, B. (2021). *After the Fall: The Rise of Authoritarianism in the World we've Made.* London: Bloomsbury.

Schmitt, C. (2005 [1922]). *Political Theology: Four Chapters on the Concept of Sovereignty.* Chicago, IL: University of Chicago Press.

Spector, A. (2021). Neoliberalism, Authoritarianism, and Resistance in the United States in the Age of Trump. In: Berberoglu, B. (ed.). *The Global Rise of Authoritarianism in the 21st Century: Crisis of Neoliberal Globalization and the Nationalist Response*. New York: Routledge.

Svolik, M. W. (2012). *The Politics of Authoritarian Rule*. Cambridge: Cambridge University Press.

Tansey, O. (2016). *The International Politics of Authoritarian Rule*. Oxford: Oxford University Press.

UN SC. (2013). Briefers Highlight: 'Prevailing Disrespect' for International Humanitarian Law as Security Council Considers Protection of Civilians in Armed Conflict. SC/11097. 20 August.

Zakaria, F. (2004). *The Future of Freedom: Illiberal Democracy at Home and Abroad*. New York, NY: W. W. Norton & Company.

1

THE FRICTION OF PRACTICE – REFLECTING ON THE MÉDECINS SANS FRONTIÈRES EXPERIENCE WITH 'AUTHORITARIAN REGIMES'

Sean Healy* and Andrew J Cunningham

Introduction

Humanitarian international non-governmental organisations (INGOs)[1] provide assistance to populations living in the midst of man-made crises, 'natural' disasters, or armed conflicts. The goal is to save lives, alleviate suffering, and help restore dignity for those suffering from a crisis. Humanitarian INGOs, however, do not implement their activities in isolation and operate within a complex global and domestic political environment. The subject of humanitarian negotiations with states has attracted considerable attention over the last decades, from both researchers and practitioners. It is easy to divine why this is the case: in most situations, humanitarians are entirely dependent on state consent if they are to do their jobs. This is not only at the level of legal principle (the requirement for 'state consent' to the delivery of humanitarian assistance that is contained in international humanitarian law) but also at the level of practice, as in hundreds of different, daily ways, humanitarians need the cooperation of government officials – for customs clearance, tax matters, travel permissions, visas, work permits, registration, international bank transfers, and so on.

One main focus of humanitarian researchers and practitioners has been to better understand and analyse state practices in relation to humanitarians and what motivates them – why and how, for example, they might seek to restrict agencies' presence in the country, what their political aims might be in relation to a given population sub-group on their territory, how their attitude to humanitarians intersects with their attitudes towards civil society as a whole, or even simply how the specific government actually operates. This line of enquiry will assist humanitarian practice if it allows humanitarians

DOI: 10.4324/9781003316541-2

to better understand a government's positions, interests, and needs and thus allows them to better prepare and conduct negotiations with governments. This is all the more needed when relations are 'difficult'.

Difficult relations is a subjective term but could certainly describe those situations where governments place barriers to access, for both humanitarian organisations and populations in need, of various levels of severity and where government-INGO negotiations are tense, slow, and often opaque. In such situations, INGOs complain of government intransigence and struggle to develop an appropriate negotiation strategy. It is also a given that each state is different and that the levels of difficulty in government relations can range from openness to mere suspicion to hostility.

To look more deeply into this topic, researchers from Médecins Sans Frontières (MSF) launched a research project to examine MSF's engagement with governments where 'humanitarian space' is restricted and where governments are suspicious or even hostile to the presence of international humanitarian actors. One aim is to develop a well-articulated and defined spectrum, from most to least hostile, upon which operational contexts can be placed. The most productive set of contexts to research are those in the middle of the spectrum, where the relationship is difficult but not untenable. Nevertheless, input from case studies of the other extremes of the spectrum is also helpful with the overall analysis.

Humanitarian engagement with states that impose restrictions varies considerably. First, there might be weaknesses in the engagement with specific state agencies. In some places, humanitarians must negotiate with specific ministries or agencies of the state that are responsible for administering, and also policing, humanitarian INGOs (such as Sudan's Humanitarian Affairs Commission). Second, there might be problems arising from states' relationships with civil societies, and restrictions on humanitarians can be seen as only a subset of restrictions being placed on civil society institutions generally. In others, there might be variations based on the place of origin (local or international), the nature of the organisation (humanitarian, development, or human rights), political complexion (perceived as pro- or anti-government), and so on. And finally, there might be problems arising from a lack of adequate contextual understanding. In some places, humanitarians are associated with specific political or religious agendas, such as foreign intervention or proselytisation, even without their full knowledge or understanding.

As well as lessons learned from specific case studies, the research project theorises the humanitarian INGO – state relationship in general. Tactical guidance on negotiations is useful but is made more robust if set against a strategic understanding of how the organisation, as an international humanitarian NGO, approaches and conceptualises sovereign states and the governments which represent them.

It should be noted that the perspective taken in this MSF research study is to examine practices rather than regimes. Glasius (2018, 517) defines authoritarian practices as:

> patterns of action that sabotage accountability to people over whom a political actor exerts control, or their representatives, by means of secrecy, disinformation and disabling voice. These are distinct from illiberal practices, which refer to patterned and organised infringements of individual autonomy and dignity. Although the two kinds of practice often go together in political life, the difference lies in the type of harm effected: authoritarian practices primarily constitute a threat to democratic processes, while illiberal practices are primarily a human rights problem.

To investigate the topic, we chose a range of case studies, from Bangladesh to the Kurdistan Region of Iraq (KRI) to Italy to Chad, to complement the traditional analytical focus on 'strong states', which are often extreme cases. This chapter reviews the research's mid-point findings and seeks to demonstrate how an organisation goes about defining the research question.

Before solving the riddle of how INGOs should best engage with states, however, it is important to understand both how states view and engage with INGOs and the global context of humanitarian action against, and within which all actors operate. The next section will review the concept of the state before the chapter addresses how INGOs approach them.

Negotiating with states – an inherently fraught endeavour[2]

There is a wide spectrum of state types, but few states are on the extremes – either deeply authoritarian or truly liberal democracies. Most states are in the middle of the spectrum. The task is to define the parameters of the spectrum of state types. Rather than an academic discussion of political concepts, this should be a practice-driven exercise as INGOs operate in the real world and interact with actual rather than ideal states. The key is to find ways to better understand the states with which organisations must work. As a starting point for this discussion, key political concepts must be described.

Defining the concept of the state is problematic. The state could more rightly be considered 'an idea or cluster of concepts, values, and ideas about social existence', than an objective reality (Vincent, 1987, 4). Each state develops in a unique historical, geographical, cultural, and religious context and will focus on different aspects of what it means to be a state. Although the modern state system has been greatly influenced by Western political and philosophical developments, there are regional and national differences which inform attitudes to the roles and responsibilities of states. This is important to keep in mind when Western-oriented INGOs encounter non-Western political heritages.

Even more than for the definition of a state, sovereignty is an ambiguous concept (Biersteker and Weber, 1996). Sovereignty can be understood as two core ideas: That there is 'no final and absolute authority exist[ing] elsewhere', that is, outside the state, and that 'there is a final and absolute political authority in the political community', that is, internally (Hinsley, 1986, 26). Therefore, an ideal state is 'sovereign' in the sense that there is no higher *external* authority and that *internally,* the state is the final decision-making body. A state can be considered a political entity which is acknowledged internationally to represent a defined geographical area and/or population. It is understood that states are autonomous, that other states should not interfere in their affairs unless under special circumstances, such as UN-mandated interventions, and that all states are equal – *de jure*, if not de facto. States can decide whether they will abide by international legal standards, treaties, and norms of behaviour of the international community of states or participate in international political structures, such as the United Nations.[3]

But domestically what is a state? In Max Weber's definition, 'a state is a human community that (successfully) claims the monopoly of the legitimate use of physical force within a given territory' (Weber, 1946). Coercive authority is an essential element holding a state together (Laski, 1935), and not coincidentally, violence is a major element in the creation of a humanitarian crisis. Another key aspect is that public and private spheres are different constructs (Dunleavy and O'Leary, 1987) and that states claim 'hegemony or predominance within a given territory over all other associations, organizations or groups within it' (Vincent, 1987, 19). A state considers itself above society and will regard its relations with civil society from a political and instrumentalist viewpoint.

For INGOs, external conceptions of statehood are less important than an understanding that political actors use coercion domestically to meet their political objectives and that the public sphere is often dominated by the state. This chapter is concerned with this domestic understanding of sovereignty, which is the most important locus of concern for the relationship between states and humanitarian INGOs.

It is also important to be clear about the use of the terms 'state' and 'government'. A government is made up of individuals who guide a state's apparatus at any given time (Vincent, 1987). Governments are 'composed of political actors who are simultaneously members of social sectors, classes, and interest groups; they have their own ideological, ethical, and religious beliefs; their own programmatic priorities; and their specific views on how best to fuse these complex personal traits with their roles as state officials' (Pempel, 1992, 118). Therefore, a government is a collection of officials holding formal power at a given time and place and is the only existing political entity which can be directly engaged with by INGOs.

Digging deeper into these concepts, Carl Schmitt discussed the idea of prerogative in relation to governmental decision-making: 'The sovereign is he who decides on the state of exception' (1985, 5). This idea of deciding on a 'state of exception' – and the related prerogative to make decisions based on this state of exception – is at the core of the interaction between states and INGOs and can be correlated to a context of humanitarian crisis. These are cases where different rules of conduct apply in reaction to an overriding emergency. Such humanitarian emergencies, therefore, create political and security environments in which governments will act outside the normal rules of state behaviour, as defined domestically and internationally.

An additional aspect of Schmitt's work which is particularly relevant to this type of research is the 'friend and enemy' distinction (2007, 26). To Schmitt, the friend and enemy distinction is independent of other judgements, such as 'good and evil', and does not 'draw upon all of those moral, aesthetic, economic, or other distinctions' (ibid, 26, 27) which are sometimes attributed to states. When considering the approach that a government takes in reacting to the presence of an external agent on its territory, Schmitt's 'friends and enemies' dichotomy may be the most useful as it allows for one actor to define another actor as a stranger, an outsider, an 'other'. The designations must be determined by the political actors themselves, establishing a conflictual relationship in the process. In humanitarian crises, which can be understood as states of exception where normal rules do not apply, INGOs, as external agents, can easily be considered to be 'enemies'.

The primary relationship under consideration in the research programme discussed in this chapter is one of negotiation. In such a negotiation structure, each side has its own objectives and interests which must be met and considered. For a humanitarian INGO a condition of being labelled an enemy and a threat is hopefully replaced by a condition of being seen as a legitimate actor with whom a government can negotiate, if not a 'friend'. The objective of negotiation is thus to create this positive discursive space. For INGOs engaged in negotiations, the primary objective is to create the 'space' – physically, legally, and morally – for an identified population in crisis to access humanitarian assistance safely and securely. Reference to humanitarian principles is often used in this negotiation and can be considered a fundamental part of humanitarian norms, if not increasingly contested. Governments are concerned with issues of national security, the social contract with their populations, their international standing, and their sovereignty, amongst other issues.

On the other side of the table are the humanitarians, but what do they stand for? Humanitarianism can be 'conceived of as an unchallenged good characterised by impartial charity for a common humanity and something which transgresses the confines of state sovereignty' (Campbell, 1998, 498). One should be reminded, though, of Schmitt's warning that 'we have come to recognize that the political is the total, and as a result we know that any decision about whether something is *unpolitical* is always a *political* decision, irrespective of who decides and what reasons are advanced' [italics in the original] (1985, 2). Given the type of work they do, INGOs are intimately involved with highly political issues, and their activities will have political consequences which will be reacted to by the main political participants in the crisis.

One framework for understanding how states deny access to humanitarian organisations describes three types of denial: Bureaucratic obstruction, the intensity of the hostilities itself (insecurity), and targeted violence against humanitarian personnel and theft (Labonte and Edgerton, 2013, 39). But the important question is why states would want to deny access to INGOs. Labonte and Edgerton argue that state behaviour is not ad hoc – denial 'can constitute a valuable policy tool for national authorities and reflects prevailing perceptions of the norms associated with humanitarian access and civilian protection' (ibid, 40). In other words, a state's political goals inform a state's policy response to humanitarian action.

In conclusion, both states and humanitarian INGOs come to a humanitarian crisis with their own normative reference points, and these will almost always be in tension. States, of course, have the upper hand in decision-making as they are sovereign actors with coercive authority over international actors. Negotiations start here.

Inward and outward forces at play for humanitarian INGOs

Within the understanding of the state and sovereignty elaborated upon above, we must situate the humanitarian sector. Humanitarianism as a concept changes over time, and the humanitarian sector faces an ever-changing set of pressures – some internal and some external. To better understand these pressures, it helps to look at them as centripetal and centrifugal forces. Centripetal forces are those which keep the humanitarian sector coherent, and centrifugal forces are those which challenge central tenets of humanitarianism. States and humanitarian actors both have a role to play in challenging or reinforcing these forces.

A non-exhaustive list of forces directed at the humanitarian section by states includes shifting interpretations of international humanitarian law (IHL); changing definitions of what constitutes criminal acts and who are criminals, inclusive of counter-terrorism laws; and fluctuating views on the space within which civil society actors must operate. These all link to state conceptions of sovereignty – what states consider within their purview to decide and have the coercive power to implement and impose unless otherwise constrained by enforceable international norms.

Philosophical debates about natural law notwithstanding, at a pragmatic level, international legal structures are state-made. IHL is what states make of it. Domestic and international political and security trends explain how IHL is interpreted and engaged with more than moral and ethical considerations. This applies as well to the issue of criminalisation of aid and aid actors. States decide what a crime is and who criminals are based on national political and security requirements. Counter-terrorism laws are a prime example. The shrinking of civic space is intimately related to all of these trends, as the balance between state and civil society actors is ever-changing. It should also be noted that there is a large collection of civil society actors outside the aid sector, implying a much larger question about how states engage with their societies.

Concerning these themes, to a large extent, the literature is less important than the practice. The important point is to follow the changes in how states actually manage these issues – nationally, regionally, and globally. The theoretical literature on sovereignty as well is not up to the task of assisting humanitarian INGOs in understanding *how* particular states interpret and operationalise these fundamental political concepts. This argues for a practice-oriented approach.

On the side of the humanitarian sector, debates have increasingly called into question the viability of the 'humanitarian project' as it is currently understood. Although sometimes driven by internal questioning, such as the protracted debates about the role of humanitarian principles, most often larger socio-economic, political, and security debates led by states and their proxies have demanded a response. The humanitarian literature is increasingly focused on issues such as the grand bargain, localisation, resilience, the nexus, decolonising aid, diversity, equity, and inclusion (DEI) – all of which demand a reinterpretation, sometimes fundamental, of how INGOs work and act. The sanctity of humanitarian principles – humanity, independence, neutrality, and impartiality – is routinely questioned; the Western identity of the majority of the large international agencies is often seen as a liability; and the contexts within which humanitarian actors work are perceived to be increasingly more dangerous. As well, serious concerns have been expressed over aid 'politicisation', when states use aid and aid actors for political purposes, and over aid 'securitisation', when aid actors are integrated into national security risk assessments (Cunningham, 2018).

Will centripetal forces within the humanitarian sector keep it a coherent whole given these disruptive forces?

Understanding the exact and specific points of friction

Having outlined some of the core beliefs of states and humanitarians and suggested some of the ways that they view each other, it is necessary to analyse the actual practices which inform the central question about state – INGO relations. Our research work, or at least its 'pointy end', focuses on 'engagement' and 'negotiation' and the actual meeting place between states and humanitarians. This section will frame the research question in reference to the findings from the survey of key concepts and debates. The issues to be explored can be summarised in the following statements:

States have their own views on how to engage with international aid actors seeking to implement projects on their territory

Key reference points which must be kept in mind are sovereignty and the nature of politics. States, represented in practice by government officials, will have political, security, social, and economic agendas in place against which international actors must negotiate. Government officials will naturally determine who are friends and who are enemies. Humanitarian organisations must analyse the context properly in order to understand how a particular state approaches international actors and frames its political and security agendas. There is a need for a proper analysis of not only what the policies, rules, and regulations are but also of the perspectives and attitudes of governments to foundational concepts such as sovereignty and politics. Although it is important to develop a generic understanding of 'statehood' as a reference point, each state is unique. This research project, therefore, frames the questioning of states against, for example, the friends and enemies dichotomy and the lenses of politicisation and securitisation, as well as understandings of politics and sovereignty.

Each state has its own historical and cultural understanding of aid

Beyond the dictates of current security policies and political demands, each country has its own history with aid and aid organisations. Current policies, however informed by contemporary events, are never made in isolation of what has gone before. The research therefore must explore these issues through methodologies such as public discourse analysis in order to understand the 'narrative arc' communicated by the state concerning aid and aid actors.

States are influenced by international trends in aid policy

States learn from each other, and so it is important to contextualise a particular government's response within a larger environment of debates. Regional and global trends inform a government's engagement with international actors. This includes trends in international and refugee law. The research must keep in mind the trends from the state's perspective, outside the inward facing debates within the aid sector. It will be important to look at the genealogy of state engagement and where each state fits on the spectrum of engagement options.

Humanitarian aid is not static as a concept, and the humanitarian norm is ever adapting

The humanitarian sector develops swiftly, and states pay attention. Much of the rhetoric coming from the aid sector is directed at and in response to states and their concerns. Aid cannot be offered in isolation, and even the most 'beneficiary'-focused policy will have implications for how government officials engage with aid agencies. Finding ways to better help people in need will not always win the favour of a government. When analysing trends in the aid sector, developing policies and approaches must be seen from the standpoint of a state – generically and specifically. In actual practice, as aid organisations decide on their perspective on emerging trends, a worldview must be articulated and communicated to a government in order to differentiate one agency from another. But to a large extent, when governments situate humanitarian organisations into their political world, a generic approach is taken. INGOs, after all, are rarely the primary concern of a government, even if the humanitarian crisis is at the forefront of the agenda.

INGOs must find the actual locus of engagement

The most important objective is to understand how any given state – within its historical and cultural heritage, in relation to its domestic and international political worldview, and against its previous engagements with INGOs responding to crises – intersects with humanitarian norms as developed over time by states, donors, and humanitarian NGOs themselves. These state and INGO norms are almost always in tension and form an ever-progressing dialectic. Analysing this dialectic – the clashing of norms resulting in a negotiated relationship – is the locus of our research. Situating properly the locus of engagement is the first step to negotiating an acceptable outcome for humanitarian organisations seeking to offer humanitarian assistance to populations living in the midst of a humanitarian crisis. Our argument, then, is for treating each case of interaction between a state and humanitarian NGOs as culturally and politically distinct and specific and to understand that interaction within its given context of differing and potentially clashing agendas between the two sets of actors. As a base-line for the research project, we performed a historical review of the most egregious cases of tension between MSF and 'strong states'. The next section will provide a brief history of MSF's engagements with governments exhibiting authoritarian practices.

The MSF experience – a historical review

MSF has its own long and complicated history of engaging with various governments considered to be 'authoritarian'. In doing so, it has often had to wrestle with a critical contradiction. As an international NGO, it needs the authorisations and permissions of such governments to work on their national territories, and so needs good working relationships with them. But as a humanitarian organisation, it provides assistance to people who have often been victimised by these very governments, and indeed, its medical teams have often directly witnessed government actors, such as militaries, commit atrocities of various kinds. This contradiction has been difficult to manage, to say the least, and has often been unresolvable.

One of the earliest, and perhaps the most archetypal, moments of crisis MSF faced with an authoritarian government occurred in 1984–1986 in Ethiopia (Binet, 2005). The military-led government of the Derg, led by Mengistu Haile Mariam, was fighting against an insurgency in the country's north, led by Tigrayan and Eritrean national liberation movements. In 1983, a famine broke out in the country, and MSF, alongside many other humanitarian organisations, worked desperately to provide relief to people who were starving. Unlike other agencies, however, MSF judged that the crisis was the result of a deliberate war-fighting strategy of the Derg and that, by silently providing assistance, humanitarian organisations were bolstering and therefore complicit in this strategy. It committed to doing no such thing, and the president of MSF France publicly denounced the Derg government's famine policy. In response, the government expelled MSF France from the country, the first such occasion in the organisation's history.

In the decades since, relations with the Ethiopian state have been through moments of calm and productive work, moments of frustration, and moments of abject crisis, regardless of which government was in power. In 2008 and 2009, during the years of Meles Zenawi's prime ministership, conflict in the Ogaden region caused widespread hunger and suffering among the civilian population and significant problems for MSF and other humanitarian organisations, including the placing of teams under house arrest and the blocking of medical supply into the region. In June 2021, during the conflict between the government of Prime Minister Abiy Ahmed and Tigrayan regional forces, three MSF employees travelling in an ambulance looking for casualties from the fighting were killed in circumstances which seemed to implicate Ethiopian government soldiers, and MSF demands for accountability met with little success. In July 2021, one of MSF's operational sections was suspended in the country for alleged breaches of administrative policy on work permits for foreigners and on the importation of communications equipment, and for charges of 'spreading misinformation' on social media about the government's handling of the conflict.

During the conflict in Darfur, in neighbouring Sudan, the government led by Omar al-Bashir imposed a strict set of controls on humanitarians, which made work in the large IDP camps on government territory difficult and even outright impossible in areas controlled by armed opposition groups, such as the East Jebel Mara. A public MSF report in 2005 on the widespread incidence of rape committed during the conflict led to the arrest of two MSF officials. And in 2009, after the indictment of Bashir by the International Criminal Court for war crimes, two operational sections of MSF were expelled from the country, as were 12 other humanitarian organisations. They were not permitted to return to the country until after the overthrow of Bashir, and a new civilian-led government took his place.

In Myanmar, MSF began its work in 1992, during the years of rule of the State Law and Order Restoration Council, a military junta. There were few international humanitarian organisations working in the country at the time, and MSF's work proceeded slowly and carefully so as not to upset the government. In 1993, MSF started working in Rakhine, home of a persecuted minority, the Rohingya, who had been stripped of their citizenship by the state, first by focusing on malaria, which was a major public health threat in the region. Large-scale treatment programmes for HIV and tuberculosis were also initiated in the states of Shan and Kachin and in the country's main city, Yangon, during a time when the government had zero willingness to itself address these diseases. Carefully worded MSF reports attest to the various restrictions the government imposed on these efforts, including in one case prohibiting entry to an entire state considered too sensitive (MSF, 2008, 2012).

During an upsurge of violence against the Rohingya in 2012–2014, MSF was suspended from operating in Rakhine for nine months by the government after confirming that it had treated victims of a massacre. The subsequent year-long process of negotiating with the government for an end to the suspension sparked intense internal debate within MSF about whether it would be forced to choose to abandon either the Rohingya in Rakhine or the HIV and tuberculosis (TB) patients under its care (Binet, 2020), although fortunately neither option eventuated. When a military campaign began in 2017 to force the Rohingya out of the country, MSF and other humanitarian organisations were in effect confined to their own compounds due to government restrictions on movement and other administrative requirements.

MSF began operating in Russia and the new states of the Former Soviet Union in the early 1990s. These were years of political and economic crisis and sometimes open conflict (in Moldova, Nagorno-Karabakh, and Tajikistan, for example) that followed the break-up of the Soviet Union. The brutal civil conflict in Chechnya laid bare the pivotal role security plays in humanitarian operations. Through the two wars and inter-war period, the threat of kidnapping and extreme violence against the population as well as humanitarian workers remained very high. MSF suffered its share of kidnappings and serious security incidents in the North Caucasus. International actors opted for a 'remote-control' working methodology, to localise as much as possible the work to decrease the risks taken by international staff, who were the most threatened with kidnappings. In this system, expatriates managed operations from a distance and only made periodic surprise 'flash-visits' to Chechnya, sometimes for only a couple of hours at a time. The security risk assessment pointed to a lesser risk to national staff and yet still mandated a very low-profile approach to operations. The context remained opaque and defined by the politics of fear. It was an open question, where the state was situated in such an environment. If Chechnya was a case where fear prevailed, it was unclear from whence threats came. In such a situation, it was impossible to know who the real negotiation partner was. Was the state a protector and partner, or a threat and a cynical manipulator? In such contexts, no actors could be trusted, and negotiations were implemented less at the organisa-tional level than personally by the staff working locally.

In Turkmenistan, a decade of work in two of the country's regions came to an end in 2010 when MSF came to the conclusion that government health authorities were pushing misinformation about the truth of the population's health and were violating medical-ethical standards of care so egregiously that remaining present would be a form of complicity. MSF issued a public report denouncing the government and withdrew from the country (MSF, 2010). Complicity has also been a question when operating in Belarus implement-ing tuberculosis (TB) programming. When does working with the Ministry of Health become problematic within a harshly controlled political environ-ment? In Uzbekistan, both during the reign of President Islam Karimov and during the partial liberalisation that has followed, MSF has worked in the western province of Karakalpakstan, first addressing the health consequences of the Aral Sea disaster and then treating tuberculosis patients, including car-rying out a clinical trial for a new TB drug. Despite the difficulties that many international NGOs have in engaging with the Uzbek government, MSF had been able to demonstrate the value of its medical relevance, sufficient to be able to work there relatively successfully (del Valle and Healy, 2013).

In Sri Lanka, over the years of civil war, MSF was faced with a government which was expert in outwardly adhering to the rules and norms of war and humanitarian negotiations. Although often difficult, negotiations resulted in (albeit limited) operational access during much of the war. The end period of the war in 2008–2009, however, brought a break-down in relations, as the GoSL was focused on ending a decades-long war and did not have the incli-nation to allow international actors to interfere with the final prosecution of the war. One lesson from the Sri Lankan experience is that states of excep-tion are real and will define the state – INGO relationship. The GoSL could effectively define when the dictates of the war effort took precedence over humanitarian norms and situate international actors in a severely limited operational and advocacy space. Another lesson is how big a role discourse plays in creating friends and enemies. The press and governmental proxies were effectively utilised to box civil society actors in when needed.

Some contexts, such as North Korea and Eritrea, have continually stymied MSF and almost all other humanitarian actors. Such totalitarian states have proven impossible to work within in any effective way, as much as INGOs attempt negotiations.

Several themes emerge from this brief historical overview. One is the significant role played by MSF's public communications in determining its relationships with these various governments. On several occasions, MSF witnessed situations it considered to be violations of basic norms of humanity, such as massacres, rape, or forced famines, and felt compelled to speak out publicly – and suffered repressive measures from the governments named as a result, which prevented it from working in a particular region or the country as a whole. This dilemma between speaking out and continued operational access has been central to generations of tortured internal debate in the organisation. While sometimes falsely dichotomised, as though they are always an either-or choice, it is easy to understand why: the ethical obligations of medical personnel in conflict zones are numerous but rarely ever clear, and it is easy for these obligations (to save lives, to speak truth to power, to provide medical care above all) to pull in different directions.

Another is the difficulty of negotiating with a government on the terms for access to particular population groups that a government considers to be an 'enemy' or at least suspect in some way. This might mean areas outright controlled by armed opposition groups (such as in Darfur, Sudan) or simply the home of discriminated-against communities (such as in Rakhine, Myanmar, the Tamils in the north of Sri Lanka, or the Chechens in Chechnya). Sometimes, this was in high-profile ways, such as by simply declaring certain regions off-limits, but often it was in less obvious but not less effective ways, such as by imposing such high administrative barriers that access became de facto too hard to achieve or making a context so dangerous for humanitarian actors as to be inaccessible. Regardless of the exact ways they have gone about it, these authoritarian governments have made their preferences known. They seem to consistently regard the very existence of such zones as dire threats to their sovereignty. They have little or no interest in acceding to the demands of non-government organisations to work there, as hard as that might be to accept for the NGOs involved.

A third theme can be found not so much in the moments of crisis named here but in the years between them. These governments have not been impossible to negotiate with. Some of MSF's largest operations worldwide have been conducted in Ethiopia, for example, and its commitment to treating tuberculosis patients in the countries of the Soviet Union has been continuously functional over decades. MSF worked in Sri Lanka for decades during the war and has remained in Russia since the early 1990s. When interests between MSF and these governments have coincided, such as when these governments have wanted MSF's medical capacities to meet a particular public health need (for example, in Belarus), then successful programmes have resulted. While the eye might be drawn to those moments when MSF publicly spoke of matters of grand humanitarian principle, the daily reality has been a much more pragmatic one. MSF has usually been quite prepared to compromise its principles when it negotiates with governments if it smooths the way towards accessing a population it wants to assist; its researchers have even published a book admitting just that (Magone, Neuman, and Weissman, 2011).

This foregoing historical review illustrates that MSF has found it difficult to negotiate with states it considers in some way 'authoritarian', and especially so during periods of conflict and crisis. This historical understanding, however, suggests more questions than answers. Where does this leave the organisation in dealing with current realities and, most importantly, preparing for the future? How can an analysis of the organisation's engagement with authoritarian regimes help future negotiations? The current research programme aims to expand the analysis and sharpen the conceptualisation of state–INGO negotiations within an environment of authoritarian and illiberal practices rather than regimes.

Not 'strong' or 'weak' states, but practises in which all states engage

For the last decade or two, MSF has avoided speaking about 'authoritarian' governments, much less 'authoritarian regimes'.[4] Instead, its analytical categories have been more vague, speaking instead of 'strong states' or sometimes 'assertive states'. In large part, this came from a growing belief that more and more governments were imposing authoritarian-style restrictions on humanitarian work and that humanitarians could face threats of control, manipulation, suppression, and even outright violence not just from dictatorships but also from democracies. The evidence seems to mount for such a conviction, whether one looks at the policies of Africa's largest democracy, Nigeria, in its war in the north-east or at those of Italy and Greece in seeking to close their southern and eastern borders to refugees.

A concept of 'strong states' also partly carried the implication that MSF had previously considered some states 'weak', or at least permissive, when it came to matters of where, how, and when humanitarians could work on their national territories, and that this was increasingly no longer the case. This is more arguable – even highly fragile states seem more than capable of enforcing their own preferences on humanitarians when situation dictates. The world's newest and possibly weakest state, South Sudan, for example, has a well-developed regime of its own to control humanitarian organisations; it even named its key institution after its ancestor in Khartoum, the Humanitarian Affairs Commission.

Hence, driven by experience, there is growing interest for forms of analysis which focus less on the type of regime that humanitarians face, be it authoritarian, democratic, or hybrid, and more on the kinds of practices they see when they engage with states, regardless of type. Following Glasius, the research project, therefore, is less focused on regimes than practices. Moving beyond the focus on the hardest cases as presented in the historical review, the present research findings from our four case studies – the Kurdish Region of Iraq, Bangladesh, Italy, and Chad – will build on this historical analysis. The findings will place the organisation better in dealing with a range of authoritarian practices in a variety of states. We can, however, already look towards what we will be able to do with such findings. While only two cases have been completed so far (the Kurdish Region of Iraq and Bangladesh) and more work is still to be done on conducting the cases and analysing the results, a few questions already arise.[5]

Both the Kurdish Region of Iraq and Bangladesh could be classified as 'hybrid' regimes which mix aspects of democratic and authoritarian functioning, and both states certainly do show a range of practices which could be classified as 'authoritarian' or 'illiberal' according to Glasius' definitions. Illiberal practices principally affect the human rights of people on the state's territory, and here humanitarians have seen a variety of examples in these two contexts, such as harsh restrictions on the freedom of movement of refugees and internally displaced people. Authoritarian practices aim at controlling and suppressing information, and in both cases, there have been severe restrictions on the freedom of the press and to some extent also on humanitarians speaking out about what they see. There were also cases where humanitarian NGOs did not need to feel the full dose of a 'practice' in order to learn a lesson; for example, in one case, some NGOs had supported a (legal) civil rights march by refugees; the government viewed this as an unwarranted interference in the politics of the country and made its displeasure known through a mix of administrative ('authoritarian') measures against the few it considered ringleaders and through a 'chilling' of relations with the humanitarian NGO sector as a whole; NGOs subsequently were much more careful about supporting refugee organisations.

However, both cases also show that the boundaries between what is and what is not an 'authoritarian' practice are not always clear. Both the Kurdish Region of Iraq and Bangladesh have administrative systems in place which, to varying extents, coordinate and control humanitarian NGOs. Each state has a rather elaborate system – formal or informal – for ensuring that all charitable funds coming from outside the country are directed towards the types of activities that it wants to see, such as immediate emergency relief, and away from those it does not, such as assistance of a longer-term nature that might create expectations among refugees that they will be allowed to stay. Certainly, humanitarian NGOs do feel this system as a bureaucratic imposition that hinders their work, but does that make it 'authoritarian'? Or rather, is it simply a form of state regulatory practice, of the kind that many states all over the world impose on charitable activities, often in cumbersome and heavy-handed ways? Or is it a form of practice ostensibly imposed on humanitarians but in service to an illiberal practice, given that its main object seems to be to support a policy which denies formal, legal refugee status to refugees on its territory? Or is this practice a mix of all of these things?

Further, the two cases completed so far show how different the perceptions of specific practices are for both government officials and humanitarian workers. Humanitarian workers tended to view any and all of the administrative measures applied to them (for example, travel permits or reporting requirements) as 'authoritarian', as a sign of suspicion or even hostility towards them by the state, and as a warning that some definitive rupture in relations was due. Government officials, however, tended to view such measures as simply them doing their assigned job; in their view, these practices were not about the state avoiding accountability but about the state ensuring the accountability of NGOs to them. In addition, it was evident that, while humanitarian workers concentrated overwhelmingly on today's problems, government officials worked at two levels, a 'tactical' level and a 'strategic' one, and while a 'tactical' level official might communicate suspicion to a humanitarian worker, a more 'strategic' level official might be seeking to communicate something quite different. Indeed, in both cases, the more senior the government official, the more long-term their vision was of the relationship with humanitarian NGOs, and the more they aligned that relationship with much wider, even historical, policy goals of the state – for example, for improved international recognition or for increased international community attention to a protracted crisis. Does this not mean we should ensure we open our eyes to the breadth of state practices, beyond simply 'authoritarian' and 'illiberal' ones?

Conclusion

One of the goals of this investigation of state practice in relation to humanitarian INGOs was to define a 'spectrum' on which various states could be placed as a heuristic device to assist practitioners in considering the various dynamics they confront when they seek to negotiate with state representatives. While more work needs to be done to achieve this goal, we can here venture some initial thoughts on how to do so.

On the basis of MSF's historical experiences, which we reviewed here, and on the case studies described above, it does seem that Glasius' description of authoritarian and illiberal practices is a useful grounding on which to construct a spectrum of state practice. Many states have exhibited behaviours designed to constrain or prevent humanitarian organisations from seeing, and then speaking about, what happens in various situations of crisis – fitting the definition of an 'authoritarian' practice. And many also have engaged in practices which restrict or deny the human rights of people living in crisis situations, such as the right to move freely or the right to equal treatment before the law, and this would fit the definition of an 'illiberal' practice.

Further, it can be said that these practices are not confined to regime types which are themselves considered 'authoritarian' – and instead do show themselves in countries considered a kind of 'hybrid' or 'mixed' regime type and even in 'democratic' regimes. The hardening of punitive border regimes and the criminalisation of humanitarian NGOs in the United Kingdom and the European Union is a clear example of the latter case. And, on the contrary, we can also see that at times 'authoritarian regimes' have engaged in 'non-authoritarian' practices and been open, welcoming, and facilitative towards humanitarian INGOs when it suits their perceived needs for their nations.

Several dependencies can perhaps also be advanced about when and how a state engages in such practices. First of all, if a state perceives that a humanitarian organisation in some way threatens its interests, for example by damaging its international reputation, then the risks of some kind of authoritarian practice increase. The intensity of its reaction might depend on how it reads this 'threat' – a threat to its perceived security (such as a suspicion that humanitarians are aiding armed opposition groups) might be treated far more harshly than a threat to its political standing (such as the raising of a controversial issue during a politically inopportune time, such as an election campaign). Further, the approach a state might take to a humanitarian INGO could be considered a product of the approach it takes to the international community as a whole and/or of the approach it takes to the civil society in its own country.

In addition to 'authoritarian' and 'illiberal' practices, however, in our view there is a further set of state practices that need to be placed on a spectrum: those related to governmental regulation of the economy and society in general and of charities and NGOs in particular. These do have some linkage to authoritarian and illiberal practices and can have major impacts on humanitarian INGOs and on people in situations of crisis – we gave several examples where administrative obstacles were placed in the way of humanitarian INGOs with the apparent motive of restricting their presence and their activities. But there will certainly be cases where such regulatory practices are only partially explained by such motivations or not explained by them at all but are rather merely the product of the growth and extension of state regulatory capacities, which in some countries has been rapid. For example, in one country, a humanitarian NGO might find its doctors denied the ability to work not because of some deliberate political motive but simply because the medical registration system imposes such restrictions on all foreign-trained doctors. Or, in another case, a humanitarian agency's problems with the tax authorities might only partially be explained by a more hostile environment for INGOs and be more closely linked to those authorities' new-found interest in closing previously existing loopholes in the tax regulations for foreigners as a whole. It cannot always be assumed that humanitarian INGOs' problems with governmental authorities are motivated by 'authoritarian' aims; sometimes, this is simply how these governments work for everyone. Figuring out what is behind each problem will have to be a matter for specific analysis on each occasion.

Another much-needed line of approach, especially for practitioners, has been to focus specifically on skill formation in the technique of negotiation. The teaching of this technique is usually polyvalent, involving a variety of aspects.[6] A key focus is on learning about interpersonal relations, about understanding that negotiations do not happen between institutions but between people – and that their relationships with each other do matter. A humanitarian negotiator who is technically correct but unsympathetic might end up failing to reach an agreement with a government official where another with a more personal touch succeeds.

Finally, we would argue that humanitarians need to understand themselves better if they are to engage better with governments. Critical self-reflection is also necessary because the uncomfortable truth might turn out to be that the government is right in a particular negotiation and that the humanitarian is not. In the Iraq and Bangladesh research, we heard many complaints from humanitarians about how bureaucratic, how corrupt, how uncaring governments were. But when we spoke to government officials we saw many of those same criticisms mirrored. Many specific examples were provided – humanitarian agencies inflate their numbers of beneficiaries so they can get more money, they say they know what they're doing, but they often don't; they claim to be all about the people, but really they are just protecting their own interests, and so on. Can we really say that criticisms such as these are all false? Doing the right thing is always harder than doing the wrong thing – harder to discern, harder to design, harder to implement. Humanitarians do not help themselves when they enter an engagement with a government filled with moral self-assurance. A much more mindful position is needed.

Notes

1 For simplicity the acronym INGO will be used to refer to the set of international non-governmental organisations which provide humanitarian assistance and of which MSF is a member.

2 Much of this section is based on arguments made in Cunningham (2018).

3 As examples, look at how North Korea and Turkmenistan engage with other states and the UN, and how some states are not signatories to core international conventions, such as the Refugee Convention. But also see the debates on the concepts of universal jurisdiction: https://www.un.org/press/en/2018/gal3571.doc.htm and customary international law: https://www.icrc.org/en/war-and-law/treaties-

customary-law/customary-law. The applicability of international law over states and state authorities is dynamic and ever developing.
4 Buth P (2010), A Line in the Sand: States' restrictions on humanitarian space. MSF, Amsterdam [Internal]. Copy on file with the authors.
5 Jacob Kumar Sarker was the co-researcher for the Bangladesh case study and Mera Jasm Bakr for the Kurdistan Region of Iraq case study.
6 As an example, see Conflict Dynamics International's normative and practitioners handbooks on negotiated access.

References

Biersteker, T. J. and Weber, C. (1996). *State Sovereignty as Social Construct*. Cambridge: Cambridge University Press.

Binet, L. (2005). Famine and forced relocations in Ethiopia 1984-86. CRASH, Paris. Available at: https://www.msf.org/speakingout/famine-and-forced-relocations-ethiopia-1984-1986

Binet, L. (2020). MSF and the Rohingya 1992-2014. CRASH, Paris. Available at: https://www.msf.org/speakingout/msf-and-rohingya-1992-2014

Campbell, D. (1998). Why Fight: Humanitarianism, Principles, and Post-structuralism. *Millennium-Journal of International Studies*, 27(3), 497–521.

Criminalisation of aid applies as much to Western democracies as elsewhere in the world: https://redcross.eu/latest-news/the-eu-must-stop-the-criminalisation-of-solidarity-with-migrants-and-refugees

Cunningham, A. J. (2018). *International Humanitarian NGOs and State Relations: Politics, Principles and Identity*. London: Routledge.

del Valle, H. and Healy, S. (2013). Humanitarian Agencies and Authoritarian States: A Symbiotic Relationship? Disasters 37(supplement 2), S188–S201

Dunleavy, P. and O'Leary, B. (1987). *Theories of the State: The Politics of Liberal Democracy*. London: Macmillan Education.

Glasius, M. (2018). What Authoritarian Is…and Is Not: A Practice Perspective. *International Affairs* 94(3), 515–533.

Hinsley, F. H. (1986). *Sovereignty*. Cambridge: Cambridge University Press.

https://www.refworld.org/docid/487de243c.html

https://www.msf.org/ethiopia-msf-seeks-answers-government-after-new-media-report-killing-its-staff

https://www.theguardian.com/global-development/2021/aug/06/ethiopia-suspends-aid-groups-for-spreading-misinformation

https://reliefweb.int/report/sudan/sudan-arrests-second-aid-worker-rape-report

https://reliefweb.int/report/sudan/harassed-and-risk-plight-humanitarian-aid-northern-sudan

https://www.latimes.com/world/la-xpm-2014-feb-28-la-fg-wn-myanmar-orders-doctors-without-borders-to-cease-operations-20140228-story.html

Labonte, M. T. and Edgerton, A. (2013). Towards a Typology of Humanitarian Access Denial. Third World Quarterly 34, 39–57

Laski, H. J. (1935). *The State in Theory and Practice*. London: George Allen and Unwin.

Magone, C., Neuman, M., and Weissman, F. (eds). (2011). *Humanitarian Negotiations Revealed: The MSF Experience*. London: Hurst.

MSF. (2008). A preventable fate: The failure of ART scale-up in Myanmar. MSF, Amsterdam. Available at: https://msf.hk/en/content/preventable-fate-failure-art-scale-myanmar

MSF. (2010). Turkmenistan's opaque health system. MSF, Amsterdam. Available at: https://www.thelancet.com/journals/lancet/article/PIIS0140673610606034/fulltext

MSF. (2012). Lives in the balance: the urgent need for HIV and TB treatment in Myanmar. MSF, Amsterdam. Available at: https://www.msf.org/report-lives-balance-urgent-need-hiv-and-tb-treatment-myanmar

NRC is the best place to start when considering the implications of counter-terrorism laws on the humanitarian sector: https://www.nrc.no/globalassets/pdf/position-papers/170622-nrc-position-paper_cve-and-humanitarian-action---fv.pdf and https://www.nrc.no/globalassets/pdf/reports/toolkit/nrc_risk_management_toolkit_principled_humanitarian_action2020.pdf

Pempel, T. J. (1992). Restructuring Social Coalitions: State, Society and Regime. In: Torstendahl, R. (ed.). *State Theory and State History*. London: Sage Publications.

Schmitt, C. (1985). *Political Theology: Four Chapters on the Concept of Sovereignty*. Chicago, IL: University of Chicago Press.

Schmitt, C. (2007). *The Concept of the Political*. Chicago, IL: University of Chicago Press.

See, for example, the view from Amnesty International: https://www.amnesty.org/en/latest/news/2019/05/un-catastrophic-failure-as-civilians-ravaged-by-war-violations-70-years-after-geneva-conventions/

See, for example, from OCHA/NRC: https://www.nrc.no/globalassets/pdf/reports/study-of-the-impact-of-donor-counterterrorism-measures-on-principled-humanitarian-action.pdf

See ICVA: https://www.icvanetwork.org/uploads/2021/08/ICVA-Report.pdf; CIVICUS: https://civicus.org/state-of-civil-society-report-2021/ and ICNL: https://www.icnl.org/

See OHCHR: https://www.ohchr.org/EN/Issues/CivicSpace/Pages/ProtectingCivicSpace.aspx

See the "MSF Speaking Out Case Studies" for a thorough archival and historical review of many of the chief episodes in this history: https://www.msf.org/speakingout

The literature on IHL is vast, but an obvious place to start is the ICRC view on trends related to IHL: https://www.icrc.org/en/document/icrc-report-ihl-and-challenges-contemporary-armed-conflicts

This is a long-standing discussion. See, for example, the case of Afghanistan in the early 2000s: https://odihpn.org/publication/the-politicisation-of-humanitarian-aid-and-its-consequences-for-afghans/

Vincent, A. (1987). *Theories of the State*. Oxford: Basil Blackwell.

Weber, M. (1946). Politics as a Vocation. In: Gerth and Wright Mills (eds.). *Max Weber: Essays in Sociology*. New York, NY: Oxford University Press.

---

* After the publication of this chapter my very good friend and long-time colleague, Sean Healy, suddenly passed away. Sean's contribution to our understanding of humanitarian action was immense. Our shared interest in state-INGO engagement had developed over the years and this is tragically one of our last collaborations. Rest in peace my friend.

HUMANiTARiAN ⌣ AUTHORiTARiAN
AUTHORiTARiAN ⌣ HUMANiTARiAN

COMMENTARY

Reflections on discourse

Tom de Kok and Andrew J Cunningham

Introduction

When analysing state engagement with humanitarian actors, methodological choices must be made. Some well-established methodologies include semi-structured interviews and standard context analysis, which involves examining the 'factors and actors' in a humanitarian context. One underutilised methodology is discourse analysis. This is not to say that analysing discourse is absent from other research methodologies; analysing the context within which states engage with international humanitarian actors often involves a historical review of state perceptions of aid, a close reading of documents, and in interviews, one will likely ask questions around what interlocutors have said in public. But although discourse analysis is sometimes incorporated into other methodologies, it is not often used as a structured approach in state engagement research or in operations. In this chapter, we discuss initial findings on the use of discourse analysis in the field as part of the research agenda proposed by Healy and Cunningham. We will explore both the positive and negative aspects of employing this methodology.

What is discourse analysis?

In general, discourse analysis 'looks at patterns of language across texts and considers the relationship between language and the social and cultural contexts in which it is used' and 'considers the ways that the use of language presents different views of the world and different understandings'. Importantly, it also 'considers how these views of the world and identities are constructed

DOI: 10.4324/9781003316541-3

through the use of discourse' (Paltridge, 2006, 2). Texts can take various forms, including written and spoken language, and they can be examined thematically (Cunningham, 2018).

In researching state engagement, the goal is to understand what the government and other key actors have said and how they have said it concerning humanitarian crises and the role of aid actors in their country. Discourse analysis is used to construct a narrative describing governmental attitudes and perceptions towards INGOs. By analysing how governments communicate, what they communicate, and the tone of their communications, researchers gain insight into not only what the government is thinking but also what they intend INGOs to understand. Discourse can be triangulated against actions, rules and regulations, context analysis findings, and information gleaned from conversations with governmental authorities. This approach allows for a comprehensive picture of governmental thoughts, messages, and intentions.

Discourse sources can include formal and informal government communication such as official minutes, policy statements, transcripts from press conferences, and text from proxies, such as friendly newspaper editors. Relevant channels of communication, such as Twitter feeds or guest editorials, can also provide valuable discourse.[1] In some cases, existing discourse analyses may be available and useful. Additionally, discourse can be expressed through actions taken by the government or proxies, such as security incidents which are meant to send a message or formal and informal laws, rules, and regulations that set parameters for INGO action (Cunningham, 2018). By examining discourse broadly, researchers and operators can gain insight into not only what is expressed but also what is assumed and implied.

Themes that can be examined in discourse analysis include:

- How does the government prefer to communicate, e.g., through accusations, argumentation, justification, or cajoling?
- What channels does the government use to communicate with international actors, such as through the press, official statements, actions, or proxies, and are these communications public or private?
- What signals (semiotics) are being communicated through discourse, such as warnings to INGOS to stay in line, to beware of angering the government, or to operate within certain boundaries? In Italy, for example, discourse about INGOs may signal to the public that 'INGOs do not reflect national values or represent a threat to the sovereignty of the nation'.
- Has the government changed its discourse over time, and if so, why? What has remained consistent?
- How does the government's international or regional discourse differ from its domestic discourse, and why?

- Who are the government proxies, such as individuals (businesspeople) or entities (newspapers)?
- What other narratives does the government contribute to, such as the Non-aligned Movement?

How discourse analysis fits into a larger process

Discourse analysis complements other research methodologies and should not be considered in isolation; rather, a robust context analysis should be inclusive of a focus on discourse.

Context analysis is an essential aspect of humanitarian operations that involves assessing various factors such as troop movements, security events, power dynamics, changing boundaries, and interdependencies within the socio-economic and political realms. It also considers the most relevant security, economic, military, political, and cultural actors in the crisis. The goal of this type of analysis is to enable organisations to interact with the humanitarian environment in an informed way and accurately measure the risks and benefits of different alternatives. However, despite its importance, context analysis alone is often insufficient for addressing the complexities of humanitarian work, even when conducted by experienced and dedicated staff.

For example, take a set of related operational questions: Is it possible or appropriate in this context to avoid tension or public differences with the government? If public differences are inevitable, is there a way to limit the procedural or administrative challenges that might arise because of these differences? These questions get at the political nature of humanitarian work and how public opinion and discourse inform a well thought out answer. The objective of context analysis, therefore, is to understand aspects of the context which are relevant to how states engage with INGOs, such as:

- How the government is structured, particularly related to engagement with INGOs – who do INGOs report to, what control mechanisms are in place, who are the informal governmental and extra-governmental actors involved, and what co-ordination mechanisms are in place within the aid community?
- What is the political culture of the country? Is it a closed and opaque system of back-channel decision-making or an open and transparent system of political contestation? Is it a formalised rule-based system or a system based on patronage? Are governmental authorities forthright or evasive when held accountable by international actors?
- What has been the historical engagement of the government with foreign aid actors? What has changed and what has remained consistent over time?
- What has been the historic engagement of INGOs with humanitarian crises in the country? How were INGOs received by the government during these crises?

- How does the country relate regionally and internationally to other states? what are the relevant themes for humanitarians to engage on? and how do they interact with this geo-political environment?

Integrating a discourse analysis methodology into the context analysis process aims to address several frequent shortcomings in the standard approach to understanding the context in complex environments. These include a fatalism that portrays unpredictability as too profound to examine for patterns or an over-reliance on gifted and dedicated locals to provide insight into operations.

Incorporating a discourse methodology into the broader project of understanding and engaging with a place has the potential to serve as an additional pillar, complementing existing approaches and enhancing overall effectiveness. This does not mean a discourse methodology will significantly alter the predictability of risks, nor will it eliminate the need for the contextual understanding that comes with being a local expert. Instead, it can help provide insights into the patterns of communication and power dynamics that may not be immediately visible through other methods.

In our view, therefore, by definition, context analysis includes an examination of discourse.

A proposed discourse methodology

To clarify, integrating a discourse methodology into context analysis involves two dynamic components that work together to inform humanitarian operations. The first component, which could be referred to as *discourse research*, examines media, common themes, the typology of raising these themes, and the historical meaning of repetitive words and gestures. The second component, *active discourse*, involves incorporating these discourse themes into interviews with key stakeholders during humanitarian operations. As thematic elements emerge in research, they are discussed with power brokers, and vice versa. This dual process involves both a survey of available materials and the utilisation of these materials to inform operational discussions in an applied context.

In the MSF research project described in Healy and Cunningham, a practical methodology was proposed which integrated context and discourse analysis. This generic and formal heuristic would rarely be implemented as stated, but is meant as a guide to the sort of steps to be taken:

- The first step is to do a standard context analysis, examining factors and actors, to provide the general background into which decisions about how to go about examining discourse are made. It should be noted, however, that often an informal discourse analysis is naturally, even unconsciously, performed by those analysing the context.

- Following this, a set of keywords to research can be developed, partly informed by the results of the context analysis exercise; examples include humanitarian organisations, humanitarian aid, aid agencies, NGOs, etc. References to a list of specific aid organisations can also be looked for. It is helpful to be as specific as possible.
- A set of research themes will then be developed, which will be informed by the context analysis, for example, government-civil society relations, laws and regulations around the work of international NGOs, and specific humanitarian issues, such as medical care provided by INGOs – this is all about homing into the concepts, words, and themes most important to examine.
- Sources of discourse will be located and researched for these themes and keywords, including government archives, statements, and documents; press articles; relevant 'think tank' products; and any other public documents that were produced by or for the government. It is recommended to go back ten years in the archives if possible.
- After data collection of discourse, categorisation and analysis of the texts and themes to find patterns and meaning behind the discourse should be done, and if needed, the context analysis report will be revised based on input from the discourse analysis exercise.
- The results of the context and discourse analysis will be both written up into a practical report which will guide the field work, such as listing primary and secondary interviewees, places to visit, and themes to explore.
- A list of people to be interviewed or engaged with can follow, as talking with people always helps clarify what the actual situation is.

It is important to highlight the dynamic between basic research and field application for several reasons. Firstly, newcomers to the concept of discourse analysis may perceive it as purely academic rather than a practical tool. Secondly, researching the most salient themes of discourse in a country is only useful when linked to context analysis as a whole. Lastly, sensitively testing and modifying the most important themes occurs in parallel with interlocutor discussions. Therefore, keeping the application in mind during research and integrating findings into meetings is essential for building an analysis that is grounded in discourse rather than solely relying on the standard contextual framework.

Methodological limitations of research on operations

For this chapter, we reflect on using discourse methodology in two vastly different contexts: Iraqi Kurdistan and Italy. Our findings reveal two key insights: First, in some contexts, a rigid application of the methodology may not be effective; second, in other contexts, there may be an overwhelming amount of discourse themes and material, which can pose its own set of challenges. Countries with a penchant for indirect references and symbolic meaning may present the most rewarding yet most difficult contexts for meaningful discourse analysis. Therefore, our findings suggest that the implementation of a discourse methodology should be done on a case-by-case basis and should be modifiable to the local context.

Discourse has to be available

Context analysis and discourse analysis together are essential to properly link context developments with the government's narrative around humanitarian aid organisations, especially before going into interviews. However, in the case of the Kurdistan Region of Iraq (KRI), there is a paucity of published information about the political situation and therefore a lack of publicly available discourse for analysis. The informal nature of political engagement in KRI means that discussions and debates happen mostly behind the scenes and are personal in orientation. This meant that the researchers had little foreknowledge of the attitudes and perspectives of the government before going into interviews, so rather than enquiring *about* attitudes, it was a question of gaining an understanding *of* them. Therefore, the researchers had to rely on follow-up informal interviews with people working in the same field to gain a better understanding of what was said during the interviews.

Discourse analysis is a skill

To effectively conduct discourse analysis in Italy, research faces a challenge that is almost diametrically opposite to that in the KRI. There is abundant discourse in Italy, but making sense of it poses a challenge. Other researchers have explained this Italian challenge as a combination of factors: numerous themes intersect with humanitarian aid; migration alone is multilayered and often simplified by academics, let alone civilians (Abbondanza, 2023); interpreting polarised Italian themes and actors through the media is prone to inaccuracies due to tropes (Filmer, 2021); the instrumentalisation of themes, like religion, is pervasive and requires cultural and historical references for interpretation (Giorgi, 2022). This picture of complexity, where there is a danger of oversimplification and thus inaccuracy, persisted throughout the research.

To provide practical examples and avoid abstraction, let's consider some positive findings from Italy and negative findings from Kurdistan that demonstrate some benefits and challenges of discourse analysis.

Positive findings

The significance of corruption discourse in understanding government relations with INGOs

Corruption discourse is a prevalent topic in Italian media, and its impact on the Italian political mindset cannot be underestimated. It dates back to the historical transition from the First to the Second Italian Republic, which did not involve a constitutional change as one might expect. Instead, a corruption scandal implicating every Italian political party marked the change of Republic and led to the judicial investigation called 'Clean Hands'. This period created a public perception that power is inevitably corrupt. Yet, contrary to the assumption that discourse builds public resistance, recent research suggests it might be normalising corruption in Italy and creating the impression that it is unavoidable and omnipresent. This normalisation is facilitated by corruption being frequently symbolised as 'rooted in' Italy or part of its 'DNA' and by corrupt individuals not being held accountable for their actions. This differs from national discourses in other countries, such as New Zealand, where corruption discourse emphasises individual responsibility (Berti, 2018).

Examining corruption discourse in Italy and uncovering trends allows for a more precise interrogation of the perception of INGOs as being corrupt. In Italy, when NGOs were accused of being traffickers, the hyperbole at play was obvious to Italians; the real message conveyed by smear attacks was that the altruistic image of INGOs must hide an undisclosed gain. Political messaging indirectly questions the motives of NGOs and fosters public suspicion. This emerged in different ways during the Italian case study.

Quantitative discourse analysis can also be useful. The well-known labels of smuggler and trafficker effectively shifted an existing stigma. While these terms appeared in right-wing media, the label 'sea taxi' was found in diverse media sources representing various political ideologies. Although it was mentioned in inverted commas when published in left-wing media, setting aside the 'criminal' narrative for something more banal, its sheer volume of exposure may have indirectly questioned humanitarian motives. Furthermore, search and rescue (SAR) boats were frequently labelled as 'Spanish', 'German', or 'French' across the media spectrum, feeding a narrative of foreign interference (Cusumano and Bell, 2021). This exemplifies McLuhan's concept of the 'medium is the message', where the content of the medium captures our attention, causing us to overlook the character of the message and its underlying implications.

In active discourse, interlocutors consistently expressed the view that investigating criminalisation messaging too literally demonstrates naivete or is off-topic. The media's criminalisation of INGOs was about othering both the problem and the solution to it. The idea of media storylines devoid of factual substance but full of Machiavellian intention was a consistent finding in interviews, regardless of political affiliation or experience.

Reconsidering the criminalisation of solidarity in Italian discourse

The popular assumption that the criminalisation of SAR work is solely attributable to Italy's populist right is inaccurate. Rather, hostility towards SAR operations off Italy is bipartisan. For example, the original code of conduct ostensibly aimed at regulating NGOs was authored by the centrist or left-centrist Democratic Party, casting doubt on their activities. Moreover, administrative obstacles, such as the number and duration of ship seizures, increased even after the polarised media discourse cooled off following Salvini's tenure but without much media attention. The overriding debate about populist criminalisation of SAR is an availability heuristic, obscuring other issues.

A discourse methodology involves investigating themes with a wide range of interlocutors as well as analysing available discourse. Interviews with civil society revealed that work aimed at addressing other social issues, such as poverty and migrant integration, paradoxically became more difficult after Salvini's tenure, even under progressively more centre-left-leaning governments. 'Things were supposed to get better, but they didn't'. However, this is not the common narrative being shared.

Follow-up interviews with parliamentarians[2] investigated the discrepancy between reality and discourse content, leading to a lopsided public (and often humanitarian) impression of a standoff between NGOs and populist Italian politics. The responses ranged from surprise to ignoring the question to providing indirect answers about the political climate. No interlocutors challenged these facts or the issues they suggested. As a result, conversations often became more substantive. Questions rooted in discourse analysis were found to establish rapport and connection more quickly than other questions.

Some negative findings

Although a simplified discourse analysis process was proposed for the research in Iraqi Kurdistan, there emerged some issues with its implementation:

- Timing is an issue. To be most productive, discourse analysis should be implemented before operational (field) research, as it will add depth to the understanding of the themes to be examined. In conjunction with a context analysis, which informs the development of a set of keywords, the discourse analysis will provide concepts to enquire about in conversations with governmental actors and their proxies. In KRI, it proved difficult, however, to organise the implementation of the discourse analysis process before the research. The researchers brought on board to help with the context analysis and networking and help with the interviews were not the ones best capable of implementing the discourse analysis.
- For the KRI, language was an issue, as a minority of Kurds speak Arabic fluently, and therefore an analysis of Federal Iraqi discourse proved difficult, necessitating bringing on board another set of researchers.
- The discursive environment in KRI was not conducive to a standard process of analysis, as there was a paucity of accessible governmental discourse and a limited media environment.

- In the KRI context, as well as in Federal Iraq, there are very limited physical archives, and therefore one is limited to digital records. In Iraq in general and KRI in particular, digital archives are shallow and very limited in their value.
- Therefore, discourse analysis was mostly limited to interpreting interview data and examining governmental actions.

A viable process for analysing discourse should be developed for such discourse poor environments, especially where multiple languages are present.

Areas for further research

The research mentioned has clarified certain aspects of using a discourse analysis methodology, but many questions remain unanswered. These questions may serve as potential areas for further research and practical considerations for implementation:

1 Can the 'emergency' culture of humanitarian INGOs accommodate the balanced approach required to engage with the opposing side of a potentially polarised debate?

2 If discourse analysis is more useful in politically complex environments, can integrating it into standard procedures offer personnel a better perspective when dealing with operational challenges and contribute to a more cogent, insightful, and long-term operational vision globally?

3 Can questions generated by discourse analysis foster understanding and address the specific demands of government officials or other power brokers, or might the meta nature of such questioning confuse and frustrate the process in some cases? Given a nuanced approach to interviewing, can a guiding methodology be developed to determine which environments to employ such a tool, who should deploy it, and what kind of training is required for INGO representatives and local counterparts?

4 How can an INGO with a high turnover rate foster this type of discourse analysis? Can it only be achieved in an ICRC-like employment model?

5 Is a discourse tool or process a purely technical proposition, or does it also address INGO culture? To what extent are semi-academic questions considered 'slow' or irrelevant, and can this attitude be addressed in the process of using discourse analysis? If a more localised, contextualised understanding of the 'other' (government or local civil society) becomes institutionalised, what existing problems in humanitarian work can also be addressed?

6 Can existing operational positions practically implement discourse analysis? What are the implications of having it conducted by external visitors

versus existing staff? How can a set of decidedly theoretical questions gain precedence, even once, let alone on an ongoing basis, in contexts where understaffing is rampant?

Conclusion

Conducting a thorough political discourse analysis in any country necessitates a variety of practical, educational, and attitudinal components. Apart from extensive knowledge of the language and politics of the country, access to more than just mass media sources, and collaboration with local researchers, an effective discourse analysis demands a critical and reflective mindset as well as a comprehensive understanding of diverse methodologies (Fairclough, 1989).

In the two case studies, meeting these complex requirements led to challenges, though they were quite distinct. Italy's abundance of discourse, fragmented politics, and implicit meanings pose difficulties. In contrast, in Kurdistan, the lack of publicly available discourse and the informal nature of political engagement hinder direct questioning and understanding of attitudes and perspectives. This does not change our view that by definition context analysis includes an examination of discourse. Concluding that the implementation of a discourse methodology needs to be flexible to the context it is applied in simply means a flexible methodology is needed.

Notes

1 For insight into the analysis of governmental discourse, see: Burton, F. and Carlen, P. (1979). *Official discourse: On discourse analysis, governmental publications, ideology and the state*. London: Routledge and Kegan Paul.
2 Particularly members of the Democratic Party.

References

Abbondanza, G. (2023). A Sea of Difference? Australian and Italian Approaches to Irregular Migration and Seaborne Asylum Seekers. *Contemporary Politics* 29(1), 93–113.

Berti, C. (2019). Rotten Apples or Rotten System? Media Framing of Political Corruption in New Zealand and Italy. *Journalism Studies* 20(11), 1580–1597.

Cunningham, A. (2018). *International Humanitarian NGOs and State Relations: Politics, Principles, and Identity*. London: Routledge.

Cusumano, E. and Bell, F. (2021). Guilt by association? The criminalisation of sea rescue NGOs in Italian media. *Journal of Ethnic and Migration Studies* 47(19), 4285–4307.

Fairclough, N. (1989). *Language and Power*. Language in social life series. London: Longman.

Filmer, D. (2021). Salvini, Stereotypes and Cultural Translation: Analysing Anglophone News Discourse on Italy's 'Little Mussolini'. *Language and Intercultural Communication* 21(3), 335–351.

Giorgi, A. (2022). Hijack or Release? On the Heuristic Limits of the Frame of Instrumentalization of Religion for Discussing the Entanglements of Populism, Religion, and Gender. *Identities* 29(4), 483–499.

Paltridge, B. (2006). *Discourse Analysis*. London: Continuum.

2

HUMANITARIAN NEGOTIATION

Challenges and compromise in hard-to-reach areas

Anaïde Nahikian and Emmanuel Tronc

Introduction

On the frontlines of volatile and protracted conflicts, the ability of organisations to obtain and maintain access to communities in crisis has long been a prevailing challenge, particularly in highly insecure environments and in 'hard-to-reach' areas. Complex, interconnected political, social, security, cultural, climatic, and economic factors escalate armed violence, contribute to the dysfunction and deterioration of essential infrastructure and services, intensify resource scarcity, and exacerbate the vulnerabilities of affected populations. The needs of communities tend to be most urgent and acute in areas facing high levels of violence and insecurity; these spaces create a grey zone in which access to populations—and populations' access to aid—is restricted.

Enduring and emerging external, internal, and inter-agency challenges create a multitude of obstacles to access. In many contexts, humanitarian organisations are challenged by suspicions of their motives or the fear that their interventions will be instrumentalised or compromised by political, diplomatic, or military objectives. They may deal with power asymmetries in their engagements, diminishing influence vis-a-vis autocratic regimes and pervasive political impunity, or face competition within the sector as NGOs vie for resources and visibility in high-risk environments, complicating trust-building efforts. Organisations also face a series of 'self-inflicted' obstacles (Tronc, et al., 2018) stemming from their own policies and approaches, including increased 'bunkerisation' in volatile contexts (Duffield, 2012; Steets, et al., 2023), incongruence between needs and programmes, discounting of local actors' capacities and expertise, and constraints and compromises linked to counter-terrorism regulations and donor state priorities that have significant

DOI: 10.4324/9781003316541-4

consequences on access. These factors challenge organisations as they aim to demonstrate their legitimacy and authority, ensure consistent and quality deployment of programmes, and negotiate their security across operational and ideological frontlines. Yet, it is in this space that we also discover the potential of humanitarian action to confront and question the norms, power, and priorities determined by influential actors (Magone, et al., 2011).

In order to overcome access obstacles, humanitarian agencies must engage with the range of actors who control territorial space and define political order—particularly those controlling critical regions or influencing the political tides of conflict—to gain and preserve access to areas that are otherwise inaccessible. As organisations are outpaced by staggering needs, humanitarian efforts can be hindered by the politicisation of aid, corruption and poor governance, and mounting criticism and rejection of international presence. The sector faces several key questions: To what extent can humanitarians define and assert the conditions of their operations when confronted with political interests considerably divergent from their own? Have the compromises made through negotiation led to the deterioration of humanitarian credibility vis-à-vis populations, authorities, and the 'international community'?

As has been observed in historical and contemporary conflicts, from Somalia to Syria, the international community—generally defined as global state powers, UN member states, and influential donors—remains unable of deterring aggression and upholding its humanitarian commitments and red lines. In the absence of a sustainable, political resolution to conflicts and as crises grow progressively protracted, the humanitarian system, which is 'increasingly characterised as chaotic, poorly managed, instrumentalised, and ill-conceived' (Gordon and Donini, 2015, 86), is compelled to fill the social and political vacuum. As such, humanitarian action illuminates the realities of the social context and the deficiencies of the state. With the deployment of aid comes an implicit acceptance of a logic of humanitarian intervention that is a reassuringly moral and arguably apolitical substitution for international diplomatic influence.

In many contexts, organisations may face power asymmetries in their engagements with dominant stakeholders (Clements, 2020), the perception of diminishing influence vis-à-vis autocratic regimes and pervasive political impunity, or competition within the sector as the marketplace (Krause, 2014) of NGOs vies for resources and visibility. These factors challenge organisations in their aims to demonstrate neutrality, impartiality, and independence, implement consistent and quality programmes, and ensure their own security across frontlines. Through a series of reactive operational and policy decisions, many international organisations have defined approaches and policies that increasingly undermine the humanitarian imperative. This is apparent in areas considered too insecure or politically sensitive, where INGOs may decide to prioritise presence with diminished space for impact, conceding to conditions imposed by state or non-state authorities, even if they severely limit operational access and do not reach those most in need.

Against this backdrop, this chapter discusses the political context of humanitarian negotiations, offers reflections on its definition and practice, and offers reflections on engaging with authoritarian regimes from research and practice. Recent decades have seen the progressive elevation of humanitarian negotiation as a domain of specialised professional practice within the sector. Once largely seen as instinctual or intuitive, or otherwise overlooked as an obvious 'part of the job' in running aid programmes, humanitarian negotiation has emerged as a catalyst for illuminating the encounters, failures, and indelible quandaries that once occupied the shadows of individual experiences and organisational histories. Humanitarian negotiation has also been branded as a distinct area of practice and served to mobilise increased institutional and donor support within the sector to define and standardise professional guidelines and focus on strategic and tactical negotiation approaches. A growing number of organisations have also led the way in providing training and capacity development to professionalise this aspect of humanitarian practice, offering inter-agency workshops and courses,[1] in addition to long-standing professional development efforts undertaken within agencies themselves, including Médecins sans Frontières (MSF), the International Committee of the Red Cross (ICRC), and the Norwegian Refugee Council, among others.

Yet, the majority of sector-wide professional development initiatives have mirrored the enduring inequities of the sector itself, prioritising access to capacity development for international humanitarian practitioners working with large, international NGOs, though increasing efforts have been made to include national staff of INGOs. Projects to promote and implement capacity development for local NGOs or to augment the access of INGO national staff to training opportunities remain comparatively neglected and underfunded. In many cases, the vision for engagement with local actors remains limited to an approach that replicates the international aid system by local actors without addressing the inherent complexities and implications of considering local staff as field-based proxies for access negotiations – physical, social, and political challenges of national staff being linked to the society in which they operate, language barriers, resource limitations, a lack of genuine leadership opportunities, and a higher 'burden of proof' for demonstrating adherence to humanitarian principles and good practices of management and accountability. Local actors are often those who endure the double standard in the way local staff are perceived and treated in the operations and engagements of INGOs versus international staff. Local staff have fewer resources and options to deal with operational difficulties and security risks than their international counterparts. These conditions undermine responsible and fruitful long-term collaboration and trust. National staff and national NGOs continue to bear the burden of frontline exposure, particularly in areas that have become too difficult for INGOs to operate, whether due to insecurity, overly restrictive regimes, or logistical obstacles.

The political context of humanitarian negotiation

The prominence of humanitarian negotiation as a professional practice may be 'attributable to two interconnected developments: the expansion of the humanitarian sector into the heart of conflict and the changing nature of contemporary armed conflict to become predominantly non-international (non-international armed conflict, or NIAC), in which the well-being of civilians invariably plays a central role' (Clements, 2020, 8). Territorial borders are more than lines drawn between states; they also trigger institutional decisions about how humanitarian assistance is delivered. The aid sector is governed by a state-centric system, requiring organisations to cooperate with state authorities for the provision of aid.[2] While Common Article 3 of the Geneva Conventions authorises an impartial humanitarian actor to offer its services to the parties to the conflict, international humanitarian law (IHL) does not grant humanitarian agencies the legal right to enter a sovereign territory without the consent of the state. It is here that we enter into the heart of the debate. In circumstances in which the state actively interferes with humanitarian operations or in which the state is unable or unwilling to grant access to areas controlled by non-state actors (e.g., non-state actors), certain humanitarian agencies have argued that it is possible, if not (morally) obligatory, to engage in humanitarian operations despite the legal requirement of state consent for access.

Some agencies will support cross-border operations. Others strictly defend cross-line operations, heeding the legal requirements to operate only with the consent of governments.

This dilemma was particularly evident in the case of Syria. As the conflict continued, two different schools of aid response endeavoured to overcome constraints and manage daily compromises on how assistance could be delivered. One avenue privileged the official way (controlled by the authorities), which allowed for access to mainly areas under government control. The alternative, cross-border action, required entering from neighbouring countries, such as Turkey or Jordan, through unofficial routes and in rebel-held areas. For some, this example illustrates the malleability of borders, a political construct, in the moral imperative of aid. NGOs continually denied access by the authorities in Damascus were compelled to work exclusively through cross-border operations to access populations in need. While this approach challenged the agency's perceived neutrality in this conflict (and resulted in security incidents of staff), the organisation deemed it essential to provide lifesaving services and to counter state strategies of containing and controlling access to assistance. In this way, adherence to international humanitarian principles and the practical realities of delivering aid in complex and volatile humanitarian contexts represent a significant challenge for the humanitarian community, which is heightened in hard-to-reach areas.

Many have argued that the so-called 'war on terror' has triggered a confluence of factors that have constrained agencies' operational space. Humanitarian actions are undertaken in 'an increasingly hostile and difficult operating environment, in which direct security threats are growing and the ability of humanitarians to act is becoming more constrained' (Collinson and Elhawary, 2012, 5). This phenomenon coincides with a changing landscape of humanitarian assistance and the rise of intrastate conflicts since the late 1980s. This period has ushered in a 'significant expansion in humanitarian action as a form of international relations and as an increasingly ordered part of a nascent global governance' (Slim, 2015, 10, 11). It has also forced the sector to reckon with the 'multi-layered, knotty, and unstable relationship between humanitarianism and politics, ethics, and power' (Barnett and Weiss, 2008, 235). Indeed, humanitarian action amplifies the realities of the social context in which it operates, particularly the deficiencies of state services, infrastructure, and capacities. This has the added effect of pushing opposition groups, ranging from civil society to non-state armed actors, to utilise the very need for aid as a demonstration of state weaknesses. The increased dominance of the security state and a return to authorities' assertive positioning and control of international assistance and public communication have resulted in donor governments' unwillingness or inability to press humanitarian and human rights issues in affected contexts.

Many have further observed that the privileged position that aid agencies once had vis-à-vis states and donors has ceased, as increasingly insular and authoritarian regimes that want to centralise or directly manage assistance and prohibit dialogue with non-state armed actors are closing the door on international aid. Arguably, this space has been further eroded by the 'blurred distinctions between the roles of military and humanitarian organisations; political manipulation of humanitarian assistance [and the] perceived lack of independence of humanitarian actors from donors or from host governments' (Magone, et al., 2011, 1, 2). Once considered a collective endeavour bolstered by Western diplomacy, access negotiations have become fragmented and dispersed, with individual agencies privileging independent deals with actors and local influencers (Duffield, 2012) and depending increasingly on national actors to support access objectives.

As critics argue that the response of the humanitarian system in hard-to-reach areas remains altogether inadequate in providing communities with assistance in a timely, responsive, and relevant way, the humanitarian sector continues to expand rapidly. This evolution has transformed its scope of operations along two key pillars: First, in the expansion and globalisation of humanitarian programmes, which now include activities such as development, resilience, and antipoverty initiatives; emergency relief; promotion of international humanitarian and human rights law; support for refugees, reconstruction efforts; and peacebuilding programmes. Second, in the complex and expansive international humanitarian architecture, one that is increasingly bureaucratic, risk-averse, and cautious of confrontation, particularly vis-à-vis authoritarian regimes. The spectrum of actors in the sector encompasses not only humanitarian organisations but also influential stakeholders such as governments, faith-based organisations, diaspora groups, nongovernmental organisations, and donors, connected through layered and intersecting networks of influence.

An emerging term for an established practice

Mancini-Griffoli and Picot elaborated the first handbook on humanitarian negotiation practice, which 'identified negotiation as a critical transferable skill in all humanitarian work, but one that was not well understood by humanitarian workers and, in general, one that was very poorly resourced by the agencies that employ them' (Slim, 2004, in Mancini-Griffoli and Picot, 9, 10). The terminology of 'frontline' was evoked by Mancini-Griffoli and Picot in their discussion of the three levels of negotiation[3] to describe 'sudden, reactive, and often also high-risk negotiations requiring quick decision-making in the face of unexpected developments' (Mancini-Griffoli and Picot, 2004, 21). The concept of humanitarian diplomacy was also defined and detailed by the ICRC and the International Federation of the Red Cross (IFRC) in two important publications in 2006 and 2011 (Harroff-Tavel, 2006; Régnier, 2011). Thrusting its history of negotiation practice out of obscurity, MSF subsequently published *Humanitarian Negotiations Revealed: The MSF Experience*, which provided an explicit and critical reflection on how the organisation navigated the contradictions and paradoxes intrinsic to its work through a series of emblematic case studies.

Despite increasing recognition of the distinct attributes and approaches of humanitarian negotiation in the sector, there are varying definitions of the term in the scholarship. While many of these definitions expand upon the purposes and attributes of humanitarian negotiation, formulating a conclusive definition remains elusive, particularly when considering the importance of integrating reflections from dynamic operational realities. Scholarship appears to deal with the types of negotiation, its challenges and obstacles, and its major objectives, but has fallen short of providing an explicit definition. Indeed, it appears that humanitarian negotiation is more easily defined by its challenges than by a conceptual framework. Mancini-Griffoli and Picot have proposed an elaborate definition of humanitarian negotiation tied to its essential purpose and characteristics:

> To ensure the impartial protection of, and the provision of assistance to, civilians affected by armed conflict and other people rendered hors de combat, as stipulated by IHL, human rights law, and refugee law. The four key characteristics of humanitarian negotiations are that they are conducted:

> - By humanitarian actors, such as members of appropriately mandated and impartial organisations like UN agencies, NGOs, or the ICRC
> - For humanitarian objectives, including humanitarian access, protection, assessment, and assistance, as set out in IHL
> - In countries affected by armed conflict, either of an international or non-international character; and
> - With the parties to the conflict, that is, those with power and responsibility for the conduct of war, for the humane treatment of civilians and those hors de combat, and for the distribution of assistance.
>
> *(Mancini-Griffoli and Picot, 2004, 19)*

The Centre of Competence on Humanitarian Negotiation (CCHN) offers the following definition:

> a set of interactions between humanitarian organisations and parties to an armed conflict, as well as other relevant actors, aimed at establishing and maintaining the presence of these organisations in conflict environments, ensuring access to vulnerable groups, and facilitating the delivery of assistance and protection activities. Negotiations may involve both state and non-state actors. They include a relational component focused on building trust with the counterparts over time and a transactional component focused on determining and agreeing on the specific terms and logistics of humanitarian operations (CCHN Field Manual, 2019, 19).

Others have offered similar, pithier definitions:

- A process of communication and relationship building undertaken with the objective of arriving at an agreed outcome around a particular set of issues, in situations where the parties are not in complete accord on those issues to begin with (Mc Hugh and Bessler, 2006, 5).
- Negotiation at its most basic is about give and take, finding or creating options that define a "win/win situation" for all parties engaged in the process (Toole, 2001, 4).

Minear folds humanitarian negotiations into the realm of diplomacy but makes the distinction between 'capital D' diplomacy and 'small d' diplomacy, which is 'more terrestrial'—even pedestrian. It covers a host of humanitarian functions of a more day-to-day sort. It functions in the middle range of activities between, on the one hand, arranging for the safe passage of humanitarian material and personnel past a given roadblock and, on the other, locating and contracting for aid agency office and warehouse space or setting up bank accounts to allow for agency transactions. It also illustrates the breakdown of traditional diplomatic channels undertaken by States, official processes, or UN Special Envoys to bring peace and promote the respect of international conventions (Minear and Smith, 2007).

Research undertaken at the Harvard Humanitarian Initiative, for example, has shown that the primary objectives of humanitarian negotiations are largely for the purposes of (1) obtaining and maintaining access and security in a given area, (2) providing humanitarian aid and supporting protection conditions for vulnerable populations, (3) ensuring an operational humanitarian space, and (4) promoting respect for IHL and humanitarian principles. As one humanitarian worker interviewed for that research explained, 'It's different from one place to the other, from one mission to the other. It depends on the context that we're working in. Most of these engagements, negotiations, discussion, dialogue [are] specifically about access, support, safety, and security most of the time'.

While humanitarian workers used terminology such as 'engagement', 'influence', 'discussion', 'relationships', 'dialogue', 'give-and-take', and 'interactions' almost interchangeably when referencing humanitarian negotiation, much of the discussion centred on the objectives, challenges, and dilemmas of humanitarian negotiation rather than defining it as such. This tendency may speak to negotiation's dynamic and evolving qualities in conflict areas and signal the emphasis that professionals place on practice-oriented terminology rather than on attempts to describe a more theoretical notion. In order to trace the practice of humanitarian negotiation as a self-conscious process, practice theory may provide useful insights to uncover 'the quotidian unfolding of international life' (Turunen, 2020, 463) and inform the ways in which humanitarian negotiation as a professional domain reveals itself precisely through its practices. What distinguishes negotiations in a humanitarian context from other types of negotiations? Scholars and experts have begun to bridge this divide (Donini, 2007; Grace, 2020; Grace and Lempereur, 2021 , in Minear and Smith; Toole, 2001) and propose several distinguishing factors.

First, unlike commercial negotiations, the volatile and high-stakes environments in which humanitarians operate often leave them with limited time and space to prepare adequately for their negotiations. Practitioners,

often proceed with limited time to read even basic information about their counterparts, with relatively scant understanding of the political issues underlying their positions, and often with limited knowledge of the sources of power and support for the belligerents. One might say that it is precisely where reflection, contact and preparation are most needed, that they are most often neglected.

(Toole, 2001, 5)

The urgency of needs has hindered deeper engagement, even if the intent is there; practitioners have expressed feeling in an eternal 'response mode' or 'stuck in lifesaving mode'. Interviewees from parallel research in South Sudan have indicated that the constant sense of urgency has also had a significant impact on staff's capacity to think strategically, beyond the day-to-day urgencies of operating across field locations. Grace confirms this in his analysis of cognitive capital, identifying three key components of preparation: Intensive contextual analysis, understanding the interests and motivations of the counterpart, and diligent preparation on the substance of the negotiation itself, including such things as 'negotiating with [non-state armed actors] on access, with community leaders on distributing humanitarian assistance, and with states on headquarters agreements' (Grace, 2020, 25). Dedicated time and space to prepare humanitarian negotiations and to learn from the lessons of past negotiations, including a sophisticated analysis of their impact on humanitarian principles and guiding frameworks to engage with others, remains out of reach for staff who are working in a purely reactive mode.

Another key difference lies in one's focus on the outcome. Negotiations concerning humanitarian issues cannot be carried out in the same way as diplomatic or commercial negotiations, which focus on results and transactional outcomes. Given the critical importance of obtaining and maintaining access to populations in need over an extended period of time, particularly in contexts enduring decades of conflict, humanitarians must cultivate relationships with the parties to the conflict, communities, and other key actors of influence in order to ensure continued access, programme implementation and delivery, safety and security, and the protection of affected populations. Ideally, these relationships can withstand staff turnover, changes in political leadership, and the volatility of armed conflict. A key component of implementing humanitarian programmes is, therefore, building and maintaining long-term relationships, or 'social capital' (Grace, 2020, 24), which emphasise the critical importance of predictability, trust-building, cultural sensitivity, personal relationships, and deference, when required, in humanitarian negotiations (Toole, 2001). In addition to forging constructive relationships, fostering trust, and building a positive reputation, social capital also includes the skills necessary for mitigating the unintended negative consequences of actions.

Finally, humanitarian actors do not engage in service of wider development goals or government ambitions for reform or legitimacy. Instead, they work in the service of populations in need to alleviate the consequences of conflict. It is important to recognise that in their engagements, while humanitarian negotiators are acting to support affected populations, their presence in the context, as well as their objective to uphold the humanitarian principles, means 'that they are also negotiating for themselves—their principles, their programmes, and the interests of their institution' (Toole, 2001, 5).

Despite these key distinctions, it is crucial to consider some of the common dimensions. An abundance of literature on the subject of mundane and commercial negotiations is available to the humanitarian world, providing valuable perspectives on the everyday negotiation processes that are equally relevant to humanitarian contexts. One of these is the importance of the role of identity. Shapiro's model of human behaviour in negotiations complements pre-existing theories by a third layer to portray persons as *homo economicus*, *homo emoticus*, and *homo identicus*, whereby human behaviour is respectively driven by three dimensions of reason, emotions, and, ultimately, identity. The latter features two facets of identity. First, the core identity—the 'spectrum of characteristics that define you as an individual or group', including the cultural background, personal beliefs, values and interests, allegiances—and second, the relational identity—'the spectrum of characteristics that define your relationship with a particular person or group' (Shapiro, 2016, 13). Shapiro argues that negotiations have the potential to compromise one of these essential parts of one's identity, which in turn may sharply raise the potential for conflict and jeopardise the success of the negotiation. Being conscious of one's—at least perceived—identity is therefore crucial in order to be able to prioritise certain characteristics of one's identity during conflict, if needed, and to quickly recognise which parts of the inner pillar may be vulnerable during negotiations.

Assessing these characteristic poses a valuable exercise on the individual level. Similarly, by applying these considerations to the macro level of humanitarian negotiations, there arises an opportunity to examine the organisational aspect within negotiations to reflect both on who is negotiating and in the name of *whom*, as the heterogeneity of humanitarian negotiations and the underlying complexity to derive a clear definition covering the subject, is further exacerbated by the diversity of the practicing humanitarian organisations with varying organisational identities. In humanitarian settings, the core identity of different humanitarian organisations plays a significant role in determining their approach and priorities. For example, some organisations may prioritise their impartial and neutral stance in providing assistance to all those in need, while others may have a specific agenda based on their cultural background, donor affiliations, or religious beliefs. Distinctions can thus be drawn between independent, principle-focused humanitarian organisations such as MSF and entities of the multilateral system, such as humanitarian agencies of the United Nations, while taking into account individual differences within each of these organisational classifications.

As such, it is paramount to consider these differences in organisational identities in the policy discourse around the subject of humanitarian negotiations.

Smaller humanitarian organisations possess a different level of flexibility, having comparatively higher autonomy, allowing them to take quick decisions when necessary in the field. Their lower, often less political, profile, partially due to their distinct relational identity, is mirrored in unique relationships with a particular government or non-state armed group, potentially leading to a higher level of trust and credibility when negotiating in the name of the affected population, arguably providing them with a comparative advantage for negotiations at the operational field level. Likewise, these distinct organisational features may also pose disadvantages. Limited resources to maintain and develop human capacity, a lower level of international protection for their staff and reduced influence – due to comparatively smaller response capacities and a reduced international backing by states – translate into the necessity to use distinct approaches in the field and simultaneously reflects in a limited possibility to successfully negotiate in mid-level operational and particularly high-level strategic frontlines.

Development of practice

Humanitarian negotiation as a domain of professional practice and analysis has mobilised considerable institutional and financial support within the sector. Many of these initiatives[4] have focused on humanitarian negotiations at the field, or 'frontline', level, notably on engagement with state authorities and non-state actors to secure safe and unimpeded access to victims of armed conflicts, promotion of international humanitarian law, and protection of civilians, including human rights. Upon recognition of humanitarian negotiation as a professional practice in and of itself, agencies have focused on strengthening their teams' capacity to negotiate access in increasingly complex environments, to develop more formal institutional guidelines, and to focus on tactical and strategic negotiation approaches, particularly relating to obtaining and maintaining humanitarian access, facilitating and implementing humanitarian assistance and protection programmes, and safeguarding staff security.[5] Various organisations across the sector have also invested in gathering and exchanging experiences and reflections on practice, both internally and across organisational lines, with a primary focus on better understanding professional approaches to dealing with the multitude of recurring challenges and dilemmas that humanitarian negotiators face.

The past 15 years have also seen increasing recognition of humanitarian negotiation as a field of both professional development and theoretical inquiry, aiming to better comprehend how humanitarians negotiate—a dimension of humanitarian work that has been largely seen as instinctual or intuitive or otherwise dismissed as 'part of the job' in running humanitarian programmes. In his analysis of the 'negotiation cognisance gap', Grace argues that despite recognition of what 'pedestrian' actions and approaches that may fall within the definitions of humanitarian negotiation, practition-ers lack awareness of the importance and role of negotiation in their work because, as a domain, it does not appear on their 'conceptual radar' (Grace, 2020, 17). He argues that while negotiation plays a role in humanitarian work generally, professionals fail to recognise it in their own practice. Recent empirical data from interviews and trainings undertaken by the authors sug-gests a shift in this perspective. In interviews and training discussions, practi-tioners of both international and local organisations expressed an increased recognition of the role and importance of negotiation in their work. This may be due in part to the expansion of negotiation-specific trainings within and across agencies, or by the simple fact that interviewing professionals about their negotiation practice inherently raises their awareness to it.

It is important to note that organisational identities are dynamic and sub-ject to evolution over time, thus requiring a constant assessment of their current state. The understanding of their core and relational identities can therefore offer valuable insights into their negotiation strategies and help to reduce the potential of conflicts during negotiations. The degree to which organisations adhere to humanitarian principles should form a critical as-pect in this evaluation process. Furthermore, individuals make a significant impact at the field level, particularly in terms of their approaches to relation-ships and issues of perception by key stakeholders. As negotiation practices become more centralised and professionalised, the trend has also been to limit the leeway individuals may have previously enjoyed in favour of a more centralised decision-making.

Negotiation in humanitarian contexts

In examining what influences the practice of humanitarian negotiation, it is important to consider the constraints of the humanitarian enterprise to-day. Humanitarianism is an ever-evolving landscape, from the frontlines of Solferino to warfare in Ukraine. The term *humanitarian* and, by extension, its essence, have been espoused by a long-standing tradition of charity and emergency assistance founded on Western values and practice (Fiori, 2013). The humanitarian space finds its origins 'in a move that combined the au-thority of the suffering produced by war with the authority of the states responsible for that suffering' (Krause, 2014) along with the constellation of agencies, actors, and actions mobilised to alleviate it. Increased attention has been devoted to defining the operational and ethical contours and limitations of the humanitarian enterprise—debating persistent paradoxes, grappling with the inherent dilemmas of aid, and considering how to adapt to emerging challenges and how to engage indirectly through local actors—as the sector continues to confront external and internal factors that compel its reactive adaptation. Humanitarian actors maintain that they are not responsible for resolving the national, political, economic, and social crises that fuel protracted armed conflicts, nor are they responsible for instituting or bolstering state competence, legitimacy, good governance, accountability, essential services, rule of law, or security sector reform, despite these being central to supporting communities' most basic needs, security, and livelihoods. Organisations providing emergency assistance do not aim to support recovery and broader development goals, or state ambitions for reform or international recognition, but rather in the service of populations, to alleviate some of the consequences of conflict. And yet, in the absence of effective and sustainable peace prospects, there remains a real risk of generating an illusion of protection and raising expectations among communities, over generations, in some cases.

The aid system remains a professional environment and marketplace of 'good projects' (Krause, 2014) that is highly competitive, bureaucratically burdensome, challenging to coordinate, and increasingly inefficient. Some have described the cartelisation of the sector, with a small number of influential actors dominating this 'market' (Collinson and Elhawary, 2012, 19). Corporate dynamics permeate agency policies and reporting lines donors' increasing scrutiny and accountability requirements have created greater restrictions on organisations; donor states at times make compromises to maintain relationships with authorities, and many agencies opt to deliver services through subcontracts and remote management. And yet, there appears to be consensus that the 'classical' humanitarian approach endures in policy and in practice, particularly in some of the most complex, volatile, and politicised conflicts where, paradoxically, the system continues to fall short.

While the aid system is larger and more diverse than ever, power remains seized by a core group of dominant actors. Global inequalities over the recent years—visible through the COVID-19 pandemic, the Black Lives Matter movement, and increasing attention in the academy to 'decolonising aid', for example—have amplified awareness of the need to address persistent colonial structures that perpetuate unequal funding and decision-making systems, as well as systemic power imbalances. At the same time, national actors also take on a greater share of the security and reputational risks associated with humanitarian interventions (Howe and Stites, 2019). A recognition of these realities led the INGOs and donor community in 2016 at the World Humanitarian Summit to call for increased direct funding to local actors, investment in local humanitarian organisations, development of more equitable partnerships between international agencies and national partners, and more inclusive coordination platforms the key areas which have been driving localisation discourse and policy, though progress appears to be minimal. This contemporary moment brings into focus the limitations, contradictions, and deficiencies of the humanitarian enterprise. As many claim that the response of the humanitarian system in acute and protracted emergencies remains altogether inadequate in providing communities with assistance in a timely, responsive, and relevant way, the humanitarian sector continues to expand rapidly. A definitive consequence of this expansion is the dislocation of international staff from the communities they aim to serve.

Critical perspectives assert that reforming the aid system is not enough. Incremental inclusionary reforms built upon foundations of Western-driven, neo-colonial structures are considered to be insufficient to rebalance the power and agency that many view to be at the heart of localisation efforts. As Barbelet writes, 'shifting power by relying on the willingness of the holder to give up power is rarely a successful strategy in any field. Power usually has to be claimed' (Barbelet, 2019, 28). Some narratives within and about the sector have speculated that the current model of the humanitarian system will inevitably be bypassed. Assertive states, increasing capacity and visibility of local organisations, and a decline in the influence and economic power of the West may result in a more diverse and wide range of alternative response possibilities in the face of ongoing emergencies. While these dynamics create an increasingly thorny environment for humanitarian negotiation to take place, they make such engagement all the more necessary. How professionals reconcile the humanitarian imperative with the compromises and consequences inherent to humanitarian negotiation remains an essential area of exploration and awakens debates on the humanitarian system's raison d'être vis-a-vis authoritarian and isolationist regimes, pervasive manipulation and exploitation of aid, and systemic failures of the ever-expanding humanitarian industry.

Reflections on principles

Humanitarian actors are not responsible for resolving the national, political, economic, and social crises that fuel protracted armed conflicts, nor are they responsible for instituting or bolstering state competence, legitimacy, good governance, accountability, essential services, rule of law, or security sector reform, despite these being central to supporting communities' most basic needs, security, and livelihoods. As explained by numerous practitioners, humanitarian agencies—particularly those who are funded by large institutional donors—try to anticipate, mitigate, and correct perceived risks in order to preserve their organisational integrity. This institutional dilemma—balancing the needs of the organisation and its independence from prevailing (and often dominant) influences with the priorities of the beneficiary population—is reflected in the literature and is common amongst many humanitarian organisations:

> On the one hand, the aid community advocates the imperative to be devoted to beneficiaries first, at any cost, making important compromises on principles (in particular impartiality and neutrality), but de facto being instrumentalised by political actors. On the other hand, this

instrumentalisation will limit the access and credibility of humanitarian actors to run principled operations on the ground in the long run … it is regrettable that humanitarians largely concede to specific conditions set by state authorities, even if they severely limit (for a certain time or indefinitely) humanitarian operational access in the field.

(Tronc, 2018, 59)

Humanitarians regularly struggle with tensions between the implementation of humanitarian principles in daily operations and the compromises this requires in order to make concrete progress, the competing needs for confidentiality and coordination between different organisations, and the challenges of adequately assessing and engaging with interlocutors in volatile environments where control of territory frequently shifts. Compromise is born when interests and norms collide, sometimes convergent, sometimes divergent. The tensions, contradictions, and dilemmas of humanitarian action are not only a consequence of the constraining and constituting effects of the world it aspires to transform but are intrinsic to the domain itself (Barnett and Weiss, 2008). Humanitarian actors weigh short-term considerations, such as gaining access and resources for immediate response, against long-term considerations, such as preserving relationships and access to the regions affected by prolonged crises, which is equally important in ensuring sustainable solutions. Striking this balance requires a nuanced and well-considered approach that takes both the urgency of the situation and the potential long-term consequences of any decisions into account. Negotiations that prioritise short-term gains over longer-term sustainability, particularly in light of increasingly protracted crises, can thus substantially compromise the effectiveness of humanitarian assistance.

Endeavouring to ensure that operations are principled is intended to establish trust that only a humanitarian objective is being pursued without any ulterior motives (Schenkenberg van Mierop, 2018). As such, the principles describe not only 'who' you are but 'how' you work. Neutrality, impartiality, and independence have commonly been at the centre of humanitarian negotiation, since humanitarians' concerns hinge first on ensuring that aid goes to the most in need and thus must demonstrate their separateness from political and military priorities and donor agendas. Aid interventions necessitate challenging negotiations with a range of actors who control territorial space and define political order—particularly those controlling critical regions or influencing the political tides of conflict—to gain and preserve access to areas that are otherwise hard to reach. Humanitarian professionals vacillate between upholding the foundational normative frameworks guiding international order, humanity, and ethics, on the one hand, and engaging in practical, agile, and responsive field operations, on the other, encountering difficult choices that engender significant short- and long-term repercussions. Humanitarian practitioners navigate circumstances over which they have little control and which increasingly challenge the norms of IHL, human rights, and humanitarian action, including the core principles of humanity, neutrality, impartiality, and independence.

In the midst of political ambiguity and pressure, humanitarian principles remain a beacon to guide practice and represent the heart of organisational identity while being essential to gaining and maintaining access to affected communities. Scholars and policy circles have raised questions about the contemporary relevance of humanitarian principles. These concerns are particularly relevant in light of the growing and diversifying humanitarian sector, the protracted and politicised conflicts preoccupying the international community, the expectations and restrictions of the international community, and, by extension, the increasingly influential and demanding donor base. It is also important to reflect on the degree to which civilians value the upholding of humanitarian principles in the midst of persistent violence, human rights violations, and enduring conflict.

While the dogma of principled humanitarian action continues to guide humanitarian interventions, the confluence of operational realities, such as deliberate and recurrent violations of [IHL], limited access, politicisation of aid, and the targeting of aid workers, continue to significantly limit international interventions. This poses a 'difficult paradox for humanitarian workers, as they find themselves inevitably negotiating in practice that which is non-negotiable in principle' (Mancini-Griffoli and Picot, 2004, 11). It is for this reason that some have criticised a broader principled approach, stating that humanitarian actors have overstated the principles as a means to resist change, claiming that they are, in turn, instrumentalising the principles in the 'defence of a non-existent ideological and structural purity of the sector' (DuBois, 2020, 8). This is an important and critical perspective that invites humanitarian organisations to re-examine their own responsibilities regarding compromises, which may be rationalised 'for good' and may create more distance from communities. The 'palliative nature of traditional humanitarianism', particularly where it escalated violence, fuelled crisis, and prolonged war, was increasingly portrayed as untenable, and the 'resort to humanitarian principles as an alibi for avoiding making difficult choices' (Gordon and Donini, 2015, 87).

Approaches to negotiating in authoritarian contexts: reflections on practice

As described above, humanitarian negotiations have become increasingly complex due to the convergence of numerous factors. One significant driver is the enduring nature of many current conflicts over years or even generations and involving multiple and fragmented parties with divergent motivations and priorities. In these environments, actors are more aware of the symbolic, economic, diplomatic, and political stakes and advantages of humanitarian intervention. Over recent decades, aid and the mediatisation of conflicts have become instruments for the parties to conflict and other influential actors to advance their political agendas. Beyond the growing influence of humanitarianism in political discourse, we have seen the emergence of a form of 'parallel' diplomacy for several years; an opening of the diplomatic field to independent and private actors, a prerogative that was previously within the exclusive competence and remit of states. This has also broadened the scope of intervention of multi-mandate humanitarian actors to include programmes related to prevention, reconciliation, or crisis resolution.

Reflections on practice have emphasised several strategic approaches to consider when negotiating in authoritarian environments. First, it is important to develop a solid understanding of how authoritarian regimes operate and, most importantly, how they perceive and inscribe humanitarian operations within their ambitions, decision-making processes, and within the scope of the responsibilities—and interests—of their ministries. Second, it is equally important to be aware of the actions that autocratic regimes perceive as 'non-neutral' or political, such as particular types of programming, access to detention centres, or protection activities, for example. This assessment includes an understanding of how a regime tolerates such interventions, particularly as this may directly impact access to beneficiaries, public communication and advocacy, and restriction of operations. Considering this analysis, some agencies may opt to engage in parallel programmes, covert delivery operations, cross-border aid, delivering assistance through intermediaries, and remote programming. Third, it is essential to learn from the experiences of others to adapt negotiation approaches accordingly. Maintaining a sector-wide perspective may also enable agencies to anticipate potential blockages. Has the regime restricted access for particular agencies? Will it engage bilaterally? What are the limits and opportunities of engaging in bilateral dialogues with authorities? Will they meet directly, or will they insist on engaging only with the UN or ICRC? Organisations should also be aware of the level of pressure that national staff face vis-à-vis the regime, as many recent cases have demonstrated that local actors may be the first targets of authorities or their representatives.

Fourth, anticipating states' approaches and decisions vis-à-vis the humanitarian system can be supported by a rich and dynamic mapping and networking approach with myriad actors of influence, including civil society organisations, academics, journalists, political advisors, community leaders, and elders, among others, with the aim to identify allies within the regime, civil society, and the international community, building momentum and creating pressure for positive outcomes. Ambassadors to the UN can also be a valuable resource in developing cooperation and fostering acceptance, though, as recent history has shown, some states may name 'hardliners' tasked with impeding humanitarian programming or objecting to UN Security Council meetings on the humanitarian situation in their country.

Finally, when engaging with authoritarian regimes, legacy matters. Authoritarian leaders remain in power for as long as they can maintain control of the political system, with far-reaching control and limited mechanisms in place to curb their power, often spanning multiple presidential terms in donor states and leadership changeovers in the humanitarian system. Regimes are attentive to a humanitarian organisation's background in the country, its operational footprint, its comportment and reputation, and its legacy. Regimes may point to organisations' operations in other contexts as evidence of or to illustrate a lack of neutrality or impartiality, etc. It is therefore important to understand how an authoritarian regime interprets humanitarian principles and whether and how this contrasts with their own policies and political constraints. Regimes may also carefully consider the funding sources of humanitarian actors, which may fuel isolationist political rhetoric claiming that humanitarian organisations are agents of imperialism or interference.

Outlook and areas of exploration

As emphasised in the introductory section of this chapter, humanitarian actors operate within volatile, ever-changing environments, requiring a capacity for adaptation to the ongoing changes brought about by both internal and external factors. It is, therefore, paramount to assess the effects of ongoing and prospective future policy shifts as well as emerging agendas on humanitarian negotiations, among them the localisation of aid. The signatures of the Grand Bargain committed themselves to make 'principled humanitarian action as local as possible and as international as necessary'.[6] The realisation of this commitment, with arguably heterogenous results so far, leads to an alternation of 'who' is conducting negotiations at the forefront of crises, and particularly conflicts, putting increased responsibility, but also pressure on local humanitarian workers. A great number of potential benefits, including increased accountability, a better understanding of the contexts and also potentially of the negotiating party, heightened legitimacy as well as sustainability of the results, must be weighed against risks, such as capacity limitations, increased security risks including for families and relatives of humanitarian workers, and potential conflicts of interests.

The discussion should, however, not be conducted in a dichotomous manner, evaluating who is potentially better suited, but instead focus on minimising risks while maximising advantageous outcomes. As such, it remains necessary to provide support beyond capacity-building to local actors and to assess and manage security risks, supporting the agenda, while simultaneously acknowledging its limits and the increased need for international actors, particularly within complex, high-risk and or international conflicts. The multiple operational challenges and obstructions of assistance, exacerbated by the war in Syria, for example, have highlighted the key role of local staff on the frontlines. It has also emphasised their absence of legitimacy and visibility within the larger aid apparatus. Another example with great potential to alter humanitarian negotiations is the current focus of an increasing collaboration of humanitarian, development, and peace actors under the so-called Triple Nexus. The implications of their increased collaboration, aiming to increase the sustainability and effectiveness of each of the three sectors, must be subjected to a thorough evaluation. This evaluation should focus on a potential erosion of principled humanitarian action and how this might affect humanitarian negotiations, especially in conflict settings, where the perception of humanitarian actors as independent and neutral remains of utmost importance. The two preceding examples, illustrative for the multitude of current policy discourses and initiatives, demonstrate the fact that the field of humanitarian negotiations will persist as a dynamic and tumultuous domain. Humanitarian negotiation is an instrument, among others, in the practice of humanitarian engagement.

The past three decades have seen a sharp increase in the humanitarian sector's recognition of the importance to reflect critically on the role and consequences of negotiations in field operations and particularly with authoritarian regimes. Yet, there still remain multiple areas of further reflection to consider: Defining and overcoming power imbalances, as well as the role and influence of third-party actors in negotiations; understanding current practices and experiences in utilising different negotiation strategies, including the use of incentives, coercion, or persuasion, and how to determine which strategy is most appropriate in a given context; better apprehending the role of technologies in facilitating negotiations with regimes, alongside the risks and opportunities; and the lasting impact of humanitarian negotiations with authoritarian regimes on the political and humanitarian landscape, including how negotiations affect the legitimacy and stability of authoritarian regimes and how they establish precedents and new standards of humanitarian practice.

While international agencies—as well as largely Western government donors—remain crucial players in most efforts to mitigate the effects of conflict and manage insecurity, and despite intentions to 'localise' their activities, they often fail to cooperate with local actors sufficiently and meaningfully in the planning and implementation of aid programming. The presence and engagement of local actors inherently influence humanitarian space and can foster a humanitarian approach that could be more effective and could generate more trust and acceptance, if implemented in line with existing local practices and priorities. Policy discourse and incremental organisational changes represent only the first steps in a potentially profound sectoral transformation. Achieving this objective implies trusting local capacities, legitimising their actions, and strengthening their technical knowledge. While it may also require strengthening awareness and practical application of the humanitarian principles and other standard processes of engagement, it also means recognising the good and effective practices already established within local contexts. To ensure effective humanitarian assistance, it is crucial that policy discourses and scholarly research continue to accompany the implementation of humanitarian negotiation practices in the field, effectively assessing established methodologies, disseminating valuable insights, and offering support in addressing ongoing and emerging issues. Critical reflections can be drawn from the experience of local actors, particularly around issues including access and reliability of data collection, gender and inclusivity in sensitive protection contexts, fostering relationships, and directly addressing the expectations and needs of communities.

Acknowledgement

Acknowledgement to Julian Watkinson for his contributions.

Notes

1 See for example, Clingendael, Conflict Dynamics International, The Centre of Competence on Humanitarian Negotiation, and the Harvard Humanitarian Initiative.
2 See, for example, United Nations General Assembly (UNGA) UNGA 1 Rule 55 (1991) and the United Nations Security Council (UNSC) Resolution 2417 (2018).
3 These levels are (1) high-level strategic, (2) mid-level operational, and (3) ground-level frontline. See Deborah Mancini-Griffoli and André Picot, *Humanitarian Negotiation: A Handbook for Securing Access, Assistance and Protection for Civilians in Armed Conflict*, Centre for Humanitarian Dialogue, October 2004: 21.
4 This includes, amongst others, activities ranging from negotiating humanitarian access to particular territories, acquiring visas and other passes for staff, ensuring the safety and security of humanitarian actors, coordinating amongst actors and stakeholders, and promoting the protection of civilians and adherence to international legal norms and principles.
5 See, for example, the creation of the Centre of Competence on Humanitarian Negotiation (CCHN) in October 2016 by the ICRC, UNHCR, WFP, MSF, and HD Centre. Other noticeable initiatives include the Harvard Humanitarian Initiative (HHI) Executive Negotiation Project (2020); the Harvard Humanitarian Initiative (HHI) Advanced Training Program on Humanitarian Action; Gerard McHugh and Manuel Bessler, Humanitarian Negotiations with Armed Groups: A Manual for Practitioners, United Nations, January 2006; and Deborah Mancini-Griffoli and André Picot, Humanitarian Negotiation: A Handbook for Securing Access, Assistance and Protection for Civilians in Armed Conflict, Centre for Humanitarian Dialogue, October 2004.
6 See The Grand Bargain—A Shared Commitment to Better Serve People in Need, Inter-Agency Standing Committee, 2016 for more information.

References

Barbelet, V. (2019). Rethinking Capacity and Complementarity for a More Local Humanitarian Action. Humanitarian Policy Group, Overseas Development Institute.
Barnett, M. and Weiss, T. (eds.) (2008). *Humanitarianism in Question: Politics, Power, Ethics*. Ithaca, NY: Cornell University Press.

CCHN Field Manual on Frontline Humanitarian Negotiation. (2019). Centre of Competence on Humanitarian Negotiation, Geneva.

Clements, A. (2020). *Humanitarian Negotiations with Armed Groups: The Frontlines of Diplomacy.* London: Routledge.

Collinson, S. and Elhawary, S. (2012). Humanitarian Space: A Review of Trends and Issues. Humanitarian Policy Group, Overseas Development Institute.

DuBois, M. (2020). *The Triple Nexus, Threat or Opportunity for the Humanitarian Principles?* Centre for Humanitarian Action.

Duffield, M. (2012). Challenging Environments: Danger, Resilience and the Aid Industry. *Security Dialogue* 43, 5, special issue: *Governing (in)security in the postcolonial world.*

Fiori, J. E. M. (2013). The Discourse of Western Humanitarianism. *Institut de Relations Internationales et Stratégiques.*

Gordon, S. and Donini, A. (2015). Romancing Principles and Human Rights: Are Humanitarian Principles Salvageable? *International Review of the Red Cross* 97(897/898), 77–111.

Grace, R. (2020). The Humanitarian as Negotiator: Developing Capacity across the Aid Sector. *Negotiation Journal* Winter, 36(1), 13–42.

Grace, R. and Lempereur, A. (2021). Four Dilemmas of Acceptance: Insights from the Field of Humanitarian Negotiation. In: *Achieving Safe Operations through Acceptance: Challenges and Opportunities for Security Risk Management.* Global Interagency Security Forum.

Harroff-Tavel, M. (2006). The Humanitarian Diplomacy of the ICRC. In: *African Yearbook on International Humanitarian Law.*

Howe, K. and Stites, E. (2019). Partners under Pressure: Humanitarian Action for the Syria Crisis. *Disasters* 43(1), 3–23.

Krause, M. (2014). *The Good Project: Humanitarian Relief NGOs and the Fragmentation of Reason.* Chicago, IL: University of Chicago Press.

Magone, C., Neuman, M., and Weissman, F. (2011). *Humanitarian Negotiations Revealed. The MSF Experience.* London: Hurst & Company.

Mancini-Griffoli, T. and Picot, A. (2004). *Humanitarian Negotiation: A Handbook for Securing Access, Assistance and Protection for Civilians in Armed Conflict.* Centre for Humanitarian Dialogue.

Mc Hugh, G. and Bessler, M. (2006). *Humanitarian Negotiations with Armed Groups: A Manual for Practitioners.* New York: United Nations Office for the Coordination of Humanitarian Affairs and the Inter-Agency Standing Committee.

Minear, L. and Smith, H. (eds.) (2007). *Humanitarian Diplomacy: Practitioners and Their Craft.* United Nations Press.

Régnier, P. (2011). The Emerging Concept of Humanitarian Diplomacy: Identification of a Community of Practice and Prospects for International Recognition. *International Review of the Red Cross* 93(884), 1211–1237.

Schenkenberg van Mierop, E. (2018). Local Humanitarian Actors and the Principle of Impartiality. Centre for Humanitarian Action.

Shapiro, D. (2016). *Negotiating the Non-negotiable: How to Resolve Your Most Emotionally Charged Conflicts.* New York, NY: Viking.

Slim, H. (2004). Preface. In Mancini-Griffoli, T. and Picot, A. (2004). *Humanitarian Negotiation: A Handbook for Securing Access, Assistance and Protection for Civilians in Armed Conflict.* Centre for Humanitarian Dialogue.

Slim, H. (2015). *Humanitarian Ethics: A Guide to the Morality of Aid in War and Disaster.* London: Hurst & Company.

Steets, J., Reichhold, U., and Sagmeister, E. (2012). *Evaluation and Review of Humanitarian Access Strategies in DG ECHO Funded Interventions.* Berlin: Global Public Policy Institute.

Straus, O. S. (1912). Humanitarian Diplomacy of the United States. *Proceedings of the American Society of International Law* 6, 45–54.

Toole, D. (2001). *Humanitarian Negotiation: Observations from Recent Experience.* Harvard Program on Humanitarian Policy and Conflict Research.

Tronc, E. (2018). The Humanitarian Imperative: Compromises and Prospects in Protracted Conflicts. In: *Pathways to Peace and Security, Special Issue: Humanitarian Challenges, Humanitarian Support and Human Protection in Armed Conflicts,* 1–54.

Tronc, E., Grace, R., and Nahikian, A. (2018). *Humanitarian Access Obstruction in Somalia: Externally Imposed and Self-Inflicted Dimensions.* Cambridge, MA: Harvard Humanitarian Initiative.

Turunen, S. (2020). Humanitarian Diplomatic Practices. *The Hague Journal of Diplomacy* 15(4), 459–487.

Veuthey, M. (2012). Humanitarian Diplomacy: Saving it When it is Most Needed. In: Vautravers A. and Fox Y. (ed.). *Humanitarian Space and the International Community.* Webster Groves, MO: Webster University.

HUMANITARIAN AUTHORITARIAN
AUTHORITARIAN HUMANITARIAN

COMMENTARY

'Security reasons'

Indira Govender

The year 2023 marks 20 years of civil war in Syria, and although I haven't followed the politics of this war or the humanitarian response to it in subsequent years, in October 2012 I was part of a two person 'diplomatic exploratory mission' to Damascus. The purpose being to negotiate legitimate access for an international NGO (INGO) into Syria from Syrian government officials via the South African office. I was a year into my position as a deputy medical coordinator for the operations in South Africa and Lesotho, the highest position occupied by a South African national in the organisation at that time. Although I was never given a clear reason for being asked to participate in this diplomatic mission, I assumed it had to do with the position I held in the in-country coordination structure. However, I quickly came to realise that my role was simply to be a brown-faced South African prop to a white man attempting to gallantly bargain with Syrian authorities on behalf of the INGO. This tactic had previously worked in another similar context: Instead of approaching from Europe, reach out to the South African ambassador in the war-torn country and negotiate access via the South African office. It may have worked the first time but the Syrian government was not as vulnerable, and whoever thought it would work in Syria clearly underestimated the lasting effects of racist and colonial legacies at thwarting the best intentions. The point of my reflection is not to debate if the INGO's presence in Syria, whether legitimate or not in the eyes of the Syrian government, was or is necessary. What I want to share is the way in which I was used as a token escort, how I was controlled and manipulated by those responsible for putting me in that position and the double standards between what was said and what was done, especially by my colleague on this mission. Moreover, my experience highlighted the stark contrast between how INGOs are perceived outside of

DOI: 10.4324/9781003316541-5

their circle of influence, public relations and self-image and how forces of imperialism and colonialism shape these perceptions, especially among those on the receiving end of such forces, regardless of the organisation's intentions.

I wasn't given much information in the run up to this mission, but a day before my departure, the information provided by another colleague based in Johannesburg created an air of top secrecy and extreme danger. I was told about the extensive surveillance and intelligence network of the Syrian government and warned against carrying any personal devices or attempting to make contact with anyone while in the country. I was made to leave my phone behind and given another one to use with an extra sim card for emergency use. I was especially warned not to associate the purpose of our visit with any of the organisation's other activities that were operational in Syria at the time, as it might directly compromise our safety or that of clandestine operations. Communication for me would be cut off once we arrived in the capital city, Damascus: No contact with anyone via phone or email, and no social media, as there was a risk these messages would be intercepted and traced, exposing the truth that we were not an independent operation but effectively a European satellite. And there was no limit to the extent of consequences we might endure, anything from being detained, imprisoned, or made to disappear by the country's intelligence network. Therefore, for the sake of securing a successful outcome, I was to put my life in the hands of my white male colleague for two weeks. My family would not hear from me once I left South Africa. I had no cash, credit card or access to money. Everything I did or wanted to do had to be approved by the man I was with; he was my only source of information or line of communication in or out of Syria.

After departing South Africa, I spent a night in Amman, Jordan, where I met my companion and learned more about the mission we were on. I had no experience with this type of situation and so I didn't ask a lot of detailed questions, suffice to say the briefing I received entailed more descriptions of how vulnerable we were to being 'monitored' by Syrian intelligence and again why it was imperative that we didn't give ourselves away.

The first thing that struck me as odd was when we checked in to the Four Seasons hotel on arrival in Damascus for 'security reasons'. It seemed slightly counter-intuitive to a humanitarian agenda from Africa to be staying at a quite conspicuously luxury hotel in the centre of Damascus, and after a few awkward nights of being among a handful of guests at the hotel, we eventually moved to more humble accommodation at a less than 5-star hotel down the road. For the duration of our stay, we remained in our hotel rooms, only going down to eat in the hotel restaurant or to have a pre-arranged meeting with someone my colleague knew. I was not allowed to go out and had very limited internet access. I was warned against using certain search terms or visiting certain websites, especially not to mention the name of the organisation in any correspondence, as we were to strictly refer to it by its alternative name to distance ourselves from European nomenclature. Ironically, my colleague was a fairly high-profile humanitarian advisor within the organisation and at the time there were no secrets about his identity that a Google search wouldn't have revealed.

Things began to unravel fairly soon into our negotiations as I heard my colleague deliver the offer of aid from comrades in South Africa, only to be met with resistance that was out of his depth. Even if I believed in the authenticity of our offer, the Syrian officials we met saw it for what it was: A charade. I think they saw beyond it too, because for the entire time we were there, we were treated with respect, no harm was brought upon us, no threats and no intimidation. If we were being watched or followed, it was never apparent. The only intimidation I was subjected to was from my colleague, who was probably anxious and desperate over the outcome of this mission and kept me on a close leash. I was frequently reminded that we were being watched or that our movements were being tracked. I was made to feel as if my verbal requests for details or explanations as to why certain decisions were being made were inappropriate or risky and, on occasion, censored. Maybe if I'd been tasked with being more than a prop to a white man trying to rebrand the NGO's assistance as an offering of *ubuntu* from an African country, I'd have more sympathy for this failed mission. All the Syrian officials who made time to meet us rejected the organisation's intervention in Syria and repeated the same story in different words. In my confined role, I took solace in witnessing how they politely refused to relent in their opinion of the organisation as a European entity trying to establish what they considered an unnecessary presence in Syria.

One of the first people we met was a Deputy Minister in the Syrian government who welcomed us warmly into his office and expressed his solidarity with South Africa. I'll never forget the picture of Che' Guevara on his desk and how he categorically refused to accept the organisation's interventions in Syria. His reasoning being that this organisation had a 'bad reputation in developing countries', a 'bad reputation in Sudan' and was already active in Syria without the government's permission. The Deputy Minister claimed to be unaware of a donation made to the Syrian government from the organisation's office in South Africa, something I found hard to believe given what I was told about the Syrian government's superior intelligence network. Discrepancies such as these made me realise the information I had been given, rather than allow me to engage in any meaningful way, was meant to control me and ensure I complied with my colleague's instructions for 'security reasons'.

A second enduring encounter was with a feminist scholar and senior advisor to the Syrian president at the time. Although she neither accepted nor denied the offer of assistance, she related a story of how another international organisation had entered Syria on the premise of providing humanitarian aid but arrived in 'big cars, getting paid big salaries, but with no material assistance for the Syrian people'. It was after this meeting that I noticed further hypocrisy from my colleague. He'd advised me to set up an alternative email address to use as a simple way to reassure my close family and friends that I was okay, with the rule being that no one must reply to any of my emails from this address because a reply might be intercepted and the sender would be hacked for information about us. I remember, on one occasion, receiving a reply and being paranoid over the consequences. But then I noticed that his alternative email inbox was full of replies from friends and people working in the Johannesburg office, with many of these emails containing the name of the organisation I was warned not to use. I confronted him about this specific point since I was given a brief not to use those words. I raised the point that his use of these words could send conflicting security messages to our team in Johannesburg, who might in turn relax their cautious approach and compromise us. I later discovered that my colleague was also scrolling through his Twitter account during our time in Damascus, while I was made to cease all contact with my family and friends for 'security reasons'.

Besides the double standards and what I refer to as deliberate omissions of information, I came to view my colleague as naïve and politically immature. Perhaps he too was a pawn in a larger game, made to believe he could negotiate this organisation's entry into Syria under the guise of an African operation? Whatever it was that drove him to try and close the deal in Damascus, my opinion of him and our mission was tainted. I secretly hoped it would fail because I started to see myself in the eyes of Syrian officials politely telling a white representative of an organisation they viewed as another vehicle of Western colonialism that he and the organisation were not welcome there. In the broader context, I wonder how conscionable it was to appropriate South Africa's reputation as a Global South ally and use it like a Trojan Horse in the name of humanitarian aid.

I hope that in the years that passed my colleague's understanding has deepened, at least enough to know that even if you're still tokenising people of colour or appropriating a nation's solidarity struggle, it just doesn't sit right to check into luxury hotels when you're a spokesperson from Southern Africa offering humanitarian aid in a crisis.

3

THE VOCABULARY OF NEGOTIATIONS

Sovereignty and authoritarian arguments
in the Security Council[1]

Maximilian Bertamini

Introduction

When reflecting on negotiations with authoritarian regimes, many of the member states of the United Nations (UN) Security Council (SC) find themselves in a position which differs from that of other negotiators. Bound by a common mandate under the UN Charter (UNCh),[2] members of the SC are required to find solutions for the maintenance of international peace and security through negotiations. Within this institutional frame, states with dramatically different styles of government meet at the negotiation table, and their views inadvertently collide. Different from the rest of the international legal system, the setting of the SC does not leave it up to its members to decide whether they want to engage in negotiations with certain types of regimes in the first place, but only how to negotiate with them. Unsurprisingly, the collisions of different perspectives on peace and security as well as on institutions have frequently resulted in deadlocks at the SC.

This chapter will take the negotiations about the various resolutions on cross-border delivery of humanitarian aid into Syria as an example to examine if and in how far such deadlocks are the result of different understandings of 'sovereignty' as a crucial item of negotiation vocabulary. Based on how different states use the concept of sovereignty in their arguments, the chapter also analyses whether some of these arguments can be classified as authoritarian.

For this purpose, the chapter will proceed as follows. First, a brief negotiation history of the resolutions in question will be provided, which sketches out the major positions and points of controversy in the SC negotiations over the course of the last years and shows how deals were eventually concluded.

DOI: 10.4324/9781003316541-6

Second, it will unearth the role of 'sovereignty' as an item of negotiation vocabulary and the implications of its use in negotiations, with a focus on whether certain invocations of sovereignty justify the label 'authoritarian'. Third, it will reflect on the possibly unintended consequences of invoking sovereignty in certain ways and how they may complicate international negotiations.

From Resolution 2165 to Resolution 2642 – a one-sided development

The SC is regularly at odds over the prolongation and modification of the much-debated aid programme, which provides for the cross-border delivery of humanitarian aid into Syria. Since the latest renewal of the delivery programme on 12 July 2022 with Resolution 2642,[3] the SC and its observers can look back at eight years of negotiation history between two very different positions, which also consistently split up the P5 like few other issues do.

Originally, the SC members were in overwhelming agreement on how to handle the situation in Syria. As a reaction to the rise of Islamist terrorist groups in Syria and the correspondingly appalling humanitarian conditions in early and mid-2014, the SC unanimously adopted Resolution 2165[4] on 14 July 2014. It contained a programme for the cross-border delivery of humanitarian assistance into Syria over four border crossing points, focusing also on regions which were controlled by the opposition to the al-Assad regime. When the SC members provided statements after the resolution was adopted, the overwhelming tone was one of mutual congratulation on such an important step towards improving and saving the lives of many Syrians and on achieving unanimity on the matter.[5] Although the Syrian representative complained about several issues concerning what the Assad regime officially considers the true reasons for Syria's dire situation, he did not criticise the Resolution directly in terms of illegality.[6]

Fast forward to 10 January 2020. The SC's unanimity in adopting resolutions that prolonged the cross-border delivery programme faces its first serious hurdles, as four of the P5 members abstained from voting. The bone of contention was the number of border-crossing points, which were eventually cut in half by Resolution 2504. On the one hand, the USA, the UK and France – alongside most of the elected members of the SC – argued for prolongations of the cross-border mechanism with as many crossing points as possible. Eventually, the US representative had to conclude:

> We fought hard to keep four of the crossing points open with a view to ensuring greater United Nations access for delivering much-needed aid. Reluctantly, for the sake of maintaining a reasonable amount of aid flows, we were

willing to compromise to authorise three crossing points for 12 months, but that compromise was not enough for the Russian Federation or for China.[7]

The supporters of upholding the scope of the aid mission held that this was the only way to even come close to fulfilling the immense humanitarian needs of the Syrian population, including the need for COVID-19 vaccines,[8] and refused to consider lifting the sanctions they imposed on members of the Syrian government.

On the other hand, Russia and the People's Republic of China (PRC), usually joined by a small minority of the respective elected SC members, pleaded for a Syrian-owned and Syrian-led solution to the problem, which entails strengthening the al-Assad regime and reducing outside influence to a minimum:

> The Syrian authorities have now restored control over the greater part of their territory, so cross-border assistance to those areas is no longer necessary.
>
> The second preambular paragraph of the draft resolution proposed by the co-penholders contain a reference to the firm commitment to the sovereignty, independence, unity and territorial integrity of Syria. In that case it is important to also consider the views of Damascus, the recipient country, as set out in a letter [...] which clearly outlines the Syrian Government's position that keeping the mechanism in its current form is unacceptable. We cannot all disregard the position of the recipient country.[9]

The states opposing the original scope of the mission profess the view that both the sanctions and the diversion of aid to terrorist organisations are the true reasons for the continuously precarious humanitarian situation in Syria. Both factions abstained (which in the UN SC counts as an affirmative vote under customary law) out of protest, some in relation to the alleged infringements on Syrian sovereignty:

> The Russian Federation abstained in the voting on resolution 2504 (2020), proposed by the co-penholders, for the sole purpose of not blocking cross-border assistance to the Syrian province of Idlib, which is the only one that still really needs that method of delivering supplies.[10]

And some in relation to the gravely reduced assistance that the Syrian population would now receive:

> The United States abstained in this evening's voting for one reason and one reason only. After months of negotiations, the text of resolution 2504 (2020) was the only path forward that would reasonably allow for the

delivery of any aid at all to the Syrian people. We could not veto such a measure, as we are committed to supporting innocent Syrians to the greatest extent possible. In abstaining, we are lending a voice to the 4 million Syrians whose welfare has been overlooked for far too long [...][11]

The United Kingdom voted to abstain in the voting on resolution 2504 (2020). We will not vote to stop vital aid reaching Syria, but neither will we vote in favour of a resolution that reduces aid provision for vulnerable populations and puts lives at risk. Although four of the five permanent members of the Security Council abstained in the voting, we obviously did not do so for the same reasons.[12]

The Syrian government, as the entity concerned, is allowed to speak on the matter on the stage of the UN as well. Of course, it has an opinion on these discussions, which it frequently made known to the SC. The Syrian regime left no doubt that it considers the Russian and Chinese positions correct and laudable in their entirety, while it rejects and criticises any proposal from the western P5 members as blatantly unlawful.

The insistence of some countries on not listening to the voice of the Syrian people and not deviating from their erroneous policies in Syria and in our Arab region has only brought terrorism and chaos, the destabilisation of security and stability, the plundering of wealth, and harm to the lives and welfare of civilians. We therefore call on those countries to conduct an honest review of the catastrophic repercussions of their policies and to put an end to their practices that violate the principles of international law, the provisions of the Charter of the United Nations and the foundations of friendly relations among States.[13]

On 11 July 2020, the aid programme had expired for the first time. Not by decision, but because the SC members, despite the continuously worsening humanitarian situation in Syria, were unable to come to terms. Eventually, Resolution 2533 was adopted with the abstention of Russia, the PRC and the Dominican Republic.[14] Of the four border-crossing points, only Bab al-Hawa remained, as pushed for by Russia and the PRC, which increasingly backed Syria's critical stance on cross-border aid. Four other attempts to agree on proposed resolutions before the assistance programme expired failed due to vetoes and lacking majorities. Meanwhile, the previously lauded cross-border aid system was criticised by Syria as blatantly illegal, and some SC members agreed that Syria's sovereignty was disregarded by the contents of the same resolutions, which had been reinstated mostly unanimously year after year before 2020. The SC, including the P5, was split into two camps, which accused each other of politicising the issue of humanitarian aid and made it almost impossible to find an agreement, holding millions of Syrians in suspense about their chances of survival.

A brief period of unanimity enabled the next prolongation on 9 July 2021 (Resolution 2585),[15] which provided for an even more reduced form of the cross-border aid programme. Yet, in July 2022, amidst the surging international tensions caused by Russia's illegal invasion of Ukraine, the humanitarian aid programme for Syria had to expire a second time, as SC members were unable to agree once more. It was only on 12 July 2022, when the already severely restricted aid programme was continued in its most reduced form yet, with one border crossing point and for a duration of only six months.

Considering where the SC started out with Resolution 2165, the eight years since then (and particularly from 2020 onwards) have been characterised by resolutions in the direction of the minority position held by Russia and China[16] and thus indirectly the position of Baschar al-Assad's Syria, regardless of its humanitarian ineffectiveness. All three regimes can (in different aspects and to varying degrees) be considered to be governed by autocratic (Marshall and Elzinga-Marshall, 2017, 45–51). More specifically, given the formally democratic but actually very limited and hardly responsible political pluralism (Linz, 1975, 264; specifically for the PRC and Syria, see Merkel, 2010, 43, 46) in these countries, the regimes can be qualified as authoritarian. These facts imply that authoritarian regimes achieved considerable success in the negotiations on humanitarian assistance to Syria, which arguably prioritises the interests of the Syrian regime in controlling its territory over the human rights and humanitarian concerns of large parts of its population.

The Syria resolutions – a tale of authoritarian success?

Whether the development of the Syria resolutions can be considered as a success for authoritarianism as such is, however, debatable.[17] The answer depends on the degree to which the arguments advanced by Russia and China in the SC can be considered authoritarian. In this section, the sovereignty-based arguments advanced by these two P5 members will therefore be analysed in terms of their authoritarian quality. For this purpose, the section first lays out a framework on how to assess the authoritarian characteristics of a sovereignty-based argument under international law. Then, it assesses the relevant arguments in light of that framework, with a focus on both the logical premises underlying the arguments and the context in which they are invoked.

A working approach to authoritarian arguments

The chapter assumes that a sovereignty-based argument can be qualified as authoritarian on the basis of conceptual and practical factors. Conceptual factors relate to underlying assumptions about the nature of sovereignty itself, while practical factors concern elements like the context in which an argument is raised. For the purposes of this chapter, the common denominator for both types of 'authoritarianisation' of arguments will be the classification of authoritarian regimes by Juan Linz. According to Linz, authoritarianism as a subset of autocracy is predominantly characterised by restricted and not responsible pluralism, which distinguishes authoritarian regimes from the much more unconstrained pluralist system of governance that is democracy (Linz, 1975, 264). As a way of governing international relations, international law qualifies as a system of governance, which therefore fits into Linz's model. How pluralistic this system of global governance is depends on how specific elements of governance (i.e. international norms) are created and applied (cf. Vereshchetin and Danilenko, 1986). These questions will be analysed shortly.[18] The degree to which international law as a system of governance is pluralistic is important for the analysis of potentially authoritarian sovereignty-based arguments because when sovereignty is invoked in an international legal argument, the argument contains an often implicit statement on the relationship between sovereignty and international law (Koskenniemi, 2007, 224–302). In so far as international law is a pluralist system of governance, the degree to which the meaning and contents of sovereignty are shaped by this system determines the degree to which a sovereignty-based argument embraces or rejects pluralism. Accordingly, the more an invocation of sovereignty is used to reject pluralistic elements of international law, the more such a use of sovereignty may be characterised as authoritarian.[19]

Pluralism in the creation of International Law

International law is a decentralised system of law-making, as the sovereign equality of states prohibits any top-down or lateral imposition of law on states. Rooted in the self-determination of peoples (Besson, 2011, para. 102; Crawford, 2006, 114), states' equality in sovereignty in and of itself poses a barrier against political monism on the international level. While not necessarily democratic, the sources of international law are by nature distant from the sovereign commands, by which national legal orders tend to operate. Sovereign equality as one of the basic principles of international law therefore predisposes the international legal order against autocracy in the sense that a plurality of equally valid national identities, perspectives and values is preserved by it (Mégret, 2020, 533–538; Voina-Motoc, 2008, 52, 53). Sovereign equality generally necessitates consent and compromise in the genesis of international law. One might label this 'horizontal pluralism' (Mégret, 2020, 538). Horizontal pluralism in international law upholds not only states' individuality in terms of their various legal cultures (e.g., civil law, common law, Islamic law), economic interests, ideologies and so on, but it also ensures that their different perspectives are valid in international negotiations and their products.[20] Especially after the large push for decolonisation in the 1960s, the numerical diversity of states increased significantly and so did the conceptions of truth at the international level (Voina-Motoc, 2008, 59–63). The decentralised structure of international law allows for all perspectives to be advanced at the same time without having to accept one universally correct view or set of values (Koskenniemi, 2007; Voina-Motoc, 2008, 59–63). As far as customary international law is concerned, one might even attest the creation of international legal norms a degree of democratic character. Once a great deal of states acts with *opinio iuris* in a certain way, the ensuing norm of customary international law will also bind those states that did not explicitly reject the application to them. Practically, this means that law-creating behaviour of a majority will be binding for the minority as well. These observations support the argument that international law is a product of legal and cultural pluralism. Arguably, however, the degree to which different subject matters of international law incorporate different ideologies and cultures differs from case to case. In that sense, not all branches of international law are equally pluralistic. While 'technical' questions, such as treaty interpretation, are hardly concerned with ideology and cultural differences, the protection of international human rights or other value-heavy fields are the centres of pluralism in the international legal order (Vereshchetin and Danilenko, 1986, 59).

This being said, the variety of views meeting at international negotiation tables is something that some consider as something that merely needs to be managed by international law (cf. Mégret, 2020, 536). And although soft law continues to increase in relevance, when it comes to the established sources and subjects of international law, the international legal system is still rather static and uniform, with only a moderate trend towards pluralism. Yet international law goes beyond the mere management of different perspectives, values and cultures. It is not an order, which just accepts any form of system and values, or lack thereof. The international legal order is not entirely relativist, but built on a form of pluralism, which focuses on communication and common understanding (cf. Berlin, 2013). It celebrates 'difference [but] remains committed to the existence of universal standards' (Appiah, 2002).

Pluralism in the application of International Law

The application of international law to states is generally dependent of their consent or, in some cases, their lack of explicit dissent to being bound. State sovereignty as the main reason *for* the pluralist nature of the creation of international law is thus also the main factor *against* its application to states. In other words, state sovereignty is the valve that regulates *if* and in how far international law as a product of pluralism is accepted or rejected as an element of legal pluralism next to the domestic legal order. Hinging on the process through which international law is created, the question of international law's applicability to states is therefore equally pluralistic in the sense that it depends not on a single commanding position, but the opinions of many individual entities. On a macro-level of applicability, there is thus some pluralism to be found as well.

On the micro-level of application, however, that is at the level that is concerned with the question of *how* international law applies to states with different normative orders, it cannot be concluded that the application of international law rules generally takes the different situations and values of states into account (think of rules like the prohibition on the use of force, which necessarily apply to all states in the same way). Yet, some pluralistic element can even be found here as well, both structurally and depending on the subject matter of the legal regime in question.

Structurally, once states accept the application of international law to them, international law coexists with the national laws of states and claims validity through direct or indirect implementation in domestic legal orders. If the sovereign equality of states was labelled the 'horizontal' pluralistic element of international law, the coexistence of international law with the domestic legal of a state could be considered an element of 'vertical' legal pluralism (Mégret, 2020, 544).

Regarding the different subject matters of international law, human rights law provides for certain margins of appreciation of states in the application of human rights standards and in the realm of socio-economic rights, where implementation is even largely subject to a state's available resources and capacities. Hence human rights law in certain areas tends to take account of the individuality of states in its application (Ibid.). Speaking of human rights, certain grave suppressions of domestic pluralism protected internationally by human rights law may be addressed by international law as well, be it through the UN or perhaps even via the Responsibility to Protect, each serving as a 'guarantor of last resort for legal pluralism' (Ibid., 549).

With the pluralistic elements in international law now defined, the next steps will be to analyse in how far the sovereignty arguments advanced in the Syria negotiations embrace or reject these elements, first at a theoretical and then at a practical level.

Conceptually authoritarian sovereignty arguments

To understand the implications embedded in different types of sovereignty-based arguments, this section will first introduce Martti Koskenniemi's distinction between 'pure fact' and 'legal' sovereignty as the analytical basis for examining in how far sovereignty-based arguments can be characterised as authoritarian. In a next step this analytical framework will be applied to the arguments made in the SC.

The different meanings of sovereignty in International Law

In his 1989 dissertation on the structure of international legal argument, Martti Koskenniemi unearthed conceptional struggles that underlie international law. It is arguably the concept of sovereignty, in which these struggles manifest most strongly. According to Koskenniemi, a distinction between two rather radical and mutually exclusive approaches to understanding the origin and nature of sovereignty in international law can be and frequently is made in international legal argument (Koskenniemi, 2007, 224–302). International legal argument tends to oscillate between these two approaches to sovereignty, namely the so-called 'pure fact approach' and the 'legal approach' (Ibid., 225). Both explain sovereignty as a legal concept, meaning that sovereignty implies rights and corresponding duties for its holders. But the two positions differ immensely when it comes to their perspectives on the relation between sovereignty and the rest of international law as well as the explanation of international law's binding force.

The pure fact approach to sovereignty operates under the assumption that states enjoy sovereignty as a matter of fact simply because they are states. Being sovereign is therefore not contingent upon law but only on statehood. While law can address facts, it does not alter or control them, which is why proponents of the pure fact view construct law from sovereignty in the form of voluntarism (Ibid., 233). Sovereignty is seen as external to and constitutive of international law, which also means that sovereignty is not something allowed or created by international law but something that law originates from and merely relates to.

This view is reflected in all international legal arguments which recur to the will of states as the original and final authority, for example, the rule that the intentions of the contracting states are the primary yardstick for the interpretation of treaties. Essentially, also those rules which propose that state consent is required for international law to be binding on states rely heavily on pure fact sovereignty (Ibid.). This position was prominently reflected in the Permanent Court of Justice's (PCIJ) Lotus judgement, where it held that:

> International law governs relations between independent States. The rules of law binding upon States therefore emanate from their own free will as expressed in conventions or by usages generally accepted as expressing principles of law and established in order to regulate the relations between these Co-existing independent communities or with a view to the achievement of common aims. Restrictions upon the independence of States cannot therefore be presumed
>
> *(PCIJ, 1927, 18)*

The pure fact approach is further reflected in rules of international law that attach weight to the interests of the state. Examples include the rule that exceptions have to be interpreted restrictively in order to not undermine the validity claim of the norm (Dörr, 2018, para. 7; European Court of Human Rights, 2000, para. 59; PCIJ, 1923, 25), the rule that restrictions on a state's freedom must not be made by analogy, and the procedural requirement that restrictions of sovereignty must be established by clear and convincing evidence (Koskenniemi, 2007, 257).

In terms of its content, pure fact sovereignty equates to a generally unrestricted freedom of action for states. In terms of international law's binding force, pure fact sovereignty considers international law binding based on the will of sovereign states, independently of justifications based on morals, reason, religion, etc. of the normative contents of the international law so created.

The separation of international law and sovereignty is a motif that runs through Chinese, Russian and Syrian statements, especially in their statements on draft resolutions S/2019/961 and S/2019/962. After the Russian representative had laid down the legal parameters for humanitarian assistance, which explicitly call for the consent of the recipient country, he emphasised that the SC members needed to '*also* consider the views of Damascus' and could not 'disregard the position of the recipient country'.[21] The Chinese representative recalled the need to respect the sovereignty of the countries concerned and then turned to the law by holding that 'cross-border humanitarian operations should *also* strictly follow international law'.[22] The Syrian representative, when invited to weigh in on the resolutions, thanked China and the PRC specifically for 'safeguarding the principles of international law and the Charter of the United Nations, chief among which is respect for the sovereignty of States *and* the rules governing humanitarian action'.[23] Most recently in the SC negotiations of July 2022, even Mexico as a democratic state expressed itself in a way that can be interpreted to distinguish between the contents of sovereignty and international law. The Mexican representative stated in relation to a new planned Turkish military operation in northern Syria that '[t]hat would be totally contrary to the provisions of international law, specifically with respect to the use of force and self-defence, and if it were to occur, it would undermine Syria's sovereignty, independence, unity and territorial integrity'.

Opposite from the pure fact view on sovereignty stands the legal view. Here, the idea is that sovereignty is a creation of international law and therefore subsequent to law (Koskenniemi, 2007, 228). In the legal view, sovereignty is essentially a descriptive term that captures the freedoms and obligations of states, which strips sovereignty of an inherent normative meaning (Ibid., 231). Instead, the legal view provides sovereignty with normative justifications and defines its scope. Under the legal view, sovereignty is not only restricted but also positively established through international law. The role of the legal approach to sovereignty becomes evident in international dispute resolution wherever two states invoke their sovereignty with regard to the same matter. Such disputes will have to be resolved by applying international law, which inevitably determines where one state's sovereignty ends and where another's begins. In fact, without recurring to international law, conflicts between two states respectively claiming sovereignty over a matter would be irresolvable through law (Ibid., 238, 239, 258).

Under the legal approach to sovereignty, international law's binding force is justified based on whether its contents are in line with considerations of fairness, morals or other sources of norm validity and not so much because states want it to be (given that their sovereignty has no inherent meaning without international law).

When arguing about the proper way to go about the cross-border delivery of humanitarian assistance to Syria, most states held that there was no way around the delivery of humanitarian aid to Syria, despite Syria's objections. For example, in reaction to the vetoes on draft resolution S/2020/654, the USA representative claimed that the continued resistance by the PRC and Russia could not be 'spun into false choices between humanitarian aid, sovereignty and sanctions'.[24] A related position was taken by the Luxembourgian representative as early as 2014, when the first resolution was adopted. She considered that 'The consent of the Syrian authorities will no longer be necessary. [...] The United Nations and its partners can distribute medical and surgical supplies without interference from Damascus'.[25] These statements make sense if sovereignty is not separate from humanitarian aid or rather the law that governs it but intertwined with it. This includes the Charter of the UN which grants the SC the right to authorise operations contrary to the will of the affected states. The consequence of this view is that only where the law gives weight to the views of a state, its views must be respected. If withholding consent is illegal (cf. Barber, 2020), then law does not endow a state with sovereignty, i.e., a free choice in that matter.

Both positions on sovereignty's relation to the law are, of course, extremes, and neither can consistently be upheld. The pure fact view would essentially leave international law in a state of non-binding nature due to the possibility to oppose sovereignty to law and the impossibility of reconciling opposing claims of sovereignty (Koskenniemi, 2007, 245, 258), while the legal view would result in states being denied any inherent sphere of liberty (Ibid., 251). It can therefore be safely assumed that the states negotiating on the matter would not subscribe to either view coherently throughout any other discussion they might have based on international law. If the negotiating states were aware of the implications of their arguments on sovereignty at all, their positions should at most be seen as rhetorical tools, which lean on theoretically exclusive positions. Overestimating and over-interpreting the role of theoretical positions on sovereignty in the arguments of the SC members would certainly distort the complex array of positions and problems intertwined within the SC negotiations on Syria. Especially the negotiations in 2022 were coined more by general tensions between Russia and other SC members. The positions taken in the SC were less technical and less theoretically charged, but rather indicative of geopolitical agendas. In practice, the position taken on sovereignty often depends on the context and moves on a spectrum from 'pure fact' to legal. This practical dimension of sovereignty-based arguments will be crucial for the upcoming analysis of practically authoritarian arguments in part 3.

For now, it remains striking that the negotiations with the most amount of controversy and tenacity – apart from those amidst the illegal war of aggression led by one of the SC's P5 – were the ones which contained theoretically charged discussions about sovereignty.

Authoritarian elements in the two views on sovereignty?

Sovereignty under the pure fact perspective equals the basis for but not the product of pluralism. It thus emphasises the pluralist nature of international law's creation and on the macro-level of its application from the perspective of state-centrism. Under the legal approach to sovereignty, sovereignty is a descriptive term for the contents and influence of products of pluralism. This approach, therefore, highlights the normative contents produced on its basis rather than the structural pluralism of international law. This means that generally neither the legal nor the pure fact approach to sovereignty can conclusively be considered a decisive rejection of pluralism. Their emphasis on some elements of pluralism in international law says little about the respective other pluralistic elements and certainly does not reject them altogether. Based on this chapter's working definition, none of the approaches to sovereignty allows a characterisation of corresponding arguments as authoritarian per se.

Yet, there is still one subtle difference regarding the importance of international law's pluralistic elements in the two views on sovereignty. This difference concerns the role of pluralistic elements in international law-making. In so far as pluralism in a political system is decisive for the distinction between several types of regimes, pluralism needs to be understood in the context of how a regime comes to its decisions. The pluralistic features of international law should therefore also be weighed according to the role that they play for the making of governance decisions. In that regard, the implications of the two views on sovereignty differ. Because pure fact sovereignty relates to international law in a way that highlights the pluralistic structure of international law, it emphasises states' possibilities to not only engage in, but also explicitly reject pluralistic decision-making on the international level. The same is true for the adoption of products of such law-making. If sovereignty means that states have an inherent and mostly unlimited sphere of liberty on which international law can be built, then sovereignty includes the possibility to never engage in any form of (by nature pluralistic) law-making on the international level. The legal approach to sovereignty highlights states' subjection to international law as the product of pluralistic decision-making. If sovereignty means whatever the applicable international law prescribes, then sovereignty presupposes the existence of some international law applicable to states. This means that states are either inherently subject to certain basic rules of international law (e.g., under some law of nature) and/or do engage in some form of law-making with other states. By comparison, the legal view on sovereignty is thus more predisposed towards pluralistic decision-making.

But again, neither view on the relationship between international law and sovereignty precludes pluralistic international decision-making per se. The pure fact view's bias towards rejecting pluralistic decision-making on the international level is very subtle. It neither precludes the possibility of pluralistic law-making, nor the possibility of states opting out of pluralistic law-making projects under the legal view. Therefore, characterising the invocation of pure fact sovereignty as containing an authoritarian element would be an overstatement.

All in all, from a conceptual perspective, sovereignty-based arguments cannot be qualified as authoritarian. Accordingly, none of the arguments raised in the SC negotiations on Syria warrant this label from a theoretical outlook. The next part of this chapter will examine if a more practical perspective leads to the same conclusion.

Practically authoritarian sovereignty arguments

At a practical level, the idea that sovereignty is the legal protection of collective political, cultural, religious, etc. self-determination is all too often misused as a shield against outside voices pointing out shortcomings or even direct violations of agreed-upon legal standards. The logic is that when the treatment of a minority, political opponents and other forms of domestic pluralism is a purely internal affair, sovereignty prohibits corresponding outside interferences. Self-determination by means of oppression and other illegal practices would then be protected.

But this is not at all how sovereignty works, not even under a pure fact view. International law is meant to provide the normative framework for the peaceful coexistence and cooperation of states. If sovereignty could be validly exercised in violation of agreed legal standards and thus in disregard of the products of international pluralism, international law would ultimately succumb to nothing but unilaterally interest-driven politics. If states could advance their sovereignty to get out of legal obligations, the influence and perspectives of other states reflected in carefully negotiated international norms would matter no longer. Such arguments are ultimately authoritarian because they do not only do away with the products of international legal pluralism in favour of horizontal pluralism, as the pure fact view does. They also do away with the whole premise that horizontal pluralism is built on. This premise is that peaceful coexistence will be achieved by granting states protection for their independent self-determination under the concept of sovereignty, which justifies a defensive and declinatory understanding of sovereignty. But this logic cannot function for already established rules. Pure fact sovereignty highlights the freedom to not engage in international law-making, but when a state does, the binding force of an agreement rests in the states' consent. Only if such consent is given in good faith and honoured independently of political changes or opportunistic considerations, can international law foster trust-building and fulfil its pacifying function.

Regarding human rights and international humanitarian law, an authoritarian carte-blanche understanding of sovereignty challenges the international legal order at its peace-oriented core. Under the UNCh, peace is understood not only as the absence of international conflict but as a more sophisticated state in which social, economic, humanitarian and ecological factors are recognised as necessary for preventing conflict and maintaining peace sustainably.[26] Any serious sovereignty-based disregard for or avoidance of already applicable legal standards which guarantee these 'softer' factors of peace is therefore not only authoritarian but a challenge to international peace and stability as such.

Of course, none of the SC members openly disregard international law. They would rather call for it to be observed next to Syria's sovereignty. But to be clear, Syria withholding its consent to a broader humanitarian programme that also reaches the opposition to Assad is illegal under the human rights law[27] applicable to Syria. This context turns the sovereignty arguments raised by the PRC, Russia and Syria from arguments implying that sovereignty is independent from the law in its content to ones that imply that sovereignty is effectively above the law.

The vocabulary of negotiations – lessons and conclusion

The different positions articulated by states in the SC (mostly in the months before Resolution 2504 of early 2020) saw states on both sides engaging in a more or less open conflict about their perspectives on how sovereignty relates to the rest of international law. In subsequent negotiations and statements, there were references to Syrian sovereignty and international law as well, but after Resolution 2533, they took place at a much more abstract level and avoided confronting the opposite perspective. Although the fact remains that the SC discussions got stuck on many other issues than 'only' the problem of legal theory elaborated above, it is undeniable that the negotiations in which this conceptual issue was addressed went noticeably less smoothly. On the theoretical level, neither view on the relationship between sovereignty and international law has strong implications for or against the role of pluralistic elements of international law. In other words, the endorsement of neither can, in and of itself, be considered an authoritarian argument or a position with an authoritarian element. On the practical level, however, the purposes for which sovereignty is sometimes invoked by states contradict the pluralistic foundation of such arguments, which effectively makes these invocations authoritarian arguments.

To do their work effectively, international negotiators should be aware of the dynamics underlying sovereignty-based arguments and understand the costs and opportunities which come with negotiating from positions charged with irreconcilable underlying perspectives. For humanitarian workers on the ground, whose ability to do their work depends on these international negotiations, understanding the sovereignty dynamics in international law is helpful as well. When faced with reservations to their work, the insights from this chapter can enable them to distinguish between internationally valid and respectable arguments on the one hand and politicised pseudo-sovereign claims on the other. This ability may be helpful for knowing what it may take to overcome reservations and what to lobby for with their governmental partners.

Because at the theoretical level, sovereignty invocations under the legal and the pure fact approach to sovereignty are not authoritarian per se, the question arises if states negotiating with authoritarian regimes have anything to gain or to lose by taking a different conceptual position on sovereignty than their authoritarian counterparts.

As part of the answer to this question, the methods of interpreting SC resolutions have a role to play. The interpretation of SC resolutions matters for the proper implementation of resolutions through states. Only if resolutions can be interpreted in a way which fulfils the SC's mandate to maintain international peace, the effectiveness of the SC as an institution can be guaranteed. Whether states may or may not take certain humanitarian measures against the will of the state concerned will depend on how a resolution is interpreted.

Different from international treaties, to which the interpretation rules from Art. 31–33 of the Vienna Convention on the Law of Treaties[28] (VCLT) apply, SC resolutions are not subject to any specific rules of interpretation. Although, like treaties, they are products of compromise and political will, they differ from international treaties in that they are drafted in fulfilment of a legally binding mandate of the SC under Art. 24(1) UNCh. While states are generally not required to engage in international negotiations or find a compromise, members of the SC, per mandate, bear a responsibility which does not allow them to remain on the side-lines. Instead, they are under pressure to find agreement in order to maintain international peace and security. Another difference to 'regular' international treaty negotiations resolutions is that SC resolutions may need to be drafted in a short period of time that does not allow negotiations to reach a point where every state is satisfied. Resolutions therefore often contain some degree of deliberate ambiguity and content that is thought to be harmless (Wood, 1998, 82). Furthermore, the resolutions of the SC do not always contain purely legal content. Consequently, SC resolutions can be characterised as 'more political' than regular international treaties, which plays a role in their interpretation in so far as the circumstances of their adoption, including the preparatory work and the considerations revealed therein, are ascribed greater weight (Ibid., 95). The history of previous resolutions can also be a factor (Papastavridis, 2007, 101, 102).

Because the negotiations matter for interpretation, whether SC member states should engage in discussions on the relationship between sovereignty and international law matters as well. In terms of opportunities, engaging in such discussions in favour of the legal approach to sovereignty could result in a greater focus on the legality of sovereignty claims. This would strengthen the contents of international law rather than its structure. To the extent that arguments for a legal approach to sovereignty are successful in the SC negotiations, legality considerations would likely influence the interpretation and application of resulting resolutions. Another opportunity for states engaging in theoretical legal discussions could be the stalemate thereby created. As pure fact sovereignty and legal sovereignty are mutually exclusive positions on the question of where sovereignty comes from and what its relation to international law is (Koskenniemi, 2007, 227), arguments based on the respective other theory may ensure that the opposite argument cannot easily be convinced. That is, unless the underlying theoretical debate on the international legal world view is settled, which is a futile endeavour due to the eventual weaknesses of both positions. Creating stalemates also means that states can potentially claim a higher price in terms of the degree to which their interests will be met in the final resolutions for abandoning the arguments resting heavily on legal theory. To avoid such stalemates and the potential price to be paid to get out of them, the negotiations might turn away from the theoretically informed arguments altogether and pragmatically focus on the areas in which consent can be easier achieved. The Chinese statement preceding the unanimous adoption of Resolution 2585 can be read to support this analysis:

> The Council should solve problems in a more pragmatic way, focus on specific goals and push all parties to find compromise solutions through dialogue and negotiations and avoid serious confrontation.[29]

When considering such a strategy, states must also be aware of its costs. Especially in the SC, these could take the form of politicising humanitarian need as a lever to force the other side to give in to its own position in order to resolve the stalemate. If both sides choose this approach, finding consent and fulfilling the SC's mandate can even be at stake altogether. Avoiding negotiations through arguments anchored in legal theory from the outset is the comparatively easier way to find consent in the SC, as one dimension of complexity would be removed from the equation. This would in turn serve the populations in need of timely SC resolutions regarding their situation. In the other pan of the scale lies the problem that giving in to or avoiding arguments touching on the relationship between sovereignty and international law may progressively create a yardstick for the interpretation of future SC resolutions based on rhetoric rather than on conviction. Such a yardstick may, in the end, not be preferred by many states, not even by those whose sovereignty rhetoric has led to its emergence. Furthermore, invoking sovereignty in an abstract way without touching upon the way it relates to international law in general leaves room for the whole spectrum of positions on the matter to be applied in the interpretation of resolutions. This may result in states acting not only uncoordinatedly, but downright refusing to act. If a state interprets the necessity to respect another state's sovereignty in a SC resolution as an obligation to not act against that state's will, then the necessary implementation of SC resolutions is in danger.

Beyond understanding the costs and opportunities related to engaging in theoretically charged debates, awareness of authoritarian misuses of sovereignty is important. Sovereignty-based arguments which twist the concept from a right to be free from influence in matters of self-determination to a right to be free from criticism and responsibility for internationally wrongful conduct must be recognised as such and rejected. The legitimacy and inviolability associated with sovereignty must not blind negotiators with regard to the limitations of claiming it. Where a state, in exercise of its sovereignty, has subjected itself to certain rules and standards vis-à-vis other states, disregard for such standards is not just an 'internal affair', but plainly illegal. Sovereignty allows to refrain from subjecting oneself to certain rules, but not to breach rules already applicable. Cutting off necessary and effective humanitarian support is not a sovereign decision, neither under the international human rights framework applicable to Syria, nor under the UNCh's sophisticated understanding of peace. And withholding consent for the provision of such essentials is arbitrary for the purposes of international humanitarian law as well.[30] The theoretical legitimacy of invoking sovereignty to avoid international cooperation must not lead to the acceptance of claiming sovereignty out of context. Sovereignty may be claimed to refuse taking part in international law-making, but not to avoid responsibility from already applicable law.

Negotiators should always assess conflicting positions diligently. Authoritarian states do not necessarily advance authoritarian arguments at the international level. Negotiators arguing with such regimes will thus have to consider if and in how far they want to take a stand against positions with a dimension of legal theory and know the costs and opportunities of doing so. Their choice will have an impact on the population in need of a resolution, the interpretation of SC resolutions and the fulfilment of the SC's mandate. When it comes to misusing sovereignty-based arguments twisting the meaning of the concept for authoritarian purposes, negotiators can and should reject them. No valid understanding of sovereignty allows to misuse the concept as a status above the law.

Notes

1 This chapter is based in part on the author's blogpost 'United in What? Some reflections on the Security Council's sovereignty rhetoric in the latest Syria resolutions' (EJIL:Talk!, 21.10.2020).
2 Charter of the United Nations, 1 UNTS XVI, 24 October 1945.
3 UN Security Council, Resolution 2585, 12 July 2022, UN Doc S/RES/2642 (2022).
4 UN Security Council, Resolution 2165, 14 July 2014, UN. Doc. S/RES/2165 (2014).
5 See the statements made on 14 July 2014 in S/PV.7216.
6 Ibid., 12–15.
7 Statement by the US American representative Mrs. Craft on 20 December 2019 in S/PV.8697, 9.
8 Statement made by the UK representative Dame Barbara Woodward on23 June 2021 in S/PV.8803: 'Without expansion, therefore, we cannot tackle the growing food crisis or overcome the impact of the coronavirus disease pandemic and fulfil the requirements of resolution 2565 (2021) to ensure equitable access to vaccines', 16.
9 Statement by the Russian representative Mr. Nebenzia on 20 December 2019 in S/PV.8697, 2, 3.
10 Statement by the Russian representative Mr. Nebenzia on 1o January 2020 in S/PV. 8700, 6.
11 Statements by the US representative Mrs. Craft on 1o January 2020 in S/PV. 8700, 9.
12 Statement by the UK representative Ms. Pierce on 10 January 2020 in S/PV. 8700, 7.
13 Statement by the Syrian representative Mr. Sabbagh on 25 June 2021 in S/PV.8805, 19.
14 See UN Doc. S/2020/698, 13 July 2020.
15 UN Security Council, Resolution 2585, 9 July 2021, UN Doc S/RES/2585 (2021).
16 See Security Council Resolutions 2504, 2533, 2585.
17 For example, other authoritarian regimes holding seats during the Syria negotiations such as Vietnam, Equatorial Guinea and Kuwait, (Marshall and Elzinga-Marshall, 2017, 45–51) have voted against the Syrian position, represented by the PRC and Russia.
18 Legal pluralism is an established branch of research in international legal academia, although its essence is hard to describe, due to the diversity of manifestations. A focus within the study and concept of international legal pluralism as a post-modern view (de Sousa Santos, 1987, 297) on international law lies in the idea of 'interlegality' in the sense that different legal orders coexist and intersect at the same time (Ibid, 290; Bianchi, 2016, 227). Through the lens of global legal pluralism, international law tends to be understood as a 'global interplay of plural voices, many of which are not associated by the state' and as a wide variety of communities, which articulate norms that have an 'impact in actual practice, regardless of the degree of coercive power those communities wield' (Schiff Berman, 2007, 308). Global

legal pluralism plays down the role that coercion, authority and legitimacy play for the genesis of norms (Bianchi, 2016, 234, 235). In this sense, an important focus of legal pluralism as a strand of international legal academia lies on the sources of international law. For the purposes of determining the degree of pluralism in international law, the focus will lie on the degree to which international law promotes, presupposes or even requires the existence and constructive coordination of different views of states in norm creation and application.

19 The classification of autocratic (including authoritarian) and democratic systems of governance used in this chapter is of course a reduced version of the more complex politological concepts. Since the classification of systems was developed for an intra-state context, the classification of 'internationally authoritarian arguments' is based more on analogy than on the proper politological categories it is inspired by. The chapter does not claim to accurately represent the definitions of all different types of regimes in detail.

20 Although the impact of such cultural pluralism should not be overestimated, according to Vereshchetin and Danilenko, 1986, 61–65.

21 Statements by the Russian representative Mr. Nebenzia on 20 December 2019 in S/PV.8697, 3, emphasis added by the author.

22 Statement by the Chinese representative Mr. Zhang Jun on 20 December 2019 in S/PV.8697, p. 5, emphasis added by the author.

23 Statement by the Syrian representative Mr. Falouh on 20 December 2019 in S/PV.8697, p. 11, emphasis added by the author.

24 UN Security Council, UN Doc. S/2020/661, Annex 21 – Statement by the Permanent Representative of the United States of America to the United Nations, Kelly Craft, p. 28.

25 Statement by the Luxembourgian representative Ms. Lucas on 14 July 2014 in S/PV.7216, p. 3.

26 UN Security Council, UN Doc. S/23500, 31. January 1992.

27 Arguably also under international humanitarian law, as a state's consent to external humanitarian action must not be withheld arbitrarily, (Barber, 2020).

28 Vienna Convention on the Law of Treaties, 23 May 1969, 1155 UNTS 331.

29 Statement by the Chinese representative Mr. Zhang Jun on 23 June 2021 in S/PV.8803, p. 15.

30 Under Art. 70(1) of the First Additional Protocol to the Geneva Conventions it says that the concerned state's consent is required, but the conditions under which such consent may be withheld are informed by other international law considerations, such as human rights law (Barber, 2020). The majority opinion does, however, still seem to be that even where consent is withheld illegally, states may not disregard it entirely (Akande and Gillard, 2016). For the SC with its power to take measures regardless of a state's consent under Chapter VII of the Charter according to Art. 2(7) UNCh, this is of little importance.

Literature

Akande, D. and Gillard, E.-C. (2016). Oxford Guidance on the Law Relating to Humanitarian Relief Operations in Situations of Armed Conflict.

Appiah, K. A. (2002). The American University in an Age of Globalisation, Lecture at the Princeton-Oxford Conference on Globalisation at Oxford University (June 15, 2002). Cited in: Burke-White, W. (2004). International Legal Pluralism. *Michigan Journal of International Law* 25(4), 963.

Barber, R. (2020). Is Security Council Authorisation Really Necessary to Allow Cross-Border Humanitarian Assistance in Syria?. EJIL:Talk!, 24.02.2020, available at:

https://www.ejiltalk.org/is-security-council-authorisation-really-necessary-to-allow-cross-border-humanitarian-assistance-in-syria/.

Berlin, I. (2013). The Crooked Timber of Humanity - Chapters in the History of Ideas (2nd ed.), edited by Henry Hardy. Princeton, NJ: Princeton University Press.

Besson, S. (2011). Sovereignty. In: Wolfrum, R. and Peters, A. (eds.). *Max Planck Encyclopaedia of Public International Law*. Oxford: Oxford University Press.

Bianchi, A. (2016). *International Law Theories*. Oxford: Oxford University Press.

Crawford, J. (2006). *The Creation of States in International Law*. Oxford: Oxford University Press.

de Sousa Santos, B. (1987). Law: A Map of Misreading. Toward a Postmodern Conception of Law. *Journal of Law and Society* 14(3), 279.

Dörr, O. (2018). Article 31. In: Dörr, O. and Schmalenbach, K. (eds.). *Vienna Convention on the Law of Treaties – A Commentary* (2nd ed.). Berlin: Springer.

Koskenniemi, M. (2007). *From Apology to Utopia – The Structure of International Legal Argument*. Cambridge: Cambridge University Press.

Linz, J. (1975). Totalitarian and Authoritarian Regimes. In: Greenstein, F. J., et al. (eds.). *Handbook of Political Science*, Vol. 3: Macro-political Theory. Reading, MA: Addison-Wesley.

Marshall, M. and Elzinga-Marshall, G. (2017). *Centre for Systemic Peace Annual Report 2017 – Conflict, Governance, and State Fragility*. Vienna.

Mégret, F. F. (2020). International Law as a System of Legal Pluralism. In: Schiff Berman, P. (ed.). *The Oxford Handbook of Global Legal Pluralism*. Oxford: Oxford University Press.

Merkel, W. (2010). *Systemtransformationen* (2nd ed.). Wiesbaden: Verlag für Sozialwissenschaften.

Papastavridis, E. (2007). Interpretation of Security Council Resolutions under Chapter VII in the Aftermath of the Iraqi Crisis. *The International and Comparative Law Quarterly* 56(1), 83.

Schiff Berman, P. (2007). A Pluralist Approach to International Law. *Yale Journal of International Law* 32(2), 301.

Vereshchetin, S. and Danilenko, G. M. (1986). Cultural and Ideological Pluralism and International Law. *German Yearbook of International Law* 29, 56.

Voina-Motoc, I. (2008). Conceptions of Pluralism and International Law. *Romanian Journal of International Law* 7, 43.

Wood, M. (1998). The Interpretation of Security Council Resolutions. In: *Max Planck Yearbook of United Nations Law*. Leiden: Martinus Nijhoff Publishers.

Jurisprudence

European Court of Human Rights, *Litwa v. Poland*, Judgment from 04 April 2000, App. No. 26629/95, ECHR 2000-III.

Permanent Court of International Justice, *Nationality Decrees Issued in Tunis and Morocco*, Advisory Opinion, PCIJ Ser. B No. 4 (1923).

Permanent Court of International Justice, *SS Lotus* (France v. Turkey), Judgment, PCIJ Series A No. 10 (1927).

COMMENTARY

A critique

Dennis Dijkzeul

In this chapter, Maximilian Bertamini asks to which extent sovereignty-based arguments in Security Council negotiations can be qualified as authoritarian. His question is important because answering it shows the extent to which the international order, and of course, in particular the Security Council, enables authoritarian positions. Contrasting authoritarian with pluralistic (democratic) arguments, Bertamini masterfully takes us to the edges of the international legal perspective.

Despite the fact that authoritarian-ruled countries, such as Syria, Russia, and China, in their contributions to Security Council debates attempt to take the high moral ground (e.g., 'protection of International Law' and 'respect for sovereignty'), they often ruthlessly follow their elites' interests. Yet, at the moment they start to debate international political and legal issues, they practise the language of International Law and show, to some extent, respect for pluralism. Clearly, such lip-service is often hypocritical. Nevertheless, hypocrisy is the compliment that vice pays to virtue, or in this case, the compliment that authoritarianism pays to International Law and pluralistic peace. In this way, Bertamini's argument resembles the defence of reason; at the moment, one starts to criticise reason in discussion with other people, one uses reason to convince them (Pinker, 2021, 39–41). Although Bertamini's defence of legal rationality is to be commended because it shows the legal limitations of authoritarianism in the Security Council, it remains dissatisfying in the sense that it cannot transcend the limits of International Law.

DOI: 10.4324/9781003316541-7

To fully explain the extent to which the Security Council allows authoritarian rulers to influence its negotiations with authoritarian arguments, we should leave the International Law perspective behind. In the remainder of this critique, I will critique the International Law perspective and use historical International Relations (IR) and Sociological approaches, and further develop Bertamini's approach. Both approaches show how International Law and sovereignty are enacted and the role that power plays in this. After all, authoritarian rulers pay careful attention to power during negotiations. In short, I will explain how the institutionalisation of the international order, including the Security Council, allows two powerful authoritarian states, China and Russia, more space to make their authoritarian arguments than other authoritarian states, in particular Syria.

International legal scholars played a central role in the founding of IR as a discipline as well as in establishing first the League of Nations and later the United Nations. They hoped that international law, international mediation, and later the functioning of international organisations could foster worldwide peace among states. IR emancipated from international law when it began to incorporate power in its analysis (see Carr, 2001 [1939]). But for a long time, IR continued to take states as its main actors (Dijkzeul and Salomons, 2021, 6).

In this respect, it is crucial to note how sovereignty, states, and international law developed together. Bryan Hehir (1998, 40) describes how the norm of non-intervention and arguments in favour of state sovereignty are closely related. In other words, the questions 'when and how to use force?' are intimately related to the way sovereign states came about (and recognised each other).[1]

> The pluralist rationale [of International Law] corresponds to three different functions that the nonintervention norm has fulfilled. First is the Westphalian emphasis on prohibiting intervention in order to reduce or prevent conflict among major states; the objective arose as a necessity to halt the interventionary pattern of war rooted in the sixteenth-century wars of religion. Second, what might be termed the liberal emphasis seeks to prevent intervention in the name of protecting self-determination and/ or communal autonomy [as with balance of power politics among the Great Powers of the nineteenth century]. Third, the anti-imperialist or postcolonial emphasis seeks to prevent the subordination of small states to the policy interest of major powers [in the twentieth century]. The rationale of the nonintervention norm, therefore, reflects the experience of diverse moments in the history of international politics since the sixteenth century. What ties these diverse themes together is the objective of curtailing the actions of powerful states that acknowledge no supreme authority.

When early modern states began to arise in Europe out of the ashes of the religious wars, they needed international law to limit war, acknowledge each other, and arrange their affairs. Put simply, states needed international law and international law needed states. You cannot have one without the other. An IR and sociology of law perspective indeed emphasises that both were enacted simultaneously over time. Bertamini's chapter implicitly acknowledges this socio-historical fact by stressing the practical aspects that make authoritarian arguments ultimately self-defeating because they undermine the international legal system they build upon. In addition, states were more afraid of external interventions leading to inter-state war than of internal chaos within a state. A dilemma that the Security Council still has to grapple with today, also in the case of Syria.

Bertamini's chapter elucidates a necessary legal fiction that actually contradicts the focus on raw power: all states are legally equal because they are all sovereign. Although the corollary principle 'one state, one vote' is a central to the functioning of the UN General Assembly and the Security Council, in practice some states are more equal than others. World politics, inside the UN Security Council and outside of it, therefore, has more Orwellian power plays than most legal scholars would like to admit.

Moreover, the necessary legal fiction of one state, one vote, and therewith state equality, was not respected when the UN Security Council itself was set up. In order to get the main victors of World War II on board, they – the United States, the Soviet Union (now Russia), the United Kingdom, France, and China – received a permanent position and a right to veto. The founders of the United Nations were afraid that otherwise the UN System would go the way of the League of Nations and become irrelevant when powerful member states refuse to participate. The position and veto power of the Permanent Five (P5) make the UN undemocratic in at least three overlapping ways.

First, it fossilised the power relations from 1945, including certain colonial structures. In comparison with the P5, other states, in particular the former colonies that became independent, simply have less clout in the UN negotiations and decision-making.

Second, whereas the UN can accept newly independent member states, when it comes to voting, the UN has no way to take the main demographic, economic, and political developments within, and among, its member states into account. In short, the 'one state, one vote' principle does not represent the demography or economic strength of states. A voting system that cannot follow demographic proportions does not look very democratic after all.

Third, when states try to go outside the UN, this weakens the Security Council. The P5 generally have more power to do so.

All three of the above ways make it easier for China and Russia to use authoritarian arguments in negotiations. Put differently, these authoritarian-led countries have greater space to use authoritarian arguments or impose their power. With their support, a small state with a disparaged, embattled government, such as Syria, also carries more weight in Security Council negotiations. Without it, Syria would lack clout and only formally receive a polite hearing.

At the same time, even the powerful P5 are generally not in a position that allows them to pursue their interests with more or less open disregard for International Law and/or the Security Council. From the examples of Iraq, Syria, the South China Sea, and Ukraine, we learn that the political and economic costs of going outside the Security Council are high and that disregard for International Law creates international opprobrium and a continuous fear of escalation. In line with Hehir, these *realpolitik* problems are still the strongest argument to respect International Law, even for authoritarian countries like China and Russia. It explains their lip service to International Law. Just like their democratic counterparts, authoritarians want to look good.

With regards to Bertamini's chapter and International Law in general, this means that international legal analysis always needs to be supplemented by IR and sociological analysis of International Law's enactment and political power. This leads to two paradoxes constitutive of our current international order. First, sovereignty is strong as a principle, but it allows for the unseemly combination of authoritarianism at home and imperfect legal pluralism abroad. Second, sovereignty is imperfectly institutionalised in the UN Security Council with, on the one hand, the P5 and their veto power and, on the other hand, the legal fiction of equality among states with one country, one vote. In the end, International Law both accommodates and contains authoritarian states. Hence, it is not irrelevant to the Security Council. It can never be fully neglected. Yet it is often only one element in broader power plays.

Note

1 See also Hendrik Spruyt (1994). *The sovereign state and its competitors.*

References

Carr, E. H. (2001 [1939]). *The Twenty Years' Crisis, 1919-1939. An Introduction to the Study of International Relations*. Basingstoke, Hampshire: Palgrave.

Dijkzeul, D. and Salomons, D. (eds). (2021). *International Organisations Revisited. Agency and Pathology in a Multipolar World*. Oxford: Berghahn Books.

Hehir, J. B. (1998). Military Intervention and National Sovereignty: Recasting the Relationship, 29–54. In: Moore, J. (ed.). *Hard Choices. Moral Dilemmas in Humanitarian Interventions*. Lanham, MD: Rowman & Littlefield.

Pinker, S. (2021). *Rationality. What It Is, Why It seems Scarce, Why It Matters*. London: Allen Lane.

4

THE XINJIANG CASE AND ITS IMPLICATION FOR THE RIGHTS DEBATE IN CHINA

What role for NGOs and humanitarian negotiations?

Claudia Astarita

Introduction

In its western region of Xinjiang, China has been accused since 2014 of having transferred over one million Uyghurs, maybe three, into mass internment camps, prisons, and other penal institutions that the government officially classifies as 'concentrated educational transformation centres'. In these camps, interned Uyghurs are suspected to be subjected to forced indoctrination, psychological stress, forced labour, and torture (Zenz, 2019).

The Uyghurs are the most numerous indigenous group in China. They are mainly located in Xinjiang, they have a Muslim background, a culture that is significantly different from that of the majority Han population, and they speak a language that belongs to the Turkic language family. The Chinese government counts about 12 million Uyghurs in Xinjiang, corresponding to 0.85% of its overall population of 1.4 billion people.

Evidence has confirmed that this re-education policy has been imposed to the whole region in 2014, and that the Uyghurs that have not been interned in camps have been placed under constant surveillance thanks to the massive instalment of Artificial Intelligence (AI) technologies (Howell and Fan, 2011). More recent discoveries have indicated that over the last few years women have been sterilised, often against their will, and children separated from their families and sent to boarding schools in order to reduce the impact of their original culture and values on their long-term development (Zenz, 2020).

Data collected by researchers and human rights practitioners that have concentrated their efforts on Xinjiang to provide regular updates on the situation in the region, have documented that hundreds of thousands of people have been dispatched into residential labour programmes in factories

DOI: 10.4324/9781003316541-8

throughout China. Official documents confirming that local authorities in Xinjiang have received the order to erase all sorts of Uyghur culture, heritage, and characteristics in the region, destroying mosques, sites of pilgrimage, and traditional neighbourhoods, as well as suppressing the Uyghur original language, history, values, and connections, have also been leaked to the media (BBC News, 2019; ICIJ, 2019).

This practice of 'de-Uyghurisation' of the region appears to have started around 2005–2006, when local authorities were still persuaded that 'complete homogenisation' of the area could be achieved by increasing the level of police and AI control in the region (Cronin-Furman, 2018). However, when resistance to this 'forced assimilation' emerged, and especially after July 2009 Urumqi riots, the China Communist Party (CCP) started reconsidering its policy opting for the creation of new 'vocational training centres' to fight both extremism, and alleviating poverty (Caksu, 2020).

From the perspective of official propaganda, violent elements in the Uyghur community had to be sidelined to assure that peace and order could be maintained in Xinjiang. Further, some of these violent elements were accused of developing connections with terrorist groups in Central Asia (Zhang, 2019).

The poorest Uyghur families were invited to integrate newly established training centres to upgrade their competences and skills and, as a consequence, strengthen their professional profile (Leibold, 2019).

Remaining consistent with this narrative, in 2019, authorities have started 'graduating' internees, moving them out of the camps. According to evidence collected by researchers such as Adrian Zenz and James Leibold, the Xinjiang based internment camps structure went through a deep restructuring in 2019. While some camps were converted into formal prisons where to transfer 're-sistant detainees', other camps were reorganised as factories, where 'graduated' detainees were formally recruited (Ruser, 2020). De facto, 'graduation' transformed the essence of detentions. Some Uyghurs were sent back home, although some seem to continue living under house arrests, or remaining separated from their families and relatives, or hosting CCP personnel in their house to confirm that 'graduate Uyghurs' have learnt and interiorised the habits a 'model Uyghur' is expected to follow in Xinjiang (Maizland, 2022).

This chapter aims at providing a better understanding of both the origins and the impact of CCP policy in Xinjiang in order to precise the state of the art of this massive 'transformation through education' campaign, as well as to decode the narrative that has been associated with it at the national level. The second section of the analysis discusses the way in which academics, media, and foreign actors have adjusted their understanding and their narrative about Xinjiang since the beginning of the current re-education campaign to disclose if any of their actions had a real impact either on the concerned region or the humanitarian crisis it is going through. Finally, the last section of the chapter delves into the world of humanitarian actions and practitioners to offer recommendations to advance the level of consciousness, the debate on rights, and humanitarian negotiations and interventions in either Xinjiang or China.

Analysing the Xinjiang case from the perspective of the CCP

The evolution of CCP policy towards minorities

To understand what is happening in Xinjiang today, it is necessary to re-enact the evolution of China's traditional ethnic policy as well as the 'anti-terrorist' dimension that was associated with it starting 2012.

Xinjiang, or 'new frontier' in Chinese, is a territory that Uyghurs identify as their homeland. The area was conquered by the Qing dynasty in the mid-18th century and absorbed into the empire as a province in the late 19th century. In 1949, it was integrated into China and renamed Xinjiang Uyghur Autonomous Region (XUAR). In 1959, Xinjiang was formally declared an historical part of China, and China's president Mao Zedong at that time was rejecting any form of territorial succession or federalism for China's minorities. Mao was persuaded that ethnocultural distinctions would have automatically disappeared following the final victory of the revolution. Despite offering some distinct legal protections for minority communities, Mao's normative ideal never changed from the one of promoting 'transformation, fusion, and unity', depicted as necessary to implement 'an inclusive state of hierarchical harmony' (Lu, 2017).

Following this logic, Han migration to the region started to be encouraged in the 1960s to facilitate a demographic shift (Rippa, 2014). In 1953, Han constituted only 6% of the population of Xinjiang. In 1982, their portion rose to 38%. Despite this massive readjustment, real integration has never been achieved, with Han migrants settling mainly in the north of the region and taking the lead in local economic development, and Uyghurs mainly concentrated in the south, around cities such as Kashgar and Khota, and progressively evolving into non-expensive employees for Han entrepreneurs (Cronin-Furman, 2018).

When Deng Xiaoping rose to power in late 1970s, Xinjiang was even more divided than what it used to be ten years before, with Uyghurs determined to maintain their cultural and linguistic traits alive. This situation pushed Hu Yaobang, the then general secretary of the CCP, to call for 'ad hoc reforms' for Xinjiang (McMillen, 1984). The Chinese fonctionnaire promoted the return of Han migrants to their hometowns while advocating for broad and unprecedented cultural, religious, and political reform. For example, the government allowed previously shuttered mosques to reopen and new mosques to be built. Uyghur-language publishing and artistic expression flourished, and Hu Yaobang even suggested making the region more autonomous within the Chinese system of governance, proposing a broader inclusion of the indigenous ethnic groups leaders to Xinjiang governance, allowing them to cultivate their own culture and language in local state institutions.

Hu Yaobang's purge in 1987 and the Tiananmen Square movement and subsequent crackdown that followed instantly closed any possibility to continue the debate on political reform in China, Xinjiang included.

The fall of the Soviet Union in 1991 came to further dissolve any remaining hope for reforms. The CCP interpreted USSR campaigns for ethnic self-determination as the driving force behind the dissolution of the country, and its new goal became avoiding China from suffering a similar fate.

Self-determination fears pushed the CCP to consider the deployment of 'anti-separatism campaigns' in Xinjiang throughout the 1990s. These campaigns were received by Uyghurs with deep dissatisfaction (Castets, 2003). Violence further escalated in 2001, right after Washington engaged in its global 'war on terror'. The US new battle against terrorism presented Beijing with the opportunity to reframe its policy in Xinjiang, linking the necessity to increase the level of control in the area to the necessity of keeping a rising terrorist threat coming from the East Turkestan Islamic Movement (ETIM), a previously unknown Uyghur group based in Afghanistan, under control (Greitens et al., 2019/2020). In 2002, the ETIM group was included into the US Terrorist Exclusion List, a list created by the United States Secretary of State to designate selected organisations as terrorist groups for immigration purposes, allowing the CCP to claim a deep-rooted complicity with terrorism and separatist militancy in Xinjiang. It was only in 2020 that the US decided to remove ETIM from the list (Soto, 2020).

New research aimed at demonising the Muslim populations as an existential threat was suddenly published, confirming the reliability of Chinese assumptions and pushing the party to reinforce its presence in the region to 'break their lineage, break their roots, break their connections, and break their origins', with the support of re-education camps and systematic surveillance (Van Schaack et al., 2021). The counterterrorism narrative also helped the Party gain the support of the whole Han population, either inside or outside Xinjiang (Garcia, 2022).

Untangling China official narrative on internment camps

A detailed analysis of Beijing's official narrative associated with internment camps is needed to better understand the general support the CCP policy for Xinjiang has received within the Chinese society.

In 2017, during the 19th Party Congress, the concept of 'forging a strong sense of collective consciousness for the Chinese nation' was included in the CCP Constitution. This addition reflected President Xi Jinping's renewed emphasis on strengthening national identity over ethnic allegiances.

The CCP started fearing a growing vulnerability of China's Uyghur population to infiltration from transnational jihadist networks in 2014, following the suicide car bombing organised by a group of Uyghurs in Beijing's Tiananmen Square. As a result, social stability and enduring peace through poverty alleviation and ethnic unity became the government's utmost priority in XUAR, to be secured with an institutionaliastion of security targeting 'three evil forces': splittism, religious extremism, and terrorism (Li, 2019).

This externally driven security strategy started evolving in August 2016, after Chen Quanguo, the former Communist Party Secretary in Tibet, was named Party Secretary in Xinjiang. In early 2017, the opening of 'concentrated transformation through education' centres in XUAR was announced, with local CCP leaders confirming that the terrorist threat in Xinjiang was more of an internal than an external problem (Zenz and Leibold, 2017).

The concept of re-education is everything but new in China. The 1957 're-education through labour' system was introduced to normalise administrative penalties and internment sentences without forcing public agencies to recur to legal procedures. Once re-education through labour was abolished, internment camps were transformed into detoxification treatment centres (Ibrahim, 2019). The 'transformation through education' system has been used first to deal with Falun Gong followers in the early 2000s and later for other 'rapid detox' campaigns related to either drug or video game addictions. In 2012, 'de-extremification' campaigns started to be organised in Xinjiang. In 2015, the existence of ad hoc camps to facilitate the success of the campaign was confirmed, with new media reports stating that Khotan City's 'de-extremification transformation through education centre' could hold up to 3,000 detainees 'deeply affected' by religious extremism (Zenz, 2018).

Chen Quanguo's arrival in 2017 marked a sharp increase in internment practices. Security strategy shifted towards collective detention, ideological re-education, and generally intensified coercion on the Uyghur community. Examples of involuntary detentions and massive re-education campaigns started growing exponentially, and the judicial framework surrounding the camps slowly started abandoning the anti-terror narrative to embrace a relatively new re-education and detoxification discourse (Zenz, 2019).

Xinjiang authorities revised the 'anti-extremism regulations' and authorised country-level officials to establish 'vocational training centres' (Sudworth, 2020). Three types of re-education facilities were included in these centres: legal system schools, rehabilitation correction centres, and centralised transformation through education training centres.

On November 24th, 2019, the International Consortium of Investigative Journalists published the 'China Cables', six documents constituting an 'operations manual' for running the camps and regulating the detainees' behaviours. The secret memo confirmed a trend of seeing former detainees remaining under surveillance even after their release and emphasised the importance of 'strict secrecy' on vocational training centres activities and dynamics (ICIJ, 2019).

Simultaneously, important efforts were developed to influence public opinion's perception of re-education. In April 2017, the Khotän Prefecture published a document entitled 'Transformation through education classes is like a free hospital treatment for the masses with sick thinking' (Zenz, 2019). The party secretary of the region's Justice Department, Zhang Yun, confirmed that approximately 30% of Xinjiang's population had been 'infected' by religious extremism. Comparing religiosity to a dangerous drug addiction, CCP's coercive internment measures were described as 'benevolent acts' and the battle against religious extremism, splittism, and terrorism became synonymous with a battle to eradicate 'malignant tumours', 'cancer cells', and a 'communicable plague'. Another party document drafted in Hotan (southern Xinjiang) stated that 'anyone infected with an ideological virus must be swiftly sent for 'residential care' of transformation-through-education classes before illness arises' (Zenz, 2019).

Pedagogical and medical discourses have been actively used in Xinjiang to legitimise the use of coercive methods (Ibrahim, 2019). These metaphors proved also ideal to convey a sense of preventive urgency necessary to justify the 2017 shift from selective to collective repression. The Chinese 'biopolitical' approach was confirmed once a 400-page CCP document was leaked to *The New York Times* in November 2019. One section of the document was aimed at offering guidelines for communication for children whose family members had been interned. Thirteen answers to the children's interrogations were proposed to Chinese officials to get suitable examples to better handle their conversation. For example, if children were asking something like, 'since it's just training, why can't (my parents) come home?', authorities were advised to use metaphors to respond to them. Grounded on the comparison of religious extremism to a virus, echoing the risks of epidemics, the suggested answer was: If you 'caught an infectious virus like SARS, you'd have to undergo enclosed, isolated treatment because it's an infectious illness'.

All leaked documents confirmed the importance of the detoxification and education narratives in justifying the internments. Analogies were regularly made with ideas such as contamination or the logic of privileging isolated treatment and quarantine as ways to fight against an infectious disease that was 'bewitching' child's relatives. As stated in the document, 'Your thoughts can be restored to health as quickly as possible only with systematic, enclosed 'inpatient treatment' in our schools that thoroughly eradicates religious extremism and terrorist ideas'.

This pervasive use of biological metaphors played a major role in portraying the state as a benevolent actor providing prompt and effective treatments. Despite arbitrary quotas and the lack of concrete legal provisions, the measures adopted in Xinjiang have been broadly accepted by the Chinese population (Su, et al., 2020).

A January 2020 article published by *The Economist* reported that many Han Chinese 'didn't mind' the internment camps targeting the Uyghurs in XUAR. A Han person interviewed for the article admitted that identifying Uyghurs as 'backward', 'untrustworthy', and 'violent' people was common among Han people in the region. Other articles depicted the disparity between Han and Uyghurs as part of everyday life in Xinjiang. A report published by *The Diplomat* explained that many Chinese Han accept 'the government line that inconveniencing the few has brought calm to the region', and most of the arrests are justified (Ingram, 2018). As the implementation of such a repressive policy in Xinjiang was followed by a drastic fall of riots, protests, or attacks, either in Xinjiang or by Uyghurs living in the rest of China, the Chinese population was even more easily convinced of the appropriateness of the Chinese methods and narratives in the region.

Discussing academic advocacy for Xinjiang

Although, within China, the official narrative about Xinjiang has always been extremely controlled and grounded on the image of a biological mission to eradicate a dangerous virus that is rapidly spreading in the region, foreign academic advocacy has played a crucial role in trying to raise international attention over what has been condemned as a forced cultural assimilation.

It was indeed through the accurate work of researcher Adrian Zenz that the sheer existence and number of people interned in the camps were disclosed in the very first place (Zenz, 2018). The same year that Zenz's initial report was published, which estimated that the camps had housed as many as one million people, Chinese diplomats stopped denying the existence of the camps and began promoting them as terrorism-fighting vocational training facilities. The German anthropologist, whose work contributed to the rare but necessary turnaround, has thereby since played a major role in exposing the repressive policies taken in Xinjiang through academic reports and has himself highlighted the unique position he has had as an academic in shaping global discourse on XUAR.

Facing China's traditional lack of transparency and local and international non-governmental organisations (NGOs) difficulties to engage into any sort of humanitarian dialogue in a sensitive area like Xinjing, international scholars specialised in Islamic studies in China such as James Leibold and David Tobin started to contribute to a shared collection of methods endorsed by the Chinese government to implement its 'fusion' policy, that is, a set of government policies aimed at assimilating ethnic minorities into the dominant Han Chinese culture, with the goal of disclosing CCP practices in Xinjiang, Tibet, and Inner Mongolia (Xiao, et al., 2020). These policies have included measures such as mandating the use of the Chinese language in schools, promoting Chinese culture and customs, and encouraging intermarriage between Han Chinese and minority groups.

A different form of 'Sinicisation' has been identified for Xinjiang, referring to the CCP's efforts to suppress the culture, religion, and population of the Uyghur Muslim minority through forced 're-education', forced labour, forced sterilisation, and forced birth control measures, as well as the destruction of mosques and cultural sites. This policy has been recognised as a conscient strategy adopted by the CCP to justify the use of extra-legal internment camps and the separation of families in Xinjiang (Tobin, 2022).

A generalised trend directly associating Turkic Muslims in Xinjiang to the notion of threat, and in particular a threat to China's ethnic and cultural homogeneity and to the country's process of modernisation, has been identified (Zhang, 2009). Accordingly, the narratives of 'us' versus 'them', of 'civilisation' versus 'savagery', started to be employed to justify the idea of proceeding with the eradication of 'inferior cultures, religions, and populations' polluting the region (Tobin, 2022). President Xi Jinping's signature slogan, 'never forget our original mission, continue our progress', to emphasise his support for a narrative shift reducing the space for diversity to promote harmony in the country, has often been quoted as a clear example of this attitude (Leibold, 2019). Under this perspective, the repressive policy adopted in Xinjiang could be justified as inevitable to continue to push China towards modernisation.

The Chinese government tends to portray the violence in Xinjiang as a conflict between civilisation and barbarism, where the CCP plays a major role in defending a shared identity against the 'inside/outside three evils' of terrorism, separatism, and extremism, presented as the main causes for regional conflict (Yau, 2022). The Chinese government has described this situation as a 'zero-sum political struggle of life or death' for the survival of the Chinese nation, further emphasising the logic that to build a unified and harmonious China, it is necessary to suppress alternative and 'backward' identities in XUAR (Tobin, 2020).

If foreign academic advocacy had no impact on Xinjiang beyond raising international awareness of the humanitarian crisis the region is experiencing, academics such as Ann-Charlotte Buntinx and Francesca Colli recently started discussing whether the debate on rights violations in Xinjiang could be further boosted by NGOs and civil society. In their most recent article, the two scholars discuss the indirect role played by western NGOs in influencing and shaping the EU's external policies and actions towards China as a result of human rights violations happening in Xinjiang. The paper introduces NGOs as actors deemed to serve as 'moral policy entrepreneurs', their focus being primarily directed towards the ethical presentation of the issue to encourage the EU to take action. Indeed, combining expertise with moral arguments about the EU's responsibility as a human rights leader, NGOs should strengthen their capacity to push the Xinjiang crisis higher on the EU's agenda and guide its response (Buntinx and Colli, 2022).

As this chapter confirms, NGOs can indeed play a much deeper role in stimulating the humanitarian debate in China. However, NGOs contributions are inevitably taking different forms according to whether civil society actors are either Chinese or foreign, and working inside or outside China.

External actions boosting advocacy: economic sanctions, media and the United Nations

The United States has been the first country to officially respond to the very first report disclosing the existence of internment camps in XUAR (Zenz and Leibold, 2017). However, despite the documented proofs about the existence of these camps, an agreement on the Uyghur Human Rights Policy Act was reached only in June 2020 (Millward, 2023). In the meanwhile, the US administration has imposed export bans and global Magnitsky sanctions to a number of Xinjiang individuals and entities.

In December 2021, President Joe Biden signed the Uyghur Forced Labor Prevention Act, a new law prohibiting imports of 'any goods, wares, articles, and merchandise mined, produced, or manufactured wholly or in part' in Xinjiang unless they could be proven not to be linked to forced labour. Canada, the United Kingdom, and the European Union have also sanctioned several Chinese entities, public and private, accused of perpetrating abuses in XUAR, and some western countries, such as Canada, the United Kingdom, the United States, Belgium, Czech Republic, France, Lithuania, and the Netherlands, have formally denounced the China Communist Party actions in Xinjiang as an act of genocide (European Parliament Resolution, 2022). 'Non-governmental and intergovernmental organisations, including the independent groups Uyghur Tribunal and the Inter-Parliamentary Alliance on China, have reached similar findings about the nature of Beijing's actions, which they have backed up with copious documentation and opinions from international jurists' (Millward, 2023).

In August 2018, the UN Committee on the Elimination of Racial Discrimination asked the Chinese government to clarify the situation in Xinjiang, without receiving any specific answer. Within the UN system, it has always been difficult to create a consensus to discuss rights violations in Xinjiang with China. When some Western countries have tried to move in this direction, as it happened in July 2019 when the UN High Commissioner on Human Rights wrote a formal letter calling on China to stop mass detentions in Xinjiang, the impact of their actions is often downsized by counter-initiatives supported by more pro-China nations within the UN (Abdeleli, 2022). For example, in October 2022, 17 UN members voted in favour of a motion to debate the contents of the UN Human Rights Council's critical report on human rights in Xinjiang, 19 members voted against, and 11 abstained. Many of those who voted 'no' were Muslim-majority countries such as Indonesia, Somalia, Pakistan, UAE and Qatar (Leduc, 2019). Among the 11 countries that abstained were India, Malaysia and Ukraine. Reluctance to condemn China on its Xinjiang policy is increasing, as this attitude is seen as detrimental to the strengthening of bilateral economic relationships (Maizland, 2022).

When UN High Commissioner Michelle Bachelet visited Xinjiang in May 2022, the UN representative was criticised for adopting Chinese official terminology to describe the current situation in Xinjiang (Wintour and Ni, 2022). However, the following August, a few minutes before midnight on the last day of Bachelet's term as UNHCR high commissioner, a final report was eventually released, expressing deep concerns regarding presumed rights violations that were taking place in Xinjiang (McMurray, 2022).

If foreign media have played a crucial role in spreading awareness on human rights violations happening in Xinjiang between 2020 and 2022 evidence seems proving that the majority of the Chinese population is not aware of XUAR re-education camps (King, et al., 2017). The 'Clubhouse' saga was particularly evocative in this respect. When the virtual chat room 'does Xinjiang have concentration camps?' was opened in the social network Clubhouse at the beginning of February 2021, the app was banned by the Chinese Government. From the few interactions in the Xinjiang chat room that have been disclosed by media, it emerged that the Chinese citizens supporting the 'anti-terrorism' approach as a justification for the existence of these camps were minoritarian, and the majority of Chinese people were simply asking questions and requiring details and clarification about the XUAR situation to the room moderators, three Chinese Han. All users emphasised that they preferred to listen to the opinions of the Room moderators rather than looking for further information on 'biased and not trustable' Western media (Byler, 2021).

NGOs in China: new roads for dialogue with the CCP

China has never been an ideal place for either domestic or international NGOs to offer an active contribution to the debate on human rights and humanitarian actions within the country (Choetsow, 2022). For this reason, it is even more valuable to assess strategies and practices they have been using to negotiate access in an environment of authoritarianism and conflict such as the one characterising China.

Although, through the years, some NGOs have succeeded in developing a working relationship with the CCP, the majority of them have been seen as potential sources of opposition and dissent. This perception has led the government to endorse tight regulations concerning their work (Chen, 2006).

On April 28, 2016, China's National People's Congress Standing Committee adopted the 'Law of the People's Republic of China on Administration of Activities of Overseas Non-Governmental Organisations in the Mainland of China'. The new law, which came into effect in January 2017, aimed at regulating foreign NGOs' activities setting out strict requirements for actors wishing to operate in China, including the need to register with the government and to declare a Chinese sponsor, such as a government agency or a state-controlled organisation.

The new law gave the government broad powers to monitor both activities and funding of foreign NGOs, as well as the right to ban any organisation identified as a threat to national security or social stability, according to the party definition of the term. The new regulation also reflected a shift towards a more security-oriented approach to international civil society as the regulatory authority for foreign NGOs in China was transferred from the Ministry of Civil Affairs to the Ministry of Public Security and local Public Security Bureaus (Civil Society Work in China: Trade-Offs and Opportunities for European NGOs, n.d.).

All these changes have confirmed a new ambition within the CCP to further increase the level of control over civil society and to suppress any form of dissent (Holbig and Lang, 2021).

To offer a more accurate understanding of the operative environment NGOs are confronted with when trying to negotiate humanitarian interventions in China, this chapter is assessing first-hand data collected through interviews with four different NGOs operators. Three of them were foreigners, some with Chinese backgrounds, and one was a Chinese working in China. The aim of the interviews has been to collect critical and unique practical insights into what it means to be humanitarian actors in China. The difficulty of reaching out to civil society practitioners and their reluctance to share their experiences in the country proved to be a significant limitation to broaden data collection, confirming the sensitivity of the topic and the limited margins for humanitarian negotiation they have been experiencing in China. To protect the identity of our interviewees, their names as well as those of the NGOs they are working for have been kept confidential.

When NGOs operate from outside China

Three members of different foreign NGOs active in China from outside the country have been interviewed for this research. The first interlocutor works for an organisation centred around an information-focused web page providing insight into the Chinese political landscape and its effects on the ability of civil society and other humanitarian actors to operate in the Chinese environment. The platform wishes to bring the voices of dissidents, activists, and humanitarian actors from within China to the outside world, providing in-depth profiles, interviews, and videos of the work carried out by a broad range of actors.

The second NGO representative works for an organisation dedicated to protecting grassroot humanitarian actors and human rights defenders and to bringing their voices to the realm of UN fonctionnaires, mechanisms, and bodies. The focus is on advocacy and on providing support to humanitarian actors on the ground by opening space for dialogue and strengthening their knowledge and skills to give them the capacity to advocate within the realm of the UN autonomously.

The last organisation, originally active in China and now coordinating their sources and actions from abroad, supports local field operations through training, assistance, and networking and provides legal support to local victims and correspondents in need. It operates on the basis of partnerships with local actors.

While the three organisations target different audiences and adopt different strategies to achieve their goals, they all share the ideal of facilitating the emergence of a solid human rights consciousness in China and, as a consequence, the spread of best practices for humanitarian negotiations.

All three NGOs have confirmed that the space for human rights debate and humanitarian actions and interventions in China is shrinking. Academic findings have confirmed this idea, noticing a major change in governance strategy with the advent of the leadership of Xi Jinping and his obsession with the notion of consolidating state security, to be achieved by increasing control and repression on the civil society and by limiting external actors operations within the country, especially when related to the humanitarian sphere (Zhu and Jun, 2021).

China has indeed strengthened its technological capacity to monitor the activities of NGOs inside and outside the country. For one of the organisations, it has become increasingly difficult to provide on-site training sessions to local actors working in China due to heightened tracking of virtual movements by the government. This is also reflected in the online space, where the organisation in question has simply decided not to hold any online training or practical experience sharing sessions due to the danger associated with participant identification and the inefficiency due to potential sudden shutdowns. The same organisation has recently experienced a new form of attack, with thousands of fake accounts illegally created under the name of the organisation used to spread disinformation, with the goal of both discrediting the NGO and its actions in the country and consequently preventing accurate information from being properly disseminated.

All hindrances faced by international humanitarian organisations working in China are reflected in the annual OHCHR report 'Cooperation with the United Nations, its representatives, and mechanisms in the field of human right'. This report collects all documented cases of reprisals against those seeking to cooperate or having cooperated with the United Nations, its representatives, and its mechanisms in the field of rights. China has been the most cited country in the last 12 years, confirming the difficult environment humanitarian actors continue to experience in the country.

The three interviewees also confirmed that, in China, it is impossible to expect to push for change on a country-level scale as transformations have to be endorsed by the CCP. For this reason, on the one hand, it is preferable to create direct channels to communicate with central and local leaders due to a perceived higher degree of openness to dialogue. On the other hand, they consider constructive exchange on humanitarian negotiations best practices as crucial to guarantee to their advocacy strategies a greater propensity of success.

Throughout different interviews, NGOs actors highlighted two main impediments to advance their actions in China: financial resources and the sensitivity of the topic approached by their campaign.

One of the interlocutors summarised the problem by stating, 'when you observe NGO operations in China, think about money money money'. The CCP has indeed progressively substituted overt tactics of repression with more subtle methods aimed at denying or limiting NGOs access to funding as well as undermining their actions on the ground (Franceschini and Nesossi, 2018).

According to an interviewee, for humanitarian organisations working in China, the most important factor impacting on the success of their campaigns is the capacity of securing funding from within the country. Indeed, the CCP perceives foreign fundings as a vital threat, comparable to a form of infiltration or an act of subversion, hiding US intention to compete 'for hearts and minds' with the CCP and subsequently undermining its grasp on its own population.

Due to the strained relationship that is currently characterising the United States and China, NGOs receiving funding from the US face additional persecution as they are viewed as a subversive tool of US foreign policy. Humanitarian actors financially supported by the United States have registered a drastic reduction of their relevance in China's humanitarian environment, especially in the context of crises (Civil Society Work in China: Trade-Offs and Opportunities for European NGOs, n.d.).

This attitude was made clear to an interviewee whose acquaintance works with disability rights in China, a topic one would rather characterise as apolitical. The NGO in question has been targeted by the CCP due to the source of their funding emanating from the United States. If the same level of scrutiny is not associated with NGOs receiving fundings from European countries, one of the interviewees believes that when US funded organisations will be completely excluded from the country, the attention of the party for NGOs funded by European entities and institutions will rise, consequently reducing their margin for engaging into humanitarian negotiations and activities in the country.

Finally, although it is true that funding coming from inside China is less scrutinised by official authorities, it is also true that it is difficult to solicit Chinese public or private entities to finance local NGOs humanitarian projects.

Interviewees have expressed deep concern for a rising awareness that all topics related to human rights and humanitarian actions have become sensitive in contemporary China. For example, NGOs working on LGBTQIA+ have recently faced more pressure than they used to experience, for two reasons. First, most of them rely heavily on international donors. Second, they have close connections with international civil society organisations, pushing the CCP to identify them as dangerous entities with problematic foreign connections (Ren and Gui, 2022). Organisations working on women's rights have experienced the same problems, and their access to funding has significantly shrunk (Bai, 2016). Additionally, due to China's conservative attitudes towards issues linked to gender and sexuality, LGBTQIA+ NGOs are often labelled as 'morally sensitive' and, as a consequence, subject to strict censorship and various restrictions.

Overall, the sensitivity on human rights and humanitarian actions debate should be understood within the light of a broader crackdown on anything that is seen as too independent or disconnected from the Party, therefore potentially representing a threat to the overall stability of the Chinese state.

Although these findings paint a grim picture of the challenges for humanitarian actors in China, the importance of continuing to nurture this debate abroad should not be contested. For example, although China's technological prowess might have a negative impact on information accessibility, the government cannot do anything to erase the first impressions people had when accessing the information when they were available. For all interviews, allowing Chinese people to ask themself why the government has decided to intervene to censor certain information or to freeze humanitarian negotiations with foreign actors at a moment of crisis is an important drive to promote social change.

Albeit China's persecution does extend beyond national borders, the possibility of installing a certain degree of anonymity when working as a humanitarian actor in China while residing outside the country can offer more protection because of the possibility of maintaining a low, possibly anonymous profile.

Throughout the research, recommendations to improve the quality and the effectiveness of humanitarian negotiations in China have been spelled out by all interviewees. It has been highlighted that a broad, solid, and reliable network of local partners is necessary to operate in China and to be identified as privileged and reliable actors at a moment of crisis. Establishing trustful connections with either universities or companies that have already settled in

China could be a useful strategy to start building this network as well as to secure local funding to finance humanitarian actions. Guaranteeing a high standard of encryption and digital security is also a must to operate in China.

The struggle of China-based NGOs

Only one China-based NGO operator agreed to arrange an informal exchange on the state of the art of humanitarian actions and humanitarian negotiation best practices in China. The long-term experience of this interlocutor has proved useful in getting a more nuanced idea of the values, the priorities, and the challenges experienced by humanitarian actors and practitioners in China.

Like the three other interviewees, the Chinese speaker confirmed that space for humanitarian negotiations in China has progressively shrunk over the last ten years. This interlocutor identified the internal memo known as Document No. 9 released by President Xi Jinping in 2013 as a turning point for people working in the humanitarian domain in China. This document has identified an independent civil society as one of the seven greatest dangers to the Chinese state (Document 9: A ChinaFile Translation, 2015; Fu, 2017).

Alongside media freedom and universal human rights, Xi Jinping has identified civil society as a threat to social stability and as an ideological challenge to the government. This memo marked the beginning of a new crackdown on civil society organisations and humanitarian activists in China and has had significant implications for the work of NGOs in the country. This drastic change can be exemplified through the arrest, in 2019, of three members of 'Changsha Funeng', who were charged with 'subversion of state power' (Kuo, 2019). The organisation, which advocates for rights of people with disabilities and other marginalised groups and combats employment discrimination against people living with HIV and hepatitis B through litigation as well as institutional discrimination associated with China's 'one child policy' and reform of the household registration (*hukou*) system, was suddenly targeted by the government, and the individuals working for it were eventually convicted and imprisoned in 2021.

This case represented a major turning point for the humanitarian community in China. For the first time, charges attributed to members of the civil society were charged with punishments comparable to those normally reserved to radical dissidents. After this case, the majority of Chinese humanitarian actors have become more careful in trying to challenge the CCP official narrative and posture (Zhu and Jun, 2021).

The Chinese interlocutor further specified that the 2017 'Law of the People's Republic of China on Administration of Activities of Overseas Non-governmental Organisations in the Mainland of China' has not only severely reduced the impact of foreign NGOs in China, but it has also pushed the majority of them out of the country, proving the effectiveness of the CCP-led crackdown (Kellogg, 2020).

The Chinese practitioner also discussed a rising interest for the CCP to solicit Chinese NGOs to identify 'reliable foreign humanitarian experts' and to identify new strategies allowing China to directly access their expertise and ideas in a neutral and securitised environment. By foreign humanitarian experts, the government refers to European practitioners, researchers, and professionals. The possibility of involving American experts is currently very limited. By neutral and securitised environment, instead, the CCP refers to closed-door meetings where foreign humanitarian actors and experts whose profiles have been pre-approved by the government are invited to participate. It is becoming more and more frequent to see local governments asking Chinese NGOs to organise 'explorative panels' on specific topics, and the participation of foreign humanitarian actors and experts is approved under the condition that no meeting proceedings will circulate beyond government circles.

For the Chinese interlocutor, the fact that the CCP is interested in keeping a window of dialogue open to listen to alternative views and to explore new operative strategies and practices should be encouraged with cautious optimism.

The Chinese interviewee clarified that the freedom humanitarian NGOs working in China can be granted depends on the area in which they act and the approach they decide to undertake. Those working within the government narrative and providing support to official public policies are inevitably better tolerated. At the moment, NGOs working in the domains of environment and poverty alleviation are generally supported as their actions fit into the national political discourse.

However, the Chinese interlocutors also highlighted that the current dynamic could further evolve. For example, gender issues used to be considered a neutral topic and they are now becoming sensitive. In the realm of education, it is easy to get official approval for projects aimed at improving the standard of scholarly equipment in remote areas, but it is not possible to imagine launching a dialogue to make the content of the actual curriculum evolve.

The funding problem evoked by the other interviewees was confirmed, although the Chinese practitioner argued that suspicion for funding coming from the EU is rapidly rising in China.

Another problem that is limiting humanitarian NGOs' impact within the country is the generalised reluctance of the society to support their actions and ambitions. Practitioners working in China tend to suffer from isolation and the ostracisation in their family and society. Because of the sensitivity of their actions, acquaintances prefer not to be associated with anyone working in this domain, aiming at avoiding any form of persecution or harassment from the government, such as attacks on one's own physical integrity or that of one's family. The absence of a supportive network has been identified as a source of intense psychological distress that could be further amplified by the limited results that practitioners can achieve. Also, humanitarian NGOs tend not to collaborate among each other, fearing that cooperative work could generate further suspicions within the party.

Conclusion

This portrait of humanitarian activism and humanitarian negotiations in China is not particularly encouraging. If foreign NGOs tend to be closely monitored by the CCP, Chinese humanitarian practitioners are not more independent in their actions. In this context, if external actions can be useful to continue to keep a high level of attention on humanitarian crises and the need to coordinate external intervention into these crises, and not only for the case of Xinjiang, change inside China can be activated only by national humanitarian actors practitioners.

Recommendations shared by the Chinese interlocutor represent a useful contribution to the debate. For example, it was argued that to achieve social change in China it is necessary to involve academia. Academic debate is something the CCP is not planning to stop, and the content of this exchange can be easily addressed to decision making circles. On the contrary, humanitarian NGOs' practices are more scrutinised, especially when their fundings are labelled as 'suspect'.

The CCP is not planning to completely cut its connection with foreign world and humanitarian experts; rather, it will continue to solicit their opinions and contributions, provided that these exchanges are kept confidential. In China, change is more likely to happen when implemented in a top-down rather than a bottom-up process, and negotiations, and in particular humanitarian negotiations, need to be driven by the government.

Trying to build broad public support for a specific humanitarian action could prove to be a double-edged sword. Addressing the general public directly could be interpreted as an immediate threat to state security, while solid arguments advanced by humanitarian experts in a clear and convincing way tend to be considered as a safe and useful strategy to propose the most suitable solution for problems, especially at a moment of crisis. Also, proposals and best practices do not have to be challenging, rather presented as options for the government to evaluate.

The Chinese interlocutor used a particularly efficient image to summarise the state of the art of humanitarian actions in the country, stating that 'working as an insider in China is like working as a nurse in a psychological hospital – you try to make them take the pills without getting beaten up. No matter how strange it might sound, it is still worth it. As far as humanitarian NGOs practitioners are concerned, we should not try to cut ourselves out even if the CCP wants to cut us out'.

References

Abdeleli, A. (2022). Why Arab and African Countries Stand with China at the UN. Swissinfo.ch. October 11. https://www.swissinfo.ch/eng/business/why-arab-and-african-countries-stand-with-china-at-the-un/47961448

Bai, G. (2016). Development of Chinese Women's NGOs since the 1995 World Women's Conference. TOAEP. https://www.toaep.org/pbs-pdf/57-bai

BBC News. (2019). Faith in Ruins: China's Vanishing Beards and Mosques. June 20. https://www.bbc.com/news/av/world-asia-china-48696184

Buntinx, A. C. and Colli, F. (2022). Moral Policy Entrepreneurship: The Role of NGOs in the EU's External Human Rights Policy towards China. *Journal of Contemporary European Studies* 30(3), 552–565.

Byler, D. (2021). 'Truth and Reconciliation': Excerpts from the Xinjiang Clubhouse. *The China Project*. March 3. https://thechinaproject.com/2021/03/03/truth-and-reconciliation-excerpts-from-the-xinjiang-clubhouse

Caksu, A. (2020). Islamophobia, Chinese Style: Total Internment of Uyghur Muslims by the People's Republic of China. *Islamophobia Studies Journal* 5(2), 175–198.

Castets, R. (2003). The Uyghurs in Xinjiang – the Malaise Grows. *China Perspectives* 49.

Chen, J. (2006). The NGO Community in China. *China Perspectives* 68, 29–40.

Choetsow T. (2022). Peace out NGOs. *Harvard International Review*. https://hir.harvard.edu/peace-out-ngos/

Civil Society Work in China: Trade-Offs and Opportunities for European NGOs. (n.d.). https://www.giga-hamburg.de/en/publications/giga-focus/civil-society-work-in-china-trade-offs-and-opportunities-for-european-ng-os

Cronin-Furman, K. (2018). China Has Chosen Cultural Genocide in Xinjiang—for Now. https://foreignpolicy.com/2018/09/19/china-has-chosen-cultural-genocide-in-xinjiang-for-now

Document 9: A ChinaFile Translation. (2015, October 30). ChinaFile. https://www.chinafile.com/document-9-chinafile-translation

European Parliament Resolution of 9 June 2022 on the Human Rights Situation in Xinjiang, including the Xinjiang Police File. https://www.europarl.europa.eu/doceo/document/TA-9-2022-0237_EN.html

Franceschini, I. and Nesossi, E. (2018). State Repression of Chinese Labor NGOs: A Chilling Effect? *The China Journal* 80, 111–129.

Fu, D. (2017). A Political Compromise? In Mobilizing without the Masses: Control and Contention in China. *Cambridge Studies in Contentious Politics*. Cambridge University Press. https://www.cambridge.org/core/books/mobilizing-without-the-masses/FE8DA14FD770D0FACF35E9979A3BB8DA

Garcia, Z. (2022). *China's Western Frontier and Eurasia: The Politics of State and Region-building*. New York: Routledge.

Greitens, S. C., Lee, M., and Yazici, E. (2019/2020). Counterterrorism and Preventive Repression: China's Changing Strategy in Xinjiang. *International Security* 44(3), 9–47.

Holbig, H. and Lang, B. (2021). China's Overseas NGO Law and the Future of International Civil Society. *Journal of Contemporary Asia* 52(4), 574–601.

Howell, A. and Fan, C. C. (2011). Migration and Inequality in Xinjiang: A Survey of Han and Uyghur Migrants in Urumqi. *Eurasian Geography and Economics* 52(1), 119–139.

Ibrahim, A. (2019). China Must Answer for Cultural Genocide in Court. *Foreign Policy*. https://foreignpolicy.com/2019/12/03/uighurs-xinjiang-china-cultural-genocide-international-criminal-court/

ICIJ. (2019). Read the China Cable Documents. https://www.icij.org/investigations/china-cables/read-the-china-cables-documents/

Ingram, R. (2018). The Uyghurs and the Han: 1 World, 2 Universes. *The Diplomat* October 4. https://thediplomat.com/2018/10/the-uyghurs-and-the-han-1-world-2-universes/

Kellogg, T. (2020). The Foreign NGO Law and the Closing of China. In: Chen, W. and Fu, H. (eds.). *Authoritarian Legality in Asia: Formation, Development and Transition*, 114–140. Cambridge: Cambridge University Press.

King, G., Pan, J., and Roberts, M. E. (2017). How the Chinese Government Fabricates Social Media Posts for Strategic Distraction, not Engaged Argument. *American Political Science Review* 3, 484–501.

Kuo, L. (2019). Staff of NGO Linked to Hong Kong Arrested in Southern China. *The Guardian* August 29. https://www.theguardian.com/world/2019/aug/29/staff-of-changsha-funeng-ngo-hong-kong-arrested-in-southern-china

Leduc, S. (2019). Muslim Countries' Silence on China's Repression of Uighurs. France 24 November 27. https://www.france24.com/en/20191127-china-communist-uighurs-xinjiang-muslim-silence-camps-repression

Leibold, J. (2019). The Spectre of Insecurity: The CCP's Mass Internment Strategy in Xinjiang. *China Leadership Monitor* 59. https://figshare.com/articles/composition/The_Spectre_of_Insecurity_The_CCP_s_Mass_Internment_Strategy_in_Xinjiang/13191050/1

Li, E. (2019). Fighting the "Three Evils": A Structural Analysis of Counter-terrorism Legal Architecture in China. *Emory International Law Review* 33, 311–365.

Lu, X. (2017). *The Rhetoric of Mao Zedong: Transforming China and Its People*. Columbia: University of South Carolina Press.

Maizland, L. (2022). China's Repression of Uyghurs in Xinjiang. *Council on Foreign Relations* September 22. https://www.cfr.org/backgrounder/china-xinjiang-uyghurs-muslims-repression-genocide-human-rights

McMillen, D. H. (1984). Xinjiang and Wang Enmao: New Directions in Power, Policy and Integration? *The China Quarterly* 99, 569–593.

McMurray, J. (2022). The UN's Report on the Uyghurs Nearly Didn't See the Light of Day, thanks to China. *The Guardian* September 1. https://www.theguardian.com/commentisfree/2022/sep/01/un-report-uyghurs-china-michelle-bachelet-human-rights-abuses

Millward, J. (2023). China's New Anti-Uyghur Campaign How the World Can Stop Beijing's Brutal Oppression. *Foreign Affairs* January 23.

New York Times. (2019). Document: What Chinese Officials Told Children Whose Families Were Put in Camps. https://www.nytimes.com/interactive/2019/11/16/world/asia/china-detention-directive.html.

OHCHR. (n.d.). OHCHR – Annual Reports on Reprisals for Cooperation with the UN. https://www.ohchr.org/en/reprisals/annual-reports-reprisals-cooperation-un

Ren, X. and Gui, T. (2022). Where the Rainbow Rises: The Strategic Adaptations of China's LGBT NGOs to Restricted Civic Space. *Journal of Contemporary China* 1–19. https://www.tandfonline.com/doi/full/10.1080/10670564.2022.2131378

Rippa, A. (2014). China's Porous (western) Borders. *The Asia Dialogue* May 26. https://theasiadialogue.com/2014/05/26/chinas-porous-western-borders

Ruser, N. (2020). Documenting Xinjiang's Detention System. *ASPI* September 25. https://cdn.xjdp.aspi.org.au/wp-content/uploads/2020/09/25125443/documenting-xinjiangs-detention-system.cleaned.pdf

Soto, J. (2020). China, ETIM, and the Politics of Terrorist Designation Lists. *American Security Project* November 19. https://www.americansecurityproject.org/china-etim-and-the-politics-of-terrorist-designation-lists/

Su, Z., Xu, X., and Xun, C. (2020). What Explains Popular Support for Government Surveillance in China? *Journal of Information Technology & Politics* 19(4), 377–392.

Sudworth, B. J. (2020). China Defends Detention of Uighur Model in Xinjiang. *BBC News* August 18. https://www.bbc.com/news/world-asia-china-53809345

Tobin, D. (2020). A "Struggle of Life or Death": Han and Uyghur Insecurities on China's North-West Frontier. *The China Quarterly* 242, 301–323.

Tobin, D. (2022). Genocidal Processes: Social Death in Xinjiang. *Ethnic and Racial Studies* 45(16), 93–121.

Van Schaack, B., et al. (2021). "Break Their Lineage, Break Their Roots:" China's Crimes against Humanity Targeting Uyghurs and Other Turkic Muslims. Human Rights Watch & Mills Legal Clinic of Stanford Law School. https://law.stanford.edu/publications/break-their-lineage-break-their-roots-chinas-crimes-against-humanity-targeting-uyghurs-and-other-turkic-muslims/

Wintour, P. and Ni, V. (2022). UN Human Rights Commissioner Criticised over Planned Xinjiang Visit. *The Guardian* May 20. https://www.theguardian.com/world/2022/may/20/un-human-rights-commissioner-xinjiang-michelle-bachelet-criticised

Xiao, E., Cheng, J., and Lin, L. (2020). Beijing Accelerates Campaign of Ethnic Assimilation. *WSJ* December 31. https://www.wsj.com/articles/beijing-accelerates-campaign-of-ethnic-assimilation-11609431781

Yau, N. (2022). China's Security Management towards Central Asia. *Foreign Policy Research Institute*. https://www.fpri.org/wp-content/uploads/2022/04/chinas-security-management-towards-central-asia.pdf

Zenz, A. (2018). New Evidence for China's Political Re-Education Campaign in Xinjiang, *China Brief, Jamestown Foundation* 18(10). https://jamestown.org/program/evidence-for-chinas-political-re-education-campaign-in-xinjiang/

Zenz, A. (2019). 'Thoroughly Reforming Them Towards a Healthy Heart Attitude': China's Political Re-education Campaign in Xinjiang. *Central Asian Survey* 38(1), 102–128.

Zenz, A. (2020). Sterilizations, IUDs, and Mandatory Birth Control: The CCP's Campaign to Suppress Uyghur Birthrates in Xinjiang. *Jamestown Foundation Report*. https://jamestown.org/wp-content/uploads/2020/06/Zenz-Internment-Sterilizations-and-IUDs-REVISED-March-17-2021.pdf

Zenz, A. and Leibold, J. (2017). Xinjiang's Rapidly Evolving Security State. *China Brief, Jamestown Foundation* 17(4). https://jamestown.org/program/xinjiangs-rapidly-evolving-security-state/

Zhang, F. (2009). Rethinking the 'Tribute System': Broadening the Conceptual Horizon of Historical East Asian Politics. *The Chinese Journal of International Politics* 2(4), 545–574.

Zhang, C. (2019). Community Engagement Under the Mass Line for Counterterrorism in China. *Studies in Conflict and Terrorism* 44(10), 1–19.

Zhu, H. and Jun, L. (2021). The Crackdown on Rights-advocacy NGOs in Xi's China: Politicizing the Law and Legalizing the Repression. *Journal of Contemporary China* 31(136), 518–538.

HUMANITARIAN AUTHORITARIAN
AUTHORITARIAN HUMANITARIAN

COMMENTARY

A personal reflection on working in China

S Mahdi Munadi

During my 10 years of involvement with China as a diplomat and an academic, I observed a significant difference in the level of military and security presence in Xinjiang compared to other provinces. I encountered Afghan individuals who married Xinjiang natives and contacted the embassy regarding their inability to see their wives as they had been in the camp. Additionally, people from Xinjiang shared their stories of hardship and oppression with me, often in Muslim restaurants in Beijing or other cities. It was challenging to hear their accounts and feel unable to offer any meaningful help, as neither my embassy (the Afghan Embassy in Beijing) nor my home country was in a position to intervene. These helpless voices were a poignant reminder of the harsh realities of China's Sinification, unification, and development policies, which Claudia's article has explicitly touched on.

The history of China's Communist Party (CCP)'s policy on ethnic groups started with classification and ethnic groups from over 400 to 55 legalised. It continued incentivising, attracting, and forcing them to comply with CCP policy under the name of unification. In this process, 10 million Uyghurs of this unification suffered the most. Claudia's work has illustrated the challenges faced by the people. She discusses the situation in Xinjiang, China, where CCP is interning over 1 million Uyghurs in mass internment camps, prisons, and other penal institutions. CCP classifies these as 'concentrated educational transformation centres', but evidence suggests that the Uyghurs are subjected to forced indoctrination, psychological stress, forced labour, and torture.

One problematic and unfair approach in national politics is the creation of unity within the population at the cost of sacrificing diversity. Regardless of who speaks out against it – people, NGOs, or anyone else – the CCP reacts

DOI: 10.4324/9781003316541-9

harshly. It is easy to understand the challenges NGOs face in China and the difficulties in carrying out humanitarian actions at different levels.

In a counter-narrative, it's possible to tolerate different colours and standards, but CCP has chosen one colour for all ethnic groups in the name of national unity and development. This approach destroys the unique characteristics that initially defined the different ethnic groups along with considerable hardship to millions.

As a Muslim in Beijing, I liked halal food restaurants. Finding such places was relatively easy before 2019. Then, I noticed a change and found no signs in Arabic or English indicating restaurants serving halal food. I discovered that the CCP had banned using Arabic or English in restaurants, food, Muslim names, etc., meaning Muslims must conform to the majority's culture. This story was disheartening to see the circle getting tighter for Muslims in China who must be like others.

Claudia's article aims to understand the origins and impact of the CCP policy in Xinjiang, especially on Uyghurs, and decode its narrative at the national level. She also discusses the role of academics, media, foreign actors, NGOs, and humanitarian negotiations in advancing the level of consciousness, asking: 'We should not try to cut ourselves out even if the CCP wants to cut us out.'

5

DAILY NEGOTIATIONS WITH STATE AGENCIES IN THE FIELD – REFLECTIONS FROM REFUGEE CAMPS IN WESTERN ETHIOPIA

Imri Schattner-Ornan

Introduction

In this short chapter, I will share some of my personal reflections on the challenges and constraints of negotiations between humanitarian international NGOs and authoritarian regimes at project level (the 'field'). This reflection is directly inspired by my experience of working with the Ethiopian ARRA in 2013 in the Benishangul-Gumuz area in Western Ethiopia. I must stress that any opinions and views expressed in this text are my own and do not in any way represent the views or attitudes of the organisation, mission, or project with which I was associated.

Ethiopia is a complex country where present conflicts, tensions, or developments can be traced to historical or long-brewing sentiments. Events that happened 40, 70, or 120 years ago are remembered and influence present situations. The record of events via documents, monuments, or ceremonies is taken seriously. This poses several disadvantages for a paper such as this. Firstly, this is a personal reflection, based on my own experience and far from perfect memory. It is informed by notes written after the experience and by retrospective remembering, which is lacking and sometimes vague. Events and developments that happened since 2013, both for me and in Ethiopia, taint these memories. Secondly, I worry about the impact that sharing these thoughts and reflections, beyond the narrow colleagues who read them already, might have on humanitarian operations in the country, on the work of the agencies with which I worked, or on individuals. So, once more, this is a personal recollection, imperfect and subjective, representing my thoughts alone.

DOI: 10.4324/9781003316541-10

This chapter is meant to be a reflection on the practice of authoritarian regimes, especially the ways a regime limits and controls international humanitarian non-governmental organisations (INGO). The focus is on practices encountered at the field level between managers, coordinators, and representatives working and living in remote sites. The objective here is specifically not to look at wider discourse at national or capital levels but at how daily interactions are impacted by authoritarian attitudes. This chapter is constructed around three elements or moments in the interaction between the actors in this setting: the Memorandum of Understanding (MoU), the Permit, and the 'Grace'.

These elements are of different kinds. The first two are physical entities, the last one a moment in a meeting, a temporal entity. The MoU and Permit have a material reality – they are objects. Objects that must be handled with care: they must be stamped, protected, recorded, and shown as proof. Beyond their existence as physical objects, these two elements are also social signifiers. They demonstrate that these actors have a relationship and that this relationship can be 'seen' in the real world by real objects. Specifically, they describe the nature of that relationship. Interestingly, the social significance of these objects exists even when the objects themselves are not materially present; it is not directly correlated to their physical relevance. That is, the MoU or Permit matter even when they are incomplete, unsigned, lacking, or absent. In some ways, an incomplete or absent Permit or MoU demonstrates their importance better than a present and complete version, as it exposes the negotiations that go into achieving these documents.

My interest in these objects, both in their materiality and social impact, mirrors similar approaches in social anthropology. I am guided in this by the work of researchers such as Navaro-Yashin (2007, 81):

> I study documents, or the material objects of law and governance, as capable of carrying, containing, or inciting affective energies when transacted or put to use in specific webs of social relation. This is not to argue that documents, or artefacts, have a subjectivity (or that they are capable of feeling), but to suggest, following the work of Marilyn Strathern (1999), that, when placed in specific social relations with persons, documents have the potentiality to discharge affective energies which are felt or experienced by persons.

The 'Grace' moment is much more fleeting. I refer to 'Grace' as a meeting, or a moment in a meeting, where one actor (the INGO) requests that the other actor (the national authority) grant something. The capacity to grant is a manifestation of practice of being the authority. In this context, requests are usually for exceptions to rules set by the same authority. It is an appeal to the discretionary power of the authority. This moment represents the relationship between, in this case, the INGO and the authority, ARRA. It symbolises the dependency of one on the decision of the other. These requests to allow exceptions to known or imagined rules capture the complexity of the entire relationship. This moment recalls Schmitt's often cited (Agamben, 2005; Nguyen, 2010) assertion that the 'Sovereign is he who decides on the exception' (Schmitt, 2005, 5).

Of course, these three elements are related: there is no Permit without an MoU, and there is no meeting without the MoU either. However, can we say that there is no appeal to 'Grace' without the Permit or the MoU? This is a bit more complicated, because if the MoU or the Permit functioned as they should, there would be no need for 'Grace' or appeal: decisions and rights would have been known and clear, not negotiable and person-dependant. At the same time, the possibility to sit together and discuss any 'Grace' is unlikely without an MoU or Permit, though not necessarily a complete one.

In sum, the paper shares experiences from the field and tries to reflect on practices, from both actors (and I focus here on the INGO and ARRA, but there are other actors involved in this context) that are shaped by authoritarian attitudes. These authoritarian attitudes are often incapsulated by a physical object, such as an MoU or a Permit. It is an invitation to consider how humanitarians' interactions at all levels, but specifically at daily field level, are shaped. I am drawn to see how these interactions are articulated around objects and moments.

Methodologically, this chapter is based on a somewhat 'bastard' approach. It is a reconstituted reflection based on a personal experience which highlights the emic and subjective point of view from a participant-observer in the most basic sense. It is 'I' who sits in the meeting, 'I' who appeal to grace or argues the points of the MoU with ARRA officials.

The initial version of this reflection was written in 2014. Since then, many things have changed in Ethiopia, good and bad. The paper refers to the political climate of the country at the time, not the current one. This paper also reflects little on the general situation of refugees in Ethiopia or the implications of being a refugee in an authoritarian state.

The Ethiopian context

Can Ethiopia be considered an 'authoritarian regime'?

Looking at the history of Ethiopia in the past 30 years, it is hard not to notice the authoritarian, top-down, and in general non-Human Rights orientation of the several governments in Ethiopia. Even if considering only the post-DERG, pre-current situation (1992–2019), the period discussed in this chapter, when Ethiopia was led by the Ethiopian's People Revolutionary Democratic Front (EPRDF), its authoritarian nature is clear (Gedamu, 2021).

Aside from numerous and regular Human Rights violations regularly monitored by organisations like Human Rights Watch (HRW, 2010, 2015) and Amnesty International (AI, 2012a, 2012b), the Ethiopian regime was authoritarian in its unwillingness or reluctance to allow for any democratic dissent and opposition and low accountability (Glasius, 2018). The EPRDF approach to governance was a single-party approach, inspired by a Marxist-Leninist ideology where the party and the state became one. As Gedamu advises (ibid, 117), 'In fact, in EPRDF-run Ethiopia, it is impossible to distinguish incumbent party politics from a government bureaucracy; in short, party rules government'.

This paper looks more at authoritarian practices than considering the wider authoritarian regimes definition. Glasius' (Glasius, et al., 2018, 9) comment that 'In authoritarian circumstances, it is never quite so clear what you can and cannot do …This results in a sense of uncertainty: you never know whether you are crossing a red line or not', is particularly useful here as we are looking at the way daily practices in such context impact individuals and organisations.

In addition, and this is well known for those who have worked in Ethiopia, Ethiopian authorities tend to be suspicious of external interventions. Of course, every intervention that 'smelled' of Human Rights advocacy was severely curtailed, and the government put specific laws and regulations in place to prevent international and local organisations from work on such issues. Infamous among those is the 2009 Charities and Societies Proclamation (GoE, 2009). Humanitarian work also, without explicit Human Rights component, was severely controlled. This attitude pre-dates the EPRDF, as can be recalled regarding the expulsion of various INGOs, such as Médecins Sans Frontiers-France, by the DERG regime during the 1984 famine crisis (Binet, 2013). In general, from my impression and those I have worked with in Ethiopia (on two occasions), it is fair to describe the Ethiopian authorities' attitude in general as opaque, obtrusive, suspicious, and overall unwelcoming of foreign NGOs (though they have been massively present in the country for many years). All of these are hallmarks of authoritarian regimes that are keen on controlling, constraining, and limiting interventions. My experience reflects those mentioned by Desportes and Hilhorst (2020, 347), referring to Ethiopia, Myanmar, and Zimbabwe:

> The challenges presented by these Low Intensity Conflicts (LIC) and authoritarian settings were not dissimilar to those faced by humanitarian workers: negotiating access; building trust; dealing with contradictory information and advice; navigating bureaucracy, daily encounters, and conversation topics; and selectively self-censoring.

From a humanitarian practitioner's perspective, an Ethiopian particularity maybe is the importance of governmental official bureaucracy. Approval is very much dependent on the provision of the correct documentation with the exact signatures, stamps, and endorsements. Not just 'authoritarian', the Ethiopian governance model can be maybe described as 'officialdom' – the reign of the government's official or the bureaucrat (BBC, 2009). Foreign agencies are constantly chasing after the correct authorisation, with the correct signature and stamp, in a maze that is not only opaque, but also often changing and, in general, is considered (from the NGO's perspective) as a tool for control rather than a tool for facilitation. Because of that, we will focus on the practice of controlling mechanisms by regimes, not just on their official discourse.

What is ARRA?[1]

The ARRA is the main Government of Ethiopia agency to deal with refugees, asylum-seekers, and returnees. In its 2013 form, it is a consequence of the 1992 EPRDF-led revolution, though it is a version of an older state's agencies and branches (ARRA, n.d.). Officially, its mandates are:

> The key mandate of ARRA is to support and maintain the physical safety of refugees as well as ensure refugees live in dignity until durable solutions are found to their plights. Moreover, ARRA takes the lead in coordinating and managing ongoing refugee programs while availing land to set up camps.
>
> The following mandates include the major activities it carries out to fulfil its responsibilities.

- Serve as a key government agency and representative on all matters of refugees and asylum-seekers
- Conduct refugee status determination exercises and deciding on refugee status
- Establish refugee camps and managing the overall coordination of camp activities
- Provide physical protection and maintain the well-being of all people of concern
- Provide and coordinate basic and social service delivery to refugees
- Coordinate country-level refugee assistance programs
- Assist and facilitate NGO partners and other stakeholder interventions in the discharge of their activities

- Facilitate and undertake repatriation movements when the causes of refugee displacement are solved (https://arra.et/mandates/)

I would highlight that Ethiopia hosts many refugees, with an estimated 800,000 registered refugees and asylum seekers in the country (UNHCR, 2021). Overall, Ethiopia is welcoming of refugees. A point well worth keeping in mind as a reminder that regimes, even authoritarian and controlling ones, can have an underlying humanitarian consideration, acknowledging the plight of refugees and their needs; ironically, at the same time, many liberal and human-rights-oriented democracies have neglected or renounced this responsibility.

ARRA's role, though clearly engaged and involved with the welfare of refugees, is also one of control and security. It is one of the organisation's major strategic objectives (ARRA, ibid):

Maintain the physical safety of refugees and avoiding potential security threats emanating from refugee themselves

(https://arra.et/major-strategic-objectives/)

Informal consensus among aid workers in Ethiopia at the time of my assignment clearly identified ARRA's position as a part of the state's security and intelligence community. As an agency constantly in contact with potentially 'dangerous' foreigners, either refugees or, differently dangerous, international relief agencies, it is clear ARRA enjoys close contacts with Ethiopia's numerous state security mechanisms.

ARRA is a federal agency, dependent directly from Addis Ababa, though with representation in states' capitals (in this case, Assosa, Benishangul-Gumuz capital). Officially, Ethiopia is a federal republic, but in practice, it is highly centralised (Gedamu, 2021). Security agencies like ARRA are controlled from the centre, with probably limited freedom or serious delegated authority to regional offices. The question of local freedom and independence is crucial because negotiations with ARRA take place at all levels: federal capital, state capital, and in each camp. To what extent those at lower levels can take initiatives and decisions, without approval from the centre remains very much unknown. This opacity is one of the main experiences of working with this agency, as well as with authoritarian regimes in general.

Experiences of working with ARRA

Working with ARRA in the field was a constant challenge. It is a case study of how regimes can translate their attitude into practice, and what approaches/

solutions humanitarian agencies can elaborate on when encountering these challenges. This will be explored by looking at specific documents and interactions.

The MoU

The MoU is a core document defining relationships between international aid agencies and states. But how are MoUs different from other documents that govern NGOs, such as registration documents, project proposals, contracts, or others? The answer to that is murky, as an MoU can be similar to these documents. In fact, it is a very flexible term, used differently by agencies and contexts, and can serve different agendas. However, there are important elements that demonstrate how an MoU, in an international humanitarian context, is different from those other documents mentioned. An MoU, unlike general registration documents, tends to be project specific. They detail the obligations and inputs of all stakeholders, either government or non-government, involved in a project (space and time specific). Unlike technical documents, such as project proposals, MoUs describe the responsibilities of all parties. Unlike contracts between providers and donors or between partners, they illustrate the collaborative nature of work, not the contractual. The MoU is an indication of collaboration, a proof of shared vision and aim, and a serious statement of commitment and intent. These are official documents, signed and approved by those legally authorised to do so, and carry a certain legal responsibility (but maybe less so than a contract or national registration documents). For such an important aspect of humanitarian bureaucracy, I retrieved little scholarly attention to them.

The MoU between the INGO, ARRA, and UNHCR for this project was a key document defining the relationship between these parties. I will refer mostly to the first two parties, as UNHCR's role in the MoU (and indeed in the project) was mostly to provide technical support and in-kind assistance or participate in monitoring, evaluation, and coordination. In general, UNHCR's role in Ethiopia is focused on responding to IDP emergencies and addressing the needs of refugees. The UN agency works closely with government authorities like ARRA and provides funding for camps to national and international NGOs. The focus below is on ARRA and the INGO, who were the more important parties in this MoU. Their responsibilities included:

For ARRA:

- Handle necessary customs duty for importation of goods needed for the project
- Facilitate access to the refugee camp for all NGO staff to enable them to support an optimal quality of care for the vulnerable refugee population

- Facilitate all taxes free importations or local procurement of all relief material, drugs, medical and logistic material, medical kits, and nutritional therapeutic supplies for the project
- Facilitate work permits, visa reception and extension, travel permit processes, or consent on short-term working permission for expatriate staff
- Support in the form of a recommendation letter to facilitate NGO importation and use of telecommunication means such as VHF, satellite phones, and VSAT
- Facilitate the availability of locations for construction of temporary medical and nutritional treatment centres, storage, offices, and staff residences
- Collaborate with NGOs and UNHCR in establishing and maintaining coordinated responses in Health and Nutritional programs
- Assist NGO in liaising with the local and regional administration
- Facilitate support from the Regional Health Bureau in delivering specific drugs and supplies (EPI vaccines, TB, HIV, and malaria treatments...) from national programs to refugee camps health facilities
- Monitor activities to be implemented by the NGO

And for the INGO:

> INGO through its own private funding and/or bilateral donor funding agreements will implement and administer jointly with ARRA, the health and nutrition programs in Benishangul-Gumuz refugee camps with an appropriate and effective response to support the intervention in a spirit of humanitarian partnership. INGO will not be making any direct payments to UNHCR, ARRA or any other party

The role of the MoU in the daily management of the project cannot be underestimated. This was the document that both sides would bring to the meeting, physically and point to what they thought the other party was not fulfilling. It was ever-present, either as a metaphor for the collaboration or as physical object used as a reminder of responsibilities.

The MoU is an agreement between partners (with UNHCR mostly as technical support/coordination), one of which is meant to support the administrative, legal, and bureaucratic requirements (ARRA) and the other to implement and administer (jointly) health and nutrition activities (INGO). There was maybe a naïve assumption by the INGO in this MoU that having such a 'symbiotic' relationship would facilitate administrative procedures; in reality, this was not the case. The MoU did not trump (or even dent) the bureaucratic mechanism of ARRA's control, to say nothing of other national authorities responsible for tax, visas, or importation. Expectations that, through a collaborative MoU with ARRA importation, visas, work permits, or tax exemptions would be facilitated never materialised. At project level, we became frustrated by what we saw as ARRA failing to deliver on the 'spirit of the MoU', by not allowing greater access to the camp and failing to push on issues like rapid drug importation clearance with other authorities, while ARRA grew frustrated with our implementation delays (related to the above) and our constant push for more access, more freedom, and more autonomy, which was not articulated in the MoU.

The larger issue here is that each party came to the MoU from a different perspective and a different expectation. From the INGO's side, this was a document that was meant to demonstrate collaboration and joint approach, which was also hoped to be used for future collaboration or consolidation of the agency's position in the country (see more on this in the section on "strategic projects" below). It was not seen as a detailed description of how to manage the project, probably because that information was captured elsewhere, in documents such as the donor's project proposal or the technical annex to the MoU. At the same time, the INGO saw the responsibilities of ARRA, listed above, as essential to the provision of the project, and failure to deliver those not just as undermining delivery but also undermining the spirit of the partnership.

From ARRA's side, the MoU seems to have had more value as a descriptor of obligations and responsibilities to what it mostly saw as a service provider. Indeed, through the project, ARRA treated the INGO as that: an external entity there to implement activities according to government priorities, guidelines, and procedures. Reference to their own obligations in the MoU and any suggested link between the INGO's incapacity to provide services as linked to ARRA's incapacity to fulfil their responsibilities were denied. For example, when the INGO's imported drugs were held by customs and ARRA was not able to press for their timely release, this caused a stockage shortage in the camps clinics. The situation led to a conflict of accusations, where each side blamed the other as unable to fulfil their responsibilities detailed in the MoU.

There were other problems and challenges working closely with ARRA, such as constant negative attitude, accusation of interferences and suspicion. But these were overall personal opinions. They demonstrated the capacity of ARRA to present a dual façade: at times harsh, abusive, and aggressive, at others conciliatory and open to discussion. All these relationships were articulated around a core document, the project's MoU. Activities in the camp or any assessments or consideration of new activities (for example, when a new influx of refugees arrived) were not considered as per humanitarian need but according to what was or was not in the original MoU. I argue that ARRA tried to reduce the humanitarian principle of the INGO to a list of activities in the MoU, ignoring the more relational, collaborative, or aspirational elements of that document, and by that aimed to maintain the INGO as a service provider with little capacity to expand activities (to new sites or new needs). This reduction to a position of a service provider with a closed mandate can be seen as a bureaucratic mechanism of control.

The Permit

If the MoU was the agreed document that served as a basis for discussion and different interpretations, the Camp Entry Permit (the Permit) was the most complicated and contentious document in the relationship. This is the document which, around its presence, or more often its absence, many of the difficult discussions between ARRA and the INGO took place. It was also the document that signified, more than anything, ARRA and the state's control on humanitarian agencies.

To enter the refugees' camps in Benishangul-Gumuz, all employees of all agencies were meant to provide a permit issued by ARRA. These were closed camps. Refugees were not meant to leave them, and locals were not allowed to enter them. They were guarded by armed state (not federal) policemen at the main gate. Though closed and protected by armed policemen, the camps were not heavily controlled. The police presence was minimal and light. There were no guard towers or patrol guards around the camps, just a presence at the main gate. The guards referred any unfamiliar entry, even if they carried the correct documentation, to the ARRA camp's coordinator office, where their entrance rights could be ascertained. Foreigners were obviously immediately directed to ARRA unless they were well known and worked in the camp regularly.

To work or even visit the camp, a permit had to be issued for the named individual by ARRA's head office in Addis Ababa. A visitor's permit lasted for the specific duration of their visit, whereas a permit for someone working in the camp could be provided for longer. These permits were essential for international staff: non-Ethiopians working for the INGO in the country for anything between 6 and 24 months while contracted and paid elsewhere; and also visiting national staff from the capital required them. Local staff, that is, nationals employed by the INGO in the field, did not require such letters (or rather, the permits were never requested or processed). For an international to receive their Permit to enter the camp, all relevant documentation about their visa and registration in the country (a lengthy process requiring submission of authenticated diplomas and work certificates) was required in the capital.

Permits are clearly means of control. In this instance, they were used to ensure ARRA controls who has access to the refugees. These are spaces from where most Ethiopians are excluded in the same way that the refugees are excluded from mixing with the general population. As suggested above, ARRA is a part of the rather nebulous security apparatus of the Ethiopian state, one that is both controlling refugees and controlling humanitarian agencies. The problem arises when these humanitarian agencies are meant to provide services and support to the refugees and are working with ARRA under a joint MoU.

In the project, ARRA refused to allow access to the camp for key international field-based workers until an official permit was delivered from the capital. For example, the INGO's international doctor was not allowed to access the clinic where she was supposed to provide services because her permit letter did not arrive on time or had a missing stamp. Likewise, the INGO's project coordinator (myself) was blocked for several weeks from entering the camp, visiting the clinic or sites where the team I was managing were providing assistance, until a permit was delivered. As can be imagined, these restrictions caused a lot of tension and friction between the partners.

For staff based in the field, the issues were resolved finally by endless negotiation. The physician and coordinator were allowed to access the clinic, but not the whole camp, until the correct authorisation was received. Visitors however were confined to meet with ARRA in their office and not allowed entry beyond a certain point unless their documents were received in advance. As mentioned, this was not only the case of international visitors but also for senior Ethiopian staff from the capital.

I am not criticising the requirement to have proper authorisation. This, by itself, is a legitimate requirement. The problem is that the Permit was an omnipresent threat. Authorisations were long and complicated to receive, constantly changing, and limited in their duration. This resulted in the humanitarian agency spending most of its time chasing these letters, authorisations, and approvals or negotiating with ARRA how to proceed without them. It also created a constant atmosphere of concern and uncertainty. Staff could be turned away from activities, or initiatives could be blocked due to these bureaucratic reasons. So, a process that is meant to ensure sustainability, transparency and equity resulted in the opposite: doubt, concern, and ambiguity. The instrument of fixed approval became the instrument of uncertainty.

From an anthropological perspective, the Permit is a fascinating object. It carries in its materiality a whole complex set of relations and expectations between the individual and the state. This can be seen for example in Cabot's (2012) work on the 'Pink Card', governing asylum seekers status in Greece. Her work demonstrates the dependency of marginalised individual on an object provided by the state and how its absence can lead to dramatic consequences. In our context, the problem is different, as it would be misleading to claim the international NGO was powerless. Because of that, the Permit is not a binary object (present or absent) but a more negotiated object. It can be partially accepted (as was the case for the physician and field coordinator) if it is 'in process', or 'under renewal'. Once the principle that a Permit is required was accepted by the INGO, the field staff could apply for a consideration (the 'Grace') even when the physical object was missing.

The 'Grace'

The 'Grace' moment is a specific kind of meeting. It is the meeting where the INGO's representatives, for example Head of Mission coming from the capital or Field Coordinator in the region meets with the camp or regional authorities and argues for a derogation. The reasons could be varied: a field visit that was unplanned, a high-level visit, a new influx of refugees to a new site, etc. This meeting has a structure: explaining why the derogation is required with references to the MoU, explaining in an apologetic way why we feel obliged to request this and cannot proceed with the usual mechanism for permits (which can take weeks), and appealing to the spirit of collaboration, the good intentions of the agency, and the consideration of the official. It is a process that re-affirms and, to an extent, symbolically re-enacts the relationship between these partners. I use the term 'Grace' to signify the discretional and exceptional nature of this request. The element of 'requesting' is important because the INGO does not claim the access requested as a right but appeals to goodwill.

The 'Grace' was not only to appeal for consent on issues like allowing temporary camp access before capital authorisations were delivered or to agree to NGO's participation in field assessments. The INGO had to constantly appeal to the arbitration and mediation of ARRA camp and regional authorities when we had conflicts with specific ARRA staff. For example, one of the ARRA's camp's doctors (Dr M) often refused to coordinate with the INGO, accusing the organisation staff to be spies and not fulfilling their MoU obligations. This relationship became extremely complicated, and the intervention of regional ARRA officials (and UNHCR) became necessary. The existence of people within ARRA, who were clearly and vocally against the presence of the organisation, and were able and willing to jeopardise the project, is worth reflecting about. In particular, the individual referred to above (Dr M) was regularly verbally abusive to the INGO staff, both national and international. He spoke openly on how INGOs in general, and this one in particular, had no role in the camps, and that all funding should be provided to ARRA directly for implementation.

It is interesting to reflect on the attitude of Dr M, as it similar to positions seen in similar situations. Consider for example the attitude of Eldar, the National HIV Coordinator, in Atlani-Duault (2007). A bureaucrat, in a post-socialist setting, refusing to acknowledge the need for involving NGO as an equal partner and arguing to maintain all the power in a context where the state is unable to fund activities, and is dependent on international organisations and NGOs. Indeed, in discussions with other ARRA officials, Dr M's approach was presented as 'old-fashioned' and out of touch with ARRA's financial situation. I think this position should be understood together with the view of the INGO as a service provider. For individuals like Dr M, it is the responsibility of the state to provide services to the refugees, not the responsibility of third sector bodies. The transfer of responsibilities and activities is both humiliating for the state and requires close control. This hint of antagonism to the demonstration of the state's incapacity to perform a core role is relevant in the reflection of the 'Grace' as a moment symbolically affirming the sovereign role. It also highlights how an authoritative agency is not necessary uniform in its approach or understanding.

A personal positioning or attitude, positive or negative, I argue, is never outside the overall organisational relations. An obstructive person who undermines the INGO and the ARRA-INGO project could probably not behave so without some support and acceptance from higher ARRA levels. Through individuals like Dr M, ARRA's management presented dual attitudes to the INGO. They could disown the person when they wanted to, but they never compelled him or others to be supportive of the international partner. The essence here is that, though relationships are individual, each person echoes trends and attitudes within their organisation. The INGO as well used dual messaging with ARRA, choosing to present reconciliatory or strict faces when it suited us. These faces are often apparent through different people (the Field Coordinator as conciliatory, the Country Medical Coordinator as strict, the Assistant Head of Mission as conciliatory, the Head of Mission as severe…). It is not personal; it is strictly business.

Whether it was for mediating personal antagonism, or appeal for a derogation to a bureaucratic requirement, or a desire to expand activities to new locations or situations, the INGO often had to appeal to the 'Grace' of ARRA officials. This process of appeal, of requesting approval or mediation to provide activities that the INGO believed were incorporated in the MoU, constantly undermined the position of the INGO and maintained it as a dependent, almost subaltern entity. This is, of course, a very interesting reversal of roles: a well-funded, internationally recognised, with a reputation for vocally expressing their positions and at time, a 'devil may care' arrogance, humanitarian organisation is constantly reminded of their temporary, unstable, and uncertain situation in the camps and country. A situation that depended, to a large extent, on the perceived goodwill of government officials. This attitude was also frustrating for us, as we knew that as ARRA was dependent on the INGO to provide essential services in the camp, as they lacked the funding to do this. But the wealth of the INGO and its access to international donors did not translate to local power in this local negotiation.

The element of what is known and what is perceived is important here. In truth, I and my colleagues did not know how ARRA functions. How and why are permits granted, to what extent the authorities encourage some ARRA staff to be abusive and what are the real limitations for the INGO are all unknown elements. The laws under which ARRA makes decisions are not just unknown to the international agency; they are virtually unknowable.

The humanitarian INGO in the field is maintained in a status of constant threat (bureaucratic threat, not violent threat) and uncertainty (See Glasius, et al., 2018). Everything depends on personal favour, which can change very quickly. The authorities, in the camp or in the regional office, advise on rules (for example, no camp entry without specific permits), but also position themselves to be those able to provide the exception of that rule, thus constantly maintaining their position as final arbitrators. This ability to provide exceptions can be presented as a field-based decision or as an appeal to higher authorities. ARRA's camp and regional offices can 'request' derogation from ARRA's central and federal levels, but such appeal maintains the humanitarian INGO in the dependency position. An appeal to higher, and more importantly distant, authorities, can serve to maintain both a friendly façade (as rejection to the appeal comes from another location) or preserve the ambiguity of where decision lies.

These situations echo Agamben's reflection (Agamben, 2005). Elements such as the arbitration of the exception as an act conferring authority, the capacity of derogation or authorisation as a sovereign act are encountered here in a meeting, not in a legal or constitutional texts. We also see other similarities: the appeal to the 'necessity' by the INGO as a reason for the exception, whilst maintaining the acceptance of the rule: 'Necessity is not the source of law, nor does it properly suspect the law; it merely releases a particular case from the literal application of the norm' (Agamben, 2005, 25). More broadly, the 'Grace' moment is a performance, almost ritualistic in its structure, affirming the relationship and the dependency of one actor on the other.

Appealing for extraordinary consideration from a local bureaucrat is a practice worth reflecting on. It evokes several interesting questions. For one, would a similar attitude be used between an INGO and a government official in a higher income or Northern Hemisphere country? To what extent does the perceived power of the organisation – its wealth, reputation, access to donors, and international media – change the dynamic in this interaction? Finally, how is this practice of appeal and favour reminiscent of, and is a reversal of, the colonial encounter? Do Western humanitarian NGOs expect that they can persuade local bureaucrats and appeal to an imagined individual favour because the local, Ethiopian (or Congolese, or Nigerian, or Yemenite…) bureaucracy is more dependent on personal power and influence? To what extent to we, the international western humanitarian practitioners, imagine our counterparts to be rational officials in a structured system or 'big men' able to manoeuvre in weak or corrupt environments?

Ironically, this moment somewhat validates ARRA's perception of the INGO as a 'dangerous' element, as it is an actor that claims, and even to an extent expects, an exceptional derogation from the rules. What legitimacy allows the INGO to expect this exception is a relevant question. Is the reference to general Humanitarian Imperative relevant or is this a reflection of wealth, position, and reputation? ARRA's distrust, and their view of the INGO as disruptive, is not without cause. The larger question here is if appealing or requesting an exception is an act that infers also some sovereignty.

To conclude this section, we should note that the 'Grace' I refer to is ARRA's exercise of power and is appealed for by the INGO. It is the favour that the authority can bestow; the belief, by the INGO, that this official, to whom we apply, possesses the power to grant exceptions, or put differently, to make bureaucratic miracles. This form of 'Grace' is linguistically and theologically rendered as 'charismatic' power in the Weberian sense (Joosse, 2014) which leads us back to Agamben's *auctoritas* (Agamben, 2005, 85). I am not suggesting that we, in the meeting, believed the ARRA official possessed divine charisma. The source of this power is either personal or bureaucratic, but which is it? This is a core question, as we cannot know if the capacity to bestow exceptions lies in the individual or its position within the hierarchy. The rules, in an authoritarian context, are to a large extent unknown, leaving appellants (the INGO) in constant ambiguity.

Relationship in practice: the daily negotiation

Chipping at the mountain

Given this complicated and often tense configuration for project implementation, we should examine what were the tactics used to create an intervention space for the INGO in the camps. It is important to notice that through continuous work and effort and by demonstrating the capacity of INGO, the engagement of its staff, and its professional quality, INGO was able to do more and be more accepted. This is possibly linked to external ARRA financial pressure, making them require INGO more than they initially expected.

The metaphor used to explain the response practices to the initial (and sometimes extended) challenges is that of slowly chipping at the mountain of limitations and procedures which is ARRA. There was no tipping point after which the relationship became smooth, but a continual investment in changing attitudes and improving relationships slowly made life and work easier. The more we met with ARRA, sat with ARRA, and talked with ARRA, the better they understood us, and the more we were able to convince them to allow us to be more engaged in the activities. More importantly, the more we knew them, the more we understood their priorities, concerns, and where the red lines were. The better we knew these, the more we were able to persuade them to participate or allow our initiatives, and the more careful we were about not crossing them.

The construction of this mutual understanding was lengthy and often limited the quick response desired by a humanitarian INGO. In practice, instead of implementing an action, procedure, or initiative in the field, it had to be discussed multiple times at several levels. The assumption was that through positive personal relations with our key partners (for example, camp medical director or regional coordinator), we were able to solve problems more rapidly on the ground. In places where we were not able to develop these, we were continuously blocked. This assumption is problematic, as ARRA's officials' individual real capacity to allow exceptions or concessions is never known.

The war of attrition

Dealing with this complicated relationship was done through chipping bit by bit at their fundamental resistance. Every time we encountered an obstacle, the issue was either escalated, bargained, presented differently, negotiated to find an intermediary solution, or conceded. Conceding sometimes meant raising the issue again, in another form, later. ARRA commented on this, advising that it is much harder to work with this INGO and that they encounter us bilaterally much more than any other organisation working in the camps.

Table 5.1 is an attempt to sum up the options available to us in the field, with their respective advantages and disadvantages.

TABLE 5.1 Field Negotiation Possibilities

Tactic	Action	Advantage	Disadvantage	In practice
Negotiation	Constant and repeated negotiation until compromise reached	Capacity to find compromise and reach ad hoc solutions	Time and energy consuming. Does not undermine dependency	Often used
Escalation	Escalation to higher levels or request arbitration by other stakeholders like UNHCR or ECHO	"Save face" as refusal originates elsewhere. Can provide neutral solution	Not solving an issue, mostly a delay tactic from both sides	Rarely used to find real solutions as they are not proven efficient
Refusal	Refusal to cooperate and threat to abandon the joint work	Clearly states red lines and important issues	Cannot be repeatedly used. Needs to be saved for serious problems	Never used by INGO
Concession	Accept ARRA's position/ limitation	Move on to other issues	Accepting limitations	Often used, and then return to the topic later

In theory, these strategies should be seen as escalating options. In practice, we were not able to regularly threaten to abandon the project unless an extremely serious incident occurred. Escalating was mostly a useful tactic to delay decisions and not commit at the field level for both parties. It was a useful mechanism not to reject other requests but to appeal to a higher authority's rejection, thus maintaining the façade of willingness to reconcile. Involving other bodies, like UNHCR or ECHO, proved useless at the field level. At the end, there was little to do but constantly negotiate or concede and maybe raise the topic again later.

The issue of conceding should not be under-evaluated. The sad reality is that the intensity of the relationship caused fatigue on both sides. This fatigue is a tool used to achieve goals, but it is a double-edged sword. Fatigue also means choosing more carefully the issues in which you are willing to invest, and to an extent, avoiding issues in which you think your likelihood of success is lower. It is a form of acceptance, which can, if not properly monitored, lead to tolerance of unacceptable practices or self-censoring (Desportes and Hilhorst, ibid). For me, this is one of the stronger arguments for constant staff turnover, providing new energy and ideas. However, constant renewal is also undermining the larger relationship between the parties, so it can also be counterproductive. Negotiation fatigue and the self-censorship that comes with it could be seen as a tactic by authorities to subversively impose control on a foreign agency.

The INGO and ARRA have, for a long time, engaged in a sort of continuous war of attrition, each side trying to tire the opponent. Both sides used similar tactics to advance their objectives in this continuous struggle. These include playing on the various approval levels, pointing out discrepancies between activities and written documents (MoU), referring to vague procedures and protocols (mostly from ARRA's side), or misunderstanding the partner. Other practices of negotiation include constant staff changes (limiting continuity) or submerging the other party with reports and written documentation. These last two approaches were used to try and further our objectives.

As can be imagined, both sides were, after some months, tired of the intensity of this partnership. Certainly, mutual tolerance increased. However, a key question arises: has this continuous effort ended up souring the relationship generally and decreasing the motivation of either organisation to continue to work together? It is possible that, though we learned, to work together in the field, the image that both organisations presented to their hierarchy was that it was a constant and exhausting effort, causing decision-makers in either structure to realise that finally it was not worth the effort. Ironically, too much investment to win this war of attrition finally meant that both sides lost interest. The greater perspective of future partnership was a causality of present collaboration.

The bigger picture: the value of Strategic Projects

The support for the refugee camps in Benishangul-Gumuz was considered, internally and unofficially, a 'strategic project'. By this, I mean a project that, though it has an intrinsic value in providing real humanitarian assistance, also has a wider value in its role in the relationship between the stakeholders. For the INGO, a successful partnership with ARRA was seen as a possible way to ensure a long-term, stable presence, in legal and bureaucratic terms, in Ethiopia. In a context of continuous administrative uncertainty and increased challenges in deploying international staff, importing medical supplies, or accessing populations, this was seen as a potential strong relationship that will allow to continue the agency's presence and be able to respond to the numerous emergencies happening in the country regularly, not to mention expected crises in neighbouring countries likely to result in refugee influx (which was the case with South Sudanese refugees in late 2013).

The existence of 'strategic projects' is not rare or exceptional in the humanitarian world. It is a survival strategy that can be useful in many situations, though it raises complex questions about ethics and humanitarian principles. However, in this case, each partner (excluding UNHCR) understood the nature of the relationship differently. For the INGO, a partnership with ARRA was a means to both provide humanitarian assistance to the refugees in the camps and leverage a federal agency for a more stable position in the country. When ARRA failed to deliver on these wider elements, the logic of this approach became questionable. For ARRA, the INGO was considered (and often referred to) as a service provider to implement activities according to ARRA's priorities and regulations, and without the claim for an equal partner. I believe that for many ARRA's staff, our requests were difficult to understand, as they were so exceptional compared to all the other service providers (mostly paid by UNHCR funds) in the camps. ARRA's authorities in the camp and region commented on this, that they have more bilateral meetings to solve issues with us than any other agency in the camp.

As a strategic project that has aimed to stabilise the INGO's presence in the country via a good working relationship with a powerful federal agency, this attempt was probably a failure. Both ARRA and this INGO learned a lot about working with each other, and I would like to believe we even learned how collaboration is possible, but at the same time both sides were exhausted by the process and became all too conscious of their respective divergences. The final sentiment seems to have been that even in routine and established settings, this collaboration was difficult, which would suggest it would be even more complicated in emergency settings.

Even if this was a 'strategic project' in some ways for us, it was not so for ARRA. They did not require or consider the need to establish a good working relationship with the humanitarian international NGO because the implementing agency was merely seen as a service provider that could be relatively easily replaced (even by a sister INGO if necessary). The investment of each partner and their aspirations from the collaboration were unequal and divergent.

Conclusion: working with authoritarian regimes

What conclusions can be drawn from this experience about humanitarian NGOs capacity to work with authoritarian regimes?

First, it is clearly essential to explore the interactions between humanitarian NGOs and authoritarian states at all levels. Specifically, it is interesting to see how the daily and continuous interactions at the project/field level are impacted by the wider national, political, and historical contexts. Actors in the field 'live out' the legacies of their organisations' histories and hierarchical attitudes. These attitudes predate the current project and the current staff. At the same time, in the field, personal relations are imagined to be able to alter attitudes and constraints. I think that any improvement in the relationship in the field is temporary, uncertain, and extremely demanding in terms of endless dialogue and demonstration of good intentions. When looking at the interactions between international humanitarian NGOs and such states, especially where there is a complicated and well-known history to these interactions, we should really pay close attention to how these are translated and acted in the field, not only in official discourse or at the capital level.

In the Ethiopian context, it is important to see how the element of 'officialdom' is omnipresent yet allows some limited local flexibility. The principle of, for example, the need for a specific permit or authorisation can never be denied, but the practice of having it can be negotiated. A document is, oddly, not necessarily binary in its existence. It can be 'in process', 'submitted', or 'on its way', allowing for an exception to be considered (a 'Grace') which provides temporary access to the camp. Exceptions can be made if they are based on acceptance of the principle and if they are not pushed too far. The very clear example for this is how international staff based in the field and working in the camp's clinic were allowed into the camp if their papers were submitted in the capital, but visiting staff could not enter without papers approved, signed, and stamped in Addis Ababa and presented physically.

An important element of this continuous discussion in the field is the need for the agency to prove its value and demonstrate its good intentions. This demonstration of good intentions also implies a desire 'not to rock the boat', not to launch new activities, or not to seek too much or too quickly to expand the partner's view of the humanitarian agency's role. This is problematic, as it can quickly result in the INGO's self-censorship and acceptance of the service provider role. In a sense, I argue that this is one of the main ways authoritarian regimes (and maybe even donors) control humanitarian agencies by reducing them to a service provider mentality with a very limited mandate and subject to constant monitoring, evaluation, and reporting mechanisms that restrict the consideration of wider issues or other needs. Likewise, living in the constant fear of approval, authorisation, and audit is a strong controlling mechanism.

Another important lesson that can be drawn from this experience is that it requires more than one successful joint project to position a humanitarian INGO in a better place vis-à-vis the authorities in Ethiopia. It is hard to know if, had the project been an unmitigated success (which it was not), such positive relationship would have ensued and would have continued in the future. But in a sense, this was not really possible, as for ARRA, this was not seen as a relationship worth investing in. Expectations for using ARRA as leverage for importation or visas were maybe over-optimistic. As ARRA did not massively facilitate issues such as drug importation or international staff permits, this caused further delays for the project, causing tensions in the field and undermining any 'strategic' value. Maybe INGOs' assumption that in an authoritarian regime, a powerful local ally is important should be questioned. Such an approach could almost 'bind' organisations to influential local stakeholders, be they government ministries, national NGOs, or even individuals.

Humanitarian NGOs should remember that even in authoritarian regimes, there can be room for negotiation and manoeuvre. In allocating space for humanitarian agencies, such regimes might try to reduce these agencies to service providers and limit their wider humanitarian mandate or consideration. This is an orientation that humanitarian organisations should resist and challenge. No MoU or solid collaboration will transform a security-oriented federal agency into a humanitarian-focused body. Agencies like ARRA will accept humanitarian relief on their own terms; it remains the role of the humanitarian NGO to then, very slowly and very laboriously, expand that space in their daily interactions. Our MoU is often a constant reminder of our fundamental misunderstandings.

Looking forward, it would be interesting to explore, via in-depth qualitative research and embedded practice, how the NGO-authorities encounter reflects historical relationships and moves beyond simplistic narratives of powerful Western NGOs and weak local authorities. This encounter is complex and changing, as the attitude towards NGOs in countries like Ethiopia is constantly evolving (sometimes negatively) and NGOs' identities, representations, and even staff change. How do elements such as nationality, gender, age, or other identity indicators impact these encounters?

Likewise, the documents used to conceptualise and negotiate humanitarian action are rich fields for further investigation and consideration. There seems to be little critical reflection in the humanitarian world about the practices of creating MoUs, Concept Notes, and such products which underlie humanitarian action. These artefacts merit attention and careful reading.

Acknowledgements

I would like to thank several people who provided essential advice and reflections on this chapter, particularly Andrew Cunningham and Bertrand Taithe for their reviews and suggestions, Dagemlidet Worku and Antoine Foucher for their comments and reflections, and the members of the INGO in the field and beyond.

Note

1 Sometime between the initial drafting of this chapter and its final publication, refugee management in Ethiopia seems to have been reformed. ARRA has been transformed to the Refugees and Returnees Service (RSS), which has new website (https://rrs.et/) and different approach. The official websites of ARRA, referred to in this section, are no longer publicly available.

References

Agamben, G. (2005). *State of Exception.* Chicago, IL: University of Chicago Press.
Amnesty International. (2012a). Ethiopia: Stifling Human Rights Work: The Impact of Civil Society Legislation in Ethiopia. *Amnesty International Report.* March 12.
Amnesty International. (2012b). Ethiopia: The 2009 Charities and Societies Proclamation as a Serious Obstacle to the Promotion and Protection of Human Rights in Ethiopia. *Statement to UN Human Rights Council* 18th June–6th July 2012.
ARRA. (n.d.) *About Us* https://arra.et/about-us/
Atlani-Duault, L. (2007). *Humanitarian Aid in Post-Soviet Countries: An Anthropological Perspective.* London: Routledge.
BBC. (2009). Ethiopia's Passion for Bureaucracy. *From Our Own Correspondent.* August 10. http://news.bbc.co.uk/1/hi/programmes/from_our_own_correspondent/8189145.stm
Binet, L. (2013). Famine and Forced Relocations in Ethiopia 1984-1986. *NGO Speaks Out Case Studies.* https://NGO-crash.org/en/publications/humanitarian-actors-and-practice/famine-and-forced-relocations-ethiopia-1984-1986
Cabot, H. (2012). The Governance of Things: Documenting Limbo in the Greek Asylum Procedure. *PoLAR: Political and Legal Anthropology Review* 35, 11–29.
Desportes, I. and Hilhorst, D. (2020). Disaster Governance in Conflict-affected Authoritarian Contexts: The Cases of Ethiopia, Myanmar, and Zimbabwe. *Politics and Governance* 8(4), 343–354.
Gedamu, Y. (2021). *The Politics of Contemporary Ethiopia: Ethnic Federalism and Authoritarian Survival.* London: Routledge.
Glasius, M. (2018). 'What authoritarianism Is…and Is Not: A Practice Perspective.' *International Affairs* 94(3), 515–533.
Glasius, M., et al. (2018). *Research, Ethics and Risk in the Authoritarian Field.* Basingstoke: Palgrave Macmillan.
GoE. (2009). *Proclamation No. 621/2009: Proclamation to Provide for the Registration and Regulation of Charities and Societies* https://www.ilo.org/dyn/natlex/docs/ELECTRONIC/85147/95159/F1985589413/ETH85147.pdf
HRW. (2010). Development without Freedom: How Aid Underwrites Repression in Ethiopia. *Human Rights Watch Report.* October 19 https://www.hrw.org/report/2010/10/19/development-without-freedom/how-aid-underwrites-repression-ethiopia

HRW. (2015). "Journalism Is Not a Crime" Violations of Media Freedoms in Ethiopia. *Human Rights Watch Report.* January 21. https://www.hrw.org/report/2015/01/21/journalism-not-crime/violations-media-freedoms-ethiopia

Joosse, P. (2014). Becoming a God: Max Weber and the Social Construction of Charisma. *Journal of Classical Sociology* 14(3), 266–283.

Navaro-Yashin, Y. (2007). Make-Believe Papers, Legal Forms, and the Counterfeit: Affective Interactions between Documents and People in Britain and Cyprus. *Anthropological Theory* 7(1), 79–96.

Nguyen, V. K. (2010). *The Republic of Therapy: Triage and Sovereignty in West Africa's Time of AIDS.* Durham, NC: Duke University Press.

Schmitt, C. (2005). *Political Theology: Four Chapters on the Concept of Sovereignty.* Chicago, IL: University of Chicago Press.

Strathern, M. (1999). *Property, Substance and Effect: Anthropological Essays on Persons and Things.* London: Athlone Press.

UNHCR. (2021). *Ethiopia Country Update 31st May 2021* https://reliefweb.int/sites/reliefweb.int/files/resources/UNHCR%20ETHIOPIA%20COVID%20and%20Operational%20Update%2010%20June%202021.pdf

COMMENTARY

Independence

Peter Buth

Of the four humanitarian principles—humanity, impartiality, neutrality, and independence—the principle of independence is perhaps the least prominent. Humanity and impartiality are often viewed as the most important core tenets. Neutrality is a practical tool, necessary to gain acceptance and access in conflicts and charged political environments, but not a value in and of itself. Independence tends to be an afterthought, yet it is the safeguard for neutrality and impartiality, for without independence, how can humanitarian organisations make decisions impartially?

Independence ensures that international non-governmental organisations (INGOs) can choose where to go, whom to help, and how to do so without undue financial or political influence from governments, donors, and warring parties. In contrast, compromised independence means that other actors have influence on an organisation's choices, which often translates into compromised neutrality and impartiality.

There are few, if any, contexts where humanitarian independence is absolute. But there are many contexts where constraints on independence are so severe that INGOs must constantly weigh and assess whether a line has been crossed. Imri Schattner-Ornan's description of Ethiopia in 2013 is one such case.

The backdrop to how multiple Ethiopian governments have viewed independent humanitarian actors is deep and complicated, and admittedly also includes occasions when there were legitimate questions about INGO neutrality. But Schattner-Ornan's experience sheds light on two of the main challenges INGOs face in many countries when striving to preserve independence from government control: (a) navigating state bureaucracy and policies designed to regulate civil society (which are typically more intrusive, coercive,

DOI: 10.4324/9781003316541-11

and arbitrary in authoritarian states); and (b) governments' political considerations and efforts to manipulate or limit aid.

From the perspective of a government granting independent actors access to a politically sensitive context, this is an issue of political risk-benefit analysis: what threats do INGOs pose (to the government), how can they mitigate these threats, and how can the government benefit from the NGO's presence? Moreover, as a rule of thumb, the more abused and marginalised the community that an NGO wants to assist, the higher tends to be the risks and fewer the benefits for governments to grant unhindered access.

In these contexts, independent access, or even the negotiation around it, is replaced by what Schattner-Ornan aptly describes as the 'grace': the regulatory framework and decision-making processes which create an operating environment that is so restrictive and complex that it makes providing humanitarian assistance with any degree of independence, agility, and flexibility virtually impossible and forces INGOs to request 'exceptions to the rule' to implement their activities.

In such politically hostile environments, the language used to frame the relationship between governments and humanitarian actors can easily distort the underlying objectives and (unequal) balance of power. The 'partnership agreement' between technical government agencies and humanitarian actors can mean very different things for those around the table: a tool of control for one and a necessary compromise for the other.

The opaqueness of authoritarian contexts calls for humanitarian agencies to take a longer-term, consistent, and strategic approach that includes investment in contextual analysis, historical knowledge of the agency's history, and institutional relationship building. A thorough understanding of the power dynamics within and among government agencies can create opportunities to exploit 'the cracks in the system', for example when interests between officials at local, regional, and federal levels differ. To know under which circumstances a request for 'grace' is more likely to be considered can help create that extra little bit of space to operate. But this is in clear tension with the DNA of most humanitarian agencies, where planning, staff contracts, and funding cycles tend to be short. Importantly, it also runs counter to the humanitarian imperative to address urgent needs. A child with malaria does not have the time to wait for treatment until an MoU is signed. For a doctor, accepting an armed escort to the clinic to attend to the patient may be an (understandable) compromise. At a broader, organisational level, however, the same compromise takes on an entirely different dimension.

The author bluntly exposes the inherent risk of compromise creep. When the alternative is to lose hard-won access altogether, any compromise to safeguard some of it can seem justifiable, especially for front-line aid workers who are faced with people in desperate need of assistance. In addition, in politically sensitive contexts, gaining access to a marginalised community is often much harder than maintaining it. Once an INGO has some degree of presence, protecting it is vital, as operational presence can create some leverage for INGOs, particularly with local stakeholders, and shutting down or expelling NGOs can incur political or reputational costs for governments.

Thus, one of the central challenges for humanitarian actors is to continually assess the risks of incrementally accepting ever more compromises and incrementally losing ever more independence. The question must constantly be posed: when do the compromises become unacceptable?

That is where the principle of independence is of critical importance—it is a yardstick that helps to expose and weigh the degree of compromises, prevent them from becoming the acceptable *norm,* and avert an unintentional slide into a situation where manipulation and harmful side effects outweigh the benefits of the humanitarian intervention.

Schattner-Ornan's chapter highlights the way that authoritarian governments use bureaucracy to control independent humanitarian action, but they are not the only ones. Migrants and refugees seeking safety in Europe, and those who try to assist them, can testify that administrative obstacles, bureaucratic tactics, and political manipulation of legal norms are also deployed—with devastating effect—in modern democracies like Italy and Greece.

6

DILEMMAS OF HUMANITARIAN NEGOTIATIONS WITH THE RISE OF THE TALIBAN IN AFGHANISTAN

S Mahdi Munadi and Rodrigo Mena

Introduction

Humanitarian negotiations are crucial in addressing complex humanitarian crises in relation to conflicts and disasters. Humanitarian negotiations can support achieving peaceful and sustainable resolutions to conflicts at the same time they are an essential part of the everyday practice of humanitarianism, taking place at every stage of the humanitarian response, from the initial assessment of needs to the delivery of assistance and the transition to long-term recovery and development (Grace, 2016; Hilhorst, 2013; Magone, et al., 2012). Humanitarian negotiations, moreover, involve a range of actors, including humanitarian organisations, governments, non-state armed groups, and local communities, and require building trust and relationships with all these actors, understanding their perspectives and priorities, and developing strategies that address the root causes of the crisis. Even in the more challenging settings, there is 'a space for negotiation, power games, and interest-seeking between aid actors and authorities' (Magone, et al., 2012, 17).

Humanitarian negotiation also occurs at different levels (macro-national, meso-regional/institutional, and micro-local) and across different dimensions (such as religion, ethnicity, power imbalances, or culture) (Mancini-Griffoli and Picot, 2004; Mena and Hilhorst, 2022). Moreover, as presented by Glasius (2018, 2023), it is important to understand that authoritarianism is not a phenomenon necessarily (or only) localised in the sphere of the state, and its manifestations are likely to occur at different levels of a society and exercised by different actors, for example, religious or private/corporate ones. In this sense, beyond state authoritarianism, we must pay attention to 'authoritarian practices' at different levels and spaces of a society (Ibid., 2018) and how,

DOI: 10.4324/9781003316541-12

therefore, authoritarian *practices* by different actors and at different levels affect humanitarian practices. Humanitarian negotiations consequently need to understand the political, cultural, and social dynamics that influence negotiations in each context, as each level of negotiation operates within a unique context that requires specific knowledge and skills to navigate.

Additionally, humanitarian negotiations need to consider factors such as religion, ethnicity, power imbalances, and culture, as these can significantly impact the negotiation process and the ability to address humanitarian crises effectively. By taking these factors into account, humanitarian actors and aid-related stakeholders can develop effective strategies to build trust, address cultural differences, and empower marginalised groups. However, humanitarian negotiations in authoritarian countries, settings, and authoritarian practices present unique challenges due to political and social factors that can impact the effectiveness of the negotiation process (Magone, et al., 2012; Mena and Hilhorst, 2022). Limited access to information, restricted freedom of speech and assembly, lack of transparency, political interference, and security concerns can all pose significant barriers to communication, information sharing, and trust-building.

Despite the importance of the above, few studies have focused on understanding the challenges of humanitarian negotiations at different levels and across multiple dimensions in authoritarian settings. To address this, in this chapter we aim to study this complexity in the case of Afghanistan in the current scenario, in which since August 2021 the Taliban are in control of the country. We develop this chapter based on a comprehensive literature review on humanitarian negotiation and the case of Afghanistan, even though both academic and professional knowledge of the country is still limited. We therefore also draw on multiple informal conversations with humanitarian actors working in or on Afghanistan, both in the United Nations (UN), international, national, and local non-governmental organisations (NGOs), donors, and some academic informants. We rely ultimately on our experience living, working, and researching in Afghanistan, as well as information gathered in previous research projects. Putting all of this together, we have developed this reflective piece on authoritarian negotiations in Afghanistan in the new scenario the country faces, with the Taliban at the head of the government, the departure of international military troops, and the Taliban in control of the entire national territory.

Humanitarian negotiation and renegotiations at different levels and across dimensions

Humanitarian negotiation is a broad term that covers multiple actions that, in the end, seek to facilitate humanitarian action. Beyond the technical aspects that negotiating with multiple actors may entail, it is a social and political process that is present throughout humanitarian action. As presented in the book *Humanitarian Negotiations Revealed: The MSF Experience* from Médecins Sans Frontières (Magone, et al., 2012), humanitarian negotiation entails a series of practices requiring preparation, research, analysis, and the development of strategies for the specific contexts in which they take place. It is important to recognise in the negotiations the role that the so-called humanitarian principles, as well as to take into account ethical considerations such as the need to protect human security and human rights.

While general humanitarian negotiations are discussed at the macro level between international agencies and organisations and national authorities, it is equally important to recognise the number of negotiations and renegotiations that occur at other times of a humanitarian crisis. In a similar vein, most studies on authoritarianism focus on the role of the state and state-level authoritarianism, missing acknowledge the significance of comprehending that authoritarian practices are not solely enacted by the state (Glasius, 2018, 2023). Rather, these practices emerge through the actions of various actors operating at different levels and within diverse spheres. These actors contribute to the production and reproduction of authoritarian practices, necessitating a comprehensive study and understanding of authoritarianism in conjunction with other practices and phenomena (Glasius, 2018). Notably, exploring the interconnections between authoritarian practices and humanitarian actions becomes particularly relevant for analysis. Humanitarian endeavours, therefore, encompass multifaceted activities directed towards mitigating human suffering, advancing human rights, and promoting social justice. At the same time, humanitarian action can intersect, coexist, or inadvertently reinforce authoritarian practices. Examining the relationship between authoritarianism, authoritarian practices, and humanitarian action sheds light on the intricacies of authoritarian systems and their impacts on societies.

A previous study in South Sudan that looked at humanitarian negotiations in the decision-making process, particularly to define the population targeted for humanitarian assistance, found that these negotiations tend to occur at three distinct levels: as macro-national, meso-regional, and micro-local (Mena and Hilhorst, 2022). Beyond defining where these negotiations take place, these groups define the actors who negotiate, at what level they make decisions, and the nature of these negotiated decisions. In more details, Mena and Hilhorst (2022) identify that negotiations and renovations unfold in at least three analytical levels and practical spaces: Level 1, negotiations and decisions regarding humanitarian action are made at the national level by multiple actors, such as donors, the UN Humanitarian Country Team, humanitarian organisations, and national authorities. Negotiations at this level are framed as seeking universality, consensus, and transparency in assistance provision. Moreover, these negotiations are usually framed as evidence-based, with decisions based on objective arguments and usually presented as transparent, by media or other communication mechanisms. Level 2 negotiations are usually made within aid agencies, government ministries or departments, and local authorities. The focus is on efficiency and accountability, and decisions are based on an analysis of the organisation's capacities, balanced against the objective of providing aid to those in the most urgent need. Negotiations are often internal to the organisation or between the organisation and its implementing partners.

Level 3 humanitarian negotiations are rooted in a narrative centring on the concepts of feasibility and efficacy. The aim is to help those who need assistance and that can be assisted. For example, at Level 1, it could have been decided to support a particular affected area; at the regional/meso level, it is decided which community in specific to work with; but at Level 3, decisions between organisations in terms of where they can access, where they have presence, and how they negotiate with local authorities and groups end up finally steering the decision of where humanitarian actions unfold and who is assisted. Decision-making at this level involves a multitude of actors, including field offices of international and local NGOs, UN agencies, governmental officials, private companies, mosques and churches, civic organisations, representatives from associations of aid recipients residing in nearby protection of civilians' sites, and security forces. Studying humanitarian negotiations at these different levels is essential to understanding the complexities of humanitarian crises and developing effective negotiation strategies in authoritarian context (Barnett and Weiss, 2008; Jaspars, 2018; Magone, et al., 2012).

While each of these three levels of decision-making and negotiations have their own unique characteristics, they do not imply that there are clear borders between these levels of action, something that other authors have also noticed (see, for example, Grace, 2016; Hilhorst and Mena, 2021; Pottier, 2006). In reality, these levels overlap, interact, and often intermingle, adding further complexity to the reality of humanitarian negotiations. Effective humanitarian aid programmes require decisions at all three levels, and actors negotiate based on the specific context of each level (Aparicio, 2015; Mena and Hilhorst, 2022). It is important to highlight that decisions made and negotiated at one level can have an impact on decisions made at other levels, and effective coordination and communication between levels is critical for successful aid programming (Boersma, et al., 2016; Pottier, 2006).

Moreover, and across the different levels, humanitarian negotiations need to consider the intersectionality of the negotiation, particularly dimensions such as religion, ethnicity, power imbalances, or culture (De Cordier, 2009; Hilhorst, 2013; Wood, et al., 2001). Religion and ethnicity, for example, can play a significant role in shaping the perspectives and priorities of the parties involved in a crisis, as well as shaping the perspectives and priorities of some particular groups. Power imbalances can also have a significant impact on the negotiation process. In an authoritarian context, the party in power commonly has significantly more power than the other actors, including humanitarian ones, which can make it challenging to develop negotiation strategies that are equitable and effective (Barnett and Weiss, 2008; Magone, et al., 2012).

The case of Afghanistan: socio-political profile and humanitarian landscape

Afghanistan is a landlocked country located in South Asia and Central Asia. It is bordered by Pakistan to the east and south, Iran to the west, Turkmenistan, Uzbekistan, and Tajikistan to the north, and China to the northeast. Afghanistan's location has been highly strategic and fought over throughout history due to its position as a land bridge between Central Asia, South Asia, and the Middle East. Afghanistan is situated at the crossroads of several ancient trade routes, including the famous Silk Road, which connected China to the Mediterranean. Control of these trade routes and the valuable resources that flowed along them, including spices, silk, and precious metals, made Afghanistan a coveted prize and reason for conflicts involving numerous empires and kingdoms throughout history.

However, the country has also faced numerous internal conflicts over the last centuries on top of a long history of foreign intervention. The Soviet Union occupied Afghanistan in 1979, and the subsequent war lasted for a decade, ending with the Soviet Union's withdrawal in 1989. Civil war followed, with different factions vying for power. The Taliban won in 1996 and ruled the country until the US-led invasion in 2001. Since then, the country has been under the control of the Afghan government, with the support of the US and its allies, until the Taliban regained power in August 2021.

To understand the humanitarian negotiations unfolding currently, it is important to understand the social, political, and economic characteristics of the country and how they are entangled with its religion, culture, and the Taliban's doctrine. Briefly, as it is not the main goal of the chapter, the following paragraphs will present some of these main characteristics and describe the current humanitarian scenario in the country, the needs of the people, and the aid sector architecture.

Providing a good social profile of a country as diverse as Afghanistan is a complex task, so we have focused on three characteristics that are essential to know in order to understand humanitarian action in the country. First, its ethnic composition and how it is embedded in the country's culture and politics. In relation to this, the linguistic diversity of the country is also important to consider. Second, the political role of the Taliban and the main characteristics of this group. Third, the country's economic dependence on external funds and internal condition that has led to economic collapse, high levels of poverty, and humanitarian needs.

To start with, Afghanistan has a relatively young population, with around 46% of the population under the age of 15 (UNICEF, 2022). The country has experienced significant population growth in recent decades, and its population is estimated to be over 42.2 million people, but getting feasible demographic statistics is difficult. There are also many different languages spoken in Afghanistan, with Dari and Pashto being the official languages and most widely spoken in the country.

Afghanistan is a diverse country with many different ethnic and linguistic groups. Pashtuns, followed by Tajiks, then Hazaras, Uzbeks, and others, including Aimaks, Baloch, and Turkmen (Sawe, 2019). Pashtuns are the largest ethnic group in Afghanistan and have a significant presence in Pakistan. They historically are identified as 'Afghan' and 'Pashtun', with the former taking on a more national connotation (Barfield, 2010, 27). *Pashtunwali*, a code of conduct, is a significant source of social solidarity within Pashtun tribes. The Taliban, which emerged in 1993 and regained power in August 2021, is closely associated with Pashtunwali and conservative tribal Pashtun customs (Thomas, 2021). They governed Afghanistan from 1996 to 2001 and have been accused of using a mix of Pashtun nationalism and radical Islamism in their policies. In terms of other groups, Tajiks are Persian-speaking Sunni Muslims engaged in farming and urban professions. Hazaras are Shia Muslims in Hazarajat, farming and breeding livestock, speak Persian. Uzbeks and Turkmen are Turkish-speaking Sunni groups from Central Asia, settled as farmers or remained nomadic. Afghan constitution also recognises tribes like Turkmen, Baluch, Pachaie, Nuristani, Aymaq, Arab, Qirghiz, Qizilbash, Gujur, Brahwui, and others.

Afghanistan's ethnic groups have been deeply affected by the struggles of having an enormous division of power, civil war, and lack of trust among each other, which affects every social sphere, including humanitarian action. These tensions remained unresolved despite establishing a republican government from 2001 to 2021, and humanitarian actors had to negotiate and navigate cultural, political divisions already in the past to be able to get access and work in different territories (Donini, 2012a; Jackson, 2018). These challenges have made it difficult for the previous government and current group to function effectively, provide essential services, and maintain law and order (Kugelman, 2019).

Moreover, these ethical differences have also, over time, mingled with regional and cross-country conflicts. During the Afghan civil war, ethnic tensions escalated into violent conflict and tension, with regional powers such as Pakistan, Iran, and Russia supporting different ethnic factions for their strategic interests. This made it difficult for Afghanistan to achieve stability and peace.

Afghanistan moreover is an Islamic country, with most of the population being Muslim. The societal pressure to adhere to Sunni Islamic traditions is intense (Barfield, 2022, 40), particularly today with the Taliban in power, being a Sunni group which was formed in the early 1990s. As such, its policies and practices are based on a strict interpretation of Sunni Islam and Pashtunwali, a traditional code of conduct followed by the Pashtun people. Highlight among these codes is to be oriented and settled by elders mainly through the Jirgas (gatherings). They have a strong sense of honour that places great emphasis on personal autonomy and resistance to state power. They famously proclaimed that they fought for Zar (gold), Zan (women), and Zamin (land), as it was considered a part of their honour to protect and dominate these resources at all costs. Additionally, they practised the obligation of hospitality (*melmastia*), which required a host to protect their guest even at the risk of their own life (Barfield, 2022, 185, 138).

The political structure of the Taliban after August 2021 is shaped by various factors rooted in their insurgency, and formal government positions alone do not determine who holds power. The Taliban is formed by different tribes, and we may assess the strength and various perceptions of its groups, but it prioritises maintaining balance and harmony among their factions since taking control. The Taliban leadership relies on the previous traditional structure and elders to exert control over territories, as the Taliban prioritise internal unity and outward image (Thomas, 2021). In the 'Taliban 1.0' regime in the 1990s, using TV and other media was banned. However, with the rise of the importance of media in power, the Taliban 2.0 has increasingly used these platforms to communicate with the local and international community and disseminate their messages. This shift in communication has allowed the Taliban to reach a broader audience and bypass traditional gatekeepers in the media. It has also provided them with a more direct line of communication with potential negotiating partners, facilitating their re-entry into Afghanistan's political mainstream (Mehran, 2022).

Regarding Afghanistan's economy, it is primarily based on subsistence farming and livestock keeping, although natural resources are becoming increasingly important. According to the United Nations Development Programme (UNDP), as of 2021, 97% of Afghanistan's population is at risk of poverty, with over half of Afghans relying on humanitarian aid. Nowadays the poverty level is deepening in Afghanistan, 'with the average income per person per day totalling less than half the poverty line' (OCHA, 2023, 18).

Before August 2021, Afghanistan's GDP depended heavily on foreign aid and public spending. According to the World Bank, grants accounted for approximately 40% of Afghanistan's GDP, and public spending comprised around 75% of the country's total economic activity (World Bank, 2021). In 2020, Afghanistan's annual budget was estimated to be $5.5 billion, according to the Republic Government. However, following the Taliban's takeover in August 2021, the Taliban announced that the country's annual budget would be significantly lower, at around $2.6 billion. Additionally, the Taliban reported that their revenue was only $2.1 billion, leaving shortfall of approximately $500 million (Zakariya, 2022). Afghanistan's current economic and humanitarian situation underscores the importance of engaging in humanitarian negotiations with the Taliban.

The other economic challenge for the country and the Taliban is the fact that the USA has frozen $7 billion of Afghanistan's assets, with half of the amount transferred to the 'Fund for the Afghan People' in Switzerland. In contrast, the other half is subject to civil proceedings related to law suits by 9/11 victims' families and others. The frozen funds are intended to support economic stabilisation in Afghanistan without providing direct funds to the Taliban administration (Byrd, 2022). However, this has caused disruptions to the flow of money between Afghanistan and other countries, and private sector funds have also been frozen in banks, preventing people from withdrawing their money. Due to disruptions in international banking transfers and liquidity issues since August 2021, the UN has transferred cash directly into Afghanistan to provide necessary financial support (UNAMA, 2023). The challenge of the banking system has reduced the private sector from investing their money, affecting the Afghan economy. The difficult economic situation in Afghanistan and the Taliban's policy banning girls' education and work have created a dilemma for aid organisations. International aid organisations and governments are grappling with how to deliver assistance.

Bringing all the above together, Barfield's (2022) perspective on the country gains importance, arguing that ethnicity in Afghanistan is nationalist, with ethnic groups having similar economic and political interests but no common ideology or separatist aspirations. While Afghanistan's neighbours may have an affinity to their ethnic groups and would like to interfere, there is currently no desire for separation among Afghanistan's ethnic groups. Instead, they seek to establish a federal political system to gain greater political autonomy. Furthermore, with the rise of the Taliban, a radical Sunni perception of Islam and Pashtunwali has again become a significant factor in the country's political landscape. These factors will continue to shape Afghanistan's political, social, and cultural landscape in the coming year.

In terms of Afghanistan's humanitarian landscape, in 2023, two-thirds of Afghanistan's population is in need of urgent humanitarian assistance due to drought, climate change, protection threats, and economic crisis (OCHA, 2023). Among them, 17 million people might face acute hunger in 2023, including 6 million at emergency levels of food insecurity. In winter and the lean season, sustained high food prices, reduced income and unemployment, and continued economic decline provide a looming forecast of people's needs in the country (OCHA, 2023). The level and multidimensional aspect of the crisis in the country is further exacerbated in consideration of the traditional gender norms and patriarchal culture imposed by the Taliban that has led to discrimination against women and girls (OHCHR, 2023). Moreover, the recent directive that prohibits women from working for NGOs has had a significant humanitarian impact on millions of people in the country, mostly by limiting their ability to travel and provide assistance to those in need (OCHA, 2023).

Under this scenario, the humanitarian situation in the country has become increasingly complex and challenging. To address this, Afghanistan has a strong humanitarian architecture, with UN agencies, coordinating bodies, and several national and international NGOs working in the country. For instance, the Cluster Approach is in Afghanistan since 2008, with the Humanitarian Country Team coordinating the six clusters.[1] Moreover, Afghanistan has the Agency Coordinating Body for Afghan Relief and Development (ACBAR) and the United Nations Office for the Coordination of Humanitarian Affairs (UNOCHA) to provide overall coordination and dialogue platforms. Other actors in the country are the International Committee of the Red Cross (ICRC), MSF, and some development agencies such as the World Bank.

Due to the fall of the Afghan Republic government in 2021, the UN launched the One-UN Transitional Engagement Framework (TEF) in 2022 (UN, 2022). TEF aims to save lives, sustain essential services, and preserve community systems and requires $8 billion for full implementation. The Humanitarian Response Plan includes a request for $4.44 billion. An additional $3.6 billion is needed for social services, community systems, and livelihood promotion, focusing on improving conditions for women and girls.

Understanding humanitarian negotiation challenges at the different levels in Afghanistan

In this section, we analyse the dilemma of humanitarian negotiations with the Taliban considering three levels: macro, meso, and micro (Mena and Hilhorst, 2022, 9). The macro-level negotiations with the Taliban involve discussions between various regional and international actors to address different issues that they prioritise. In the international context, the primary goal of negotiations is to address critical humanitarian concerns like access to food, water, and healthcare, as well as human rights, particularly women's rights, which are often violated by the Taliban. In contrast, neighbouring countries like Pakistan, China, Uzbekistan, and Iran are more concerned about addressing security issues, particularly with terrorist groups that operate in Afghanistan. This was expressed by their foreign ministers in a Joint Statement of the Second Informal Meeting on Afghanistan between Foreign Ministers of China, Russia, Pakistan, and Iran.

> The Ministers emphasized their deep concerns regarding the terrorism-related security situation in Afghanistan, pointed out that all terrorist groups, namely the Islamic State Khorasan Province (ISIS-KP), Al-Qaeda, the Eastern Turkistan Islamic.
>
> *(Chinese Ministry or Foreign Affairs, 2023-04-14)*

Tajikistan's President Emomali Rahmon has again expressed concern over security threats posed by Afghanistan to the region and has called for a "security belt" to be built around the country.

(Ariananews, October 19, 2022)

Meso-level negotiations in Afghanistan could include internal discussions within aid agencies or government ministries and negotiations between organisations and their implementing partners. These negotiations may focus on resource allocation, programme design and implementation, and coordination with other organisations. With the Taliban in control of most parts of the country, it will be necessary for meso-level negotiations to ensure that local communities can access the resources they need.

Micro-level negotiations in Afghanistan will be critical for addressing immediate humanitarian needs or conflicts. This could include discussions between aid workers and local communities to provide emergency relief, or negotiations between families or tribes to resolve disputes or prevent violence. With the situation in Afghanistan still uncertain and many people in need of assistance, micro-level negotiations will be necessary to provide support at the local level.

It's important to note that the situation in Afghanistan is complex and evolving, and negotiations at all levels will be necessary to address the country's full range of humanitarian needs. The international community will closely watch the Taliban's approach to negotiations and governance, and there will likely be ongoing discussions at all three levels as the situation continues to develop.

The macro level of humanitarian negotiations in Afghanistan: balancing humanitarian principles and political realities

Negotiations between regional states and the Taliban have predominantly focused on security and political aspects, while the humanitarian aspect has not been at the core of these discussions. However, the approach has been different for international humanitarian organisations.

According to an aid coordinator interviewed in Afghanistan in March 2023, aid organisations usually coordinate through ACBAR and OCHA, and some others, such as the ICRC and MSF, communicate directly. They have varying levels of communication with the Taliban. At the higher level, humanitarian organisations communicate with the Ministry of Economy if this is with whom they are registered and with the Ministry of Foreign Affairs, and for specific types of assistance such as health, education, and immigration, they communicate directly with the related line ministry. The Taliban's appointed ministers are considered to be macro-level decision-makers, but their actions are often influenced by the vague decrees of the Taliban leader, who emphasises religious and traditional values to control women in Afghanistan. Furthermore, the absence of a unified structure for providing humanitarian assistance in Afghanistan means that ministers negotiate everything in their own way. As a result, decisions are often renegotiated at the meso and micro levels.

While many assert that humanitarian negotiations should consider principles such as humanity, impartiality, neutrality, and independence, or even the framework of human rights approaches (Magone, et al., 2012; Mancini-Griffoli and Picot, 2004), the political situation in Afghanistan makes it difficult to fully adhere to these principles. Like in many countries, aid is often instrumentalised and used for political or security reasons (Dijkzeul and Hilhorst, 2016; Donini, 2012b; Hilhorst and Mena, 2021), which is also the case in Afghanistan. Therefore, at the macro level, there doesn't appear to be a clear and standardised principle for negotiating humanitarian assistance for Afghanistan, apart from countries' national interests that often take precedence. While public statements do mention finding ways to provide humanitarian aid, they are typically accompanied by concerns about security challenges.

Even though the UN organisations do not have direct access to countries' intentions towards Afghanistan, their dependence on donations from these countries makes them susceptible to their influence. Additionally, their operations face the dilemma of how to manage aid to avoid being seen as legitimising authoritarian practices or human right violation carried by the Taliban such as the ban of women from education.

Kelly's (2021) review on 'Lessons learnt from humanitarian negotiations with the Taliban, 1996–2001' identifies several lessons on negotiating with the Taliban, including the importance of clarifying ultimate objectives, measurable principled actions, understanding local culture, politics, and economics, and the difficulty of arranging joint action among humanitarian actors. Additionally, the review emphasises the importance of dialogue, 'quiet diplomacy', and negotiating skills training to ensure a good working relationship with counterparts. This approach changed in Taliban 2.0, as it uses the media as an essential approach to diplomacy and communication. In the past, the Taliban relied on traditional methods of communication, such as face-to-face meetings and negotiations through intermediaries. The Taliban took apart government-controlled TV stations, made it illegal to watch television completely, prohibited music, and punished individuals who broke these regulations. The movement expanded its traditional approach and now uses the media to project its power and control information (Mehran, 2022). Despite this fact that the Taliban oriented towards 'open diplomacy', the practitioners indicated that 'quiet diplomacy' is still effective. Through quiet communication, it's possible to see some of the

Taliban officials violate their Amir's order when everything is secret and not publicised.

Humanitarian aid to Afghanistan and its interconnection with politics

Despite Afghanistan remaining the world's largest humanitarian crisis in 2023 (UN News, 2023), providing humanitarian aid under the Taliban regime poses significant challenges within the context of economic sanctions, a lack of political recognition, a volatile banking system, tensions around Taliban policies, and political differences within the region and beyond, all affecting the delivery of aid and humanitarian negotiations.

Aid of all types has played a critical role in Afghanistan's affairs; it is often subject to political influence from other countries or is used to legitimise a region's authority. In Afghanistan and the surrounding region, humanitarian aid is frequently politicised due to political and geopolitical factors. The history of Afghanistan illustrates how foreign aid has shaped the country's political system and government, and NGOs have also played a role in politics through their humanitarian aid efforts (Baitenmann, 1990). Therefore, humanitarian negotiation for humanitarian assistance is connected with the country's policies.

Bizhan (2018) also argues in 'Aid Paradoxes in Afghanistan: Building and Undermining the State' that the relationship between aid and state-building is complex, with the effects of aid on weak states being influenced by various factors such as the interests of donors, aid delivery methods, and the pre-existing institutional and socio-political conditions of the recipient. Providing aid for humanitarian and developmental purposes has impacted regimes' politics by consolidating power and causing their downfall. As indicated by Bizhan (2018, 39), in 'Afghanistan, external revenue has been made available under geostrategic considerations. Sources of state revenue have thus profoundly impacted state building'.

After the USA and NATO withdrew from Afghanistan, neighbouring countries felt initial relief from the conflict. However, concerns about security challenges posed by terrorist groups that have found refuge under the Taliban persist (Shah, 2021). Countries in the Samarkand Declaration of the Fourth Meeting of Foreign Ministers of Afghanistan's Neighbouring States in 2023/04/14 pointed out that all terrorist groups, namely the Islamic State of Iraq and the Levant (ISIL), Al-Qaeda, the Eastern Turkistan Islamic Movement (ETIM), the Tehreek-e-Taliban Pakistan (TTP), the Balochistan Liberation Army (BLA), Jundallah, Jaish al-Adl, Jamaat Ansarullah, the Islamic Movement of Uzbekistan (IMU), and other terrorist organisations based in Afghanistan continue to pose a serious threat to regional and global security. The international community has urged the Taliban to address their concerns and establish an inclusive government, and protect human rights, particularly those of women and minorities. No country has officially recognised them as the legitimate government of Afghanistan. Some regional countries like China and Uzbekistan have signed long-term contracts with the Taliban, suggesting closer ties and cooperation on economic projects and resource extraction (Panda, 2021). While most neighbouring countries have reopened their embassies in Kabul and are in dialogue with the Taliban, Tajikistan has been more cautious, increasing its military presence along the border due to concerns about the Taliban's policies towards Tajik ethnic groups (Panda, 2021).

Regional countries have assisted in Afghanistan, but the aid has predominantly been given to the Taliban. For example, China provided 7.5 million in humanitarian assistance to Afghanistan after an earthquake in June 2022 and delivered a dozen batches of aid (Zhang, 2022). Uzbekistan provided 3,700 tons of humanitarian aid to Afghanistan to help people in the chilly winter (Xinhua, 2021). In contrast, the USA and the EU have provided aid through international humanitarian organisations. The USA provided $1.1 billion in humanitarian assistance (Blinken, 2022; USAID, 2022), while the EU announced an aid package worth €1 billion to deal with the aftermath of the Taliban takeover of Afghanistan (*Euronews*, 2021).

Some regional countries, like China, have chosen to hand over cash and goods as humanitarian assistance directly to the Taliban for distribution, which raises concerns about how the aid is being spent. In October 2022, the Taliban implemented a 'food for work' scheme that requires recipients of humanitarian aid to engage in manual labour on public works projects. The Taliban claims that this programme is an extension of its pre-existing 'food for work' initiative. In addition, due to economic constraints, the Taliban has resorted to utilising foreign wheat aid to pay the wages of public sector workers (Azadi, 2022). This is one way that the Taliban is using humanitarian aid to justify their rule in Afghanistan.

In summary, providing humanitarian aid to Afghanistan is crucial for people in need; however, it often becomes politicised due to political and geopolitical factors, or the regime uses it to legitimise its authority. Afghanistan's history shows that foreign aid has significantly impacted its political system and government, and the relationship between aid and state-building is intricate. The recent political turmoil in Afghanistan highlights the complex connection between aid and politics, with neighbouring countries and international organisations engaging with the Taliban for stability and human rights protection. Spending more assistance through organisations reduces the potential for politicisation, but corruption and waste can still occur. When aid is provided directly to the Taliban, it can become politicised and strengthen their power. However, the complexity of politics and security in Afghanistan suggests that the connection between humanitarian assistance and political and security ambitions may only sometimes be straightforward or transparent.

Dilemmas in humanitarian negotiations with the Taliban in Afghanistan

The rise of the Taliban in Afghanistan has led to an increase in challenges and difficulties for multiple aid actors and humanitarian negotiations. The issues with regards to human rights violations with the Taliban (see OHCHR, 2023) put many actors in the dilemma that negotiating with them means to recognise their authority and way of acting. On the other hand, failing to negotiate could result in an exacerbation of the humanitarian crisis in the country. This dilemma raises ethical and practical questions for the UN and other aid actors, and their approach to these negotiations will have significant consequences for the people of Afghanistan.

However, this issue is not unique to the UN or any other organisation operating in Afghanistan. As early as 1999, the UN developed a Strategic Framework for Afghanistan to improve international assistance and human rights policies. The primary goal of the framework was to enhance cooperation between the political strategy of the UN in Afghanistan and international aid activities to increase the effectiveness and consistency of the international assistance programme. The framework also stressed the importance of eliminating discrimination based on gender, tribe, ethnicity, language, religion, or political affiliation among international aid organisations operating in Afghanistan. The framework's objective was to cease hostilities, seek a regional political consensus supporting the peace process, and facilitate direct negotiations between all parties to reach a political settlement (OCHA, 1999).

The Taliban's December 2022 decree, which banned Afghan women from working for certain types of aid agencies, has presented a significant challenge for approximately 400 female employees of the UN and many others from different organisations (AFP and *Le Monde*, 2023). This restrictive measure not only infringes upon fundamental human rights principles but also hampers the progress and development of Afghan society (UN, March 2023). Despite extensive negotiations and pressure from regional and international actors, including the UN Secretary-General's warning regarding the severe impact of the Taliban's decision on millions of people in Afghanistan, the Taliban has remained firm in its stance. Consequently, the UN has decided to permit its female employees to work remotely from home while maintaining its operations in Afghanistan (Jawad, 2023).

Providing humanitarian aid in a country where the Taliban's influence is increasing has raised concerns among women whose rights have been diminished (OHCHR, 2023). To address this situation, Afghan women activists have demanded that broader political dialogue with the Taliban and advocating for inclusive governance and protecting human rights (especially for women and girls) be a condition for aid to improve rights protections and governance in the long term. Viken and Kaplan (2021) reflected the strong voice of Afghans inside and outside of Afghanistan in their report, supporting conditionality of aid as leverage to push Taliban while they concern that it would aggravate the poverty situation in Afghanistan.

Humanitarian action in Afghanistan is also risky and complex. The humanitarian, economic, and security consequences of the situation, particularly the ban on women from working in the aid sector (with exception of medical workers), have created the dilemma between aid actors of how to act under this scenario (Suhrke, 2021). Five top NGOs have halted their work in Afghanistan after the Taliban government banned women from working for them, further exacerbating the situation (BBC News, 2022). UN Secretary-General António Guterres, in his statement at the end of a two-day meeting about Afghanistan in Doha, called the current ban on Afghan women working for the UN and national and international NGOs unacceptable and stated that it puts lives in jeopardy (UNAMA, May 3). This was an important factor in the decision to not invite the Taliban to the Doha meeting in May 2023, and countries seem to be more unified against Taliban policies on women following UN Security Council Resolution 2681 (2023) condemning the ban on women working.

The international community's inability to pursue or pressure the Taliban and the lack of alternatives in Afghanistan would exacerbate the humanitarian crisis in Afghanistan. Failing to address the humanitarian and economic crisis could lead to mass migration and significant economic and security repercussions for the region (OCHA, 2023). To address this situation, conversations with multiple actors pointed to the need to engage in a broader political dialogue with the Taliban, promote inclusive governance, and strategically protect human rights while establishing effective mechanisms for long-term improvement of rights protection and governance (Suhrke, 2021).

While the UN representatives' negotiations with Taliban officials may be practical in conveying aid, they have yet to be able to have an influential role in changing Taliban policy on human rights, which them has led the question of the role of humanitarian action to steer these processes. Although the Taliban has been present in diplomatic efforts and dialogues with multiple parties, in practice there is a reluctance to make significant concessions on human rights, especially women's rights, and therefore humanitarian action has been affected and needs to grow.

The meso level of negotiations in Afghanistan: navigating humanitarian principles and political realities

Identifying the real meso-level actors within the Taliban structure is challenging. Taliban has substituted the head of these institutions and most of lower ranking employees are working in the former republic institutions. Therefore, the former institutions of the republic, including ministries and their representatives, are crucial in negotiating the facilitation of humanitarian assistance. General directors and provincial representatives of the ministries play a key role in facilitating aid delivery. In conversations with practitioners on the ground, it became evident that negotiations conducted at the macro level are frequently renegotiated at the meso level – except for sensitive orders. With the Taliban controlling most parts of the country, aid organisations face significant obstacles in assisting those in need. Meso-level negotiations are an essential aspect of humanitarian work in Afghanistan, as they involve discussions between aid agencies and their implementing partners and internal discussions within government ministries, regional authorities, and key stakeholders. This section examines the meso-level negotiations taking place in Afghanistan and explores how aid agencies can navigate humanitarian principles and political realities to deliver assistance to those in need.

According to Donini (2007), humanitarian organisations working in Afghanistan have taken varied approaches to engage with the Taliban 1.0 in the 1990s. These approaches can be classified into three categories. The first category was the principled approach, which involved insisting on changes in Taliban policies and threatening to withdraw aid. The second category was the accommodationist approach, which involved making pragmatic arrangements with the authorities to deliver aid. The third category was the 'duck-and-weave' approach, which involved avoiding Taliban authorities and working directly with communities. In the case of Afghanistan at present, all these strategies can still be found.

A complicated process that reinforces the dilemma of aid instrumentalisation described at the macro level is when aid organisations have to negotiate and accept the management of a certain amount of assistance by the Taliban to deliver the remaining aid. In some provinces of Afghanistan, this has resulted in either halting the entire distribution process or accepting assistance from the Taliban. This is due to the presence of Taliban fighters on the ground who are not in direct contact with their leaders. The Taliban are attempting to transition their fighters into formal state security forces, but this process is slow and challenging, particularly in remote areas where many need more formal training. In cities and larger towns, some Taliban fighters have taken on roles in police and civil service offices. However, the Taliban face difficulties in managing challenges in urban areas and regions with non-Pashtun ethnic communities, where they struggle to exert influence with their fighters (Watkins, 2022).

Another challenge shows that the renegotiations necessary for humanitarian action not only mean translating and operationalising decisions taken at the macro level but also between actors and processes at the meso level. For instance, Taliban officials often contradict each other, making it difficult to establish a consensus, in part because seniority does not necessarily equate to influence and decision-making processes are based ongoing discussions with actors that change their positions and roles. To address this, some aid actors have attempted to secure written agreements with the Taliban, but the results have been inconsistent, and the agreements have frequently been disregarded (Kelly, 2021, 11). For example, female employees in public health NGOs continue to work and educate despite uncertainty surrounding whether the Taliban will enforce a ban on their employment.

Nowadays, in March 2023, multiple humanitarian actors in the country shared with us that negotiations for providing services, especially health services, have been relatively more accessible, and the Taliban's health acting minister have been seen as helpful. While this is seen as the results of negotiation at the macro level, these decisions and processes have had to be reaffirmed and corroborated at the regional level. Often, these negotiations are not associated with the larger decision of what aid to give but rather with the specifics of where and how to give it, which again opens the door to the instrumentalisation of humanitarian action. In fact, a report indicates that in some instances, the Taliban has diverted humanitarian assistance to specific groups, resulting in aid activities being halted in two provinces (UN News, 2023). Moreover, these negotiations show that the Taliban agencies and people do not have a unified and consistent approach in all parts of Afghanistan, making it more difficult for aid actors to prepare for the negotiations and discussions.

Negotiating humanitarian principles and political realities at the micro level in aid delivery in Afghanistan

Local actors in villages, representing diverse ethnic groups and operating under different provincial governors, have the potential to influence the negotiations for aid distribution. At a micro or practical level, provincial representatives and councils bear the primary responsibility for implementing and delivering humanitarian assistance. According to a humanitarian coordinator with whom we talked in March 2023, effective communication with local communities is crucial for successful aid delivery, especially to agree on how decisions made at higher levels can be better implemented in their particular contexts.

Important has been for us to understand that humanitarian actors in the country acknowledge that at the micro level many decisions taken at higher levels can be disregarded or completely reinterpreted, which reinforces the notion that authoritarianism is not only at the level of regimes – such as the Taliban – but is manifest in practices that are constantly being (re)negotiated at the local level. The lack of governance of the territories also means a lack of accountability for actions. Moreover, given the level of conflict and differences between ethnic or different groups within the Taliban itself, many prefer not to follow through on decisions taken as a way to avoid exacerbating the conflict.

Authorities and actors at the micro level are also in closer contact with affected people and recognise not only the importance but also the necessity of humanitarian action for the survival of those affected and to sustain people's livelihoods. Without it, a large part of the population could suffer long-term negative effects, illness, or even death. Therefore, while some individuals in different levels may be willing to help, they may be hesitant to do so officially due to potential consequences or an informal accountability mechanism. As indicated above, writing and record keeping are highly avoided practices, which hinders the process not only of accountability but also of learning about the humanitarian business, actions taken, and what is happening in the territories.

Another difficulty that constantly needs to be negotiated at this level is that of the biased distribution of aid in Afghanistan due to competition between ethnic groups, tribes, religions, and social classes. Cases of favouritism and external influence, such as the Taliban, can undermine the effectiveness of aid distribution. During informal talks with local humanitarian actors in the north of Afghanistan, it was indicated that some people (including Taliban relatives) are receiving more aid than others, while others are receiving only the aid that is left. This is seen as a compromise to be able to reach some communities, but at the same time, it shows that authoritarianism also unfolds at the micro level. And if considered that the vast majority of NGO employees in Afghanistan are from the country, differences in language, ethnicity, or political views have a major influence not only on their actions but also on the impact and range of action of their humanitarian practices.

In the same vein, negotiating aid delivery in Afghanistan at this level is also complex due to political and cultural realities. Aid organisations must engage with local communities while trying to adhere to humanitarian principles. A way of addressing these challenges is to communicate and negotiate with institutions like the council of elders and the mosque, which provide legitimacy and access to the territories affected.

What this case shows at this level is how much humanitarian action in Afghanistan can be impacted by social and cultural dimensions, affecting strongly at the moment of negotiating humanitarian outcomes and means. Successful aid distribution requires coordination and effort from all stakeholders; however, the discriminatory policies of the Taliban towards women, ethnic and religious minorities have further complicated the process. This, combined with the lack of recognition by Afghan minorities and the international community, presents an additional challenge.

Reflections and conclusions

The case of Afghanistan as we have seen shows well how humanitarian action is based on negotiations that occur at multiple levels and moments; how decisions at the macro and national levels are renegotiated down to meso moments of decision-making, whether at the regional level in terms of locations or at the institutional level in terms of actors. Moreover, at the micro level, at the level of the affected communities or locations, these decisions are renegotiated in shaping the humanitarian assistance that is ultimately provided. Along with reinforcing this knowledge already presented in the literature, the Afghanistan case contributes two important extra elements to consider: The importance of a multidimensional analysis, especially the role of ethnicity, and the importance of bringing to the analysis of negotiations that authoritarian theocratic states are different from authoritarian states based on political ideologies.

The case of humanitarian negotiations and renegotiations in Afghanistan provides us with other interesting insights into humanitarian governance and how authoritarian states and authoritarian practices are perceived. In the literature and those with whom we spoke it is thought that authoritarian states have a high capacity to impose and implement ideas decided at the macro level in any place of the territory. However, the fragility of governance, of clear structures of government and governance, of processes and policies, results in a lack of mechanisms to effectively translate macro decisions (e.g., at the ministerial level as we have seen here) to meso and micro levels by the authorities in place. In other words, authoritarian decisions cannot always effectively be translated into humanitarian practices, and not at all levels, creating extra room for manoeuvring and challenges for humanitarian actors. This invites humanitarian actors to focus more on humanitarian practices at different levels and by different actors rather than humanitarian regimes, an exercise that will provide the nuances and granularity that seem to be needed to (re)negotiate humanitarian practices.

Moreover, and reinforcing the previous, authoritarian states such as Afghanistan present highly diverse contexts with diverse and distributed authorities, authoritarianisms, and authoritarian practices, which oblige humanitarian actors to reflect and adapt their practices to each particular context. They must negotiate and renegotiate with authorities and authoritarianisms at the macro, meso, and micro levels and navigate conflicts in the power differences and power struggles that exist in each of these settings. Conversely, countries with more functional and effective democracies and governance systems might have more mechanisms so that what is decided at the ministerial level, for example, is translated into public policies that allow for a more controlled translation of those decisions into implementation. This is not to deny the possible presence of corruption, (re)negotiation, or a humanitarian arena of interest and struggles in non-authoritarian settings, but the case of Afghanistan shows that this scenario is the norm for action.

The case also shows that the combination of the rise of the Taliban and ongoing ethnic conflict in Afghanistan has created significant challenges for humanitarian negotiations in the country. Providing aid and support to vulnerable populations is complicated by the uncertainty and new challenges posed by the Taliban's return to power and the difficulty in building trust and cooperation between different ethnic groups. The rise of the Taliban, moreover, has generated a highly impoverished scenario, where geopolitical issues are involved which have had a major impact on the country, such as the freezing of funds or the disruption of economic trade routes, worsening the humanitarian crises, both in terms of people in need and the acuteness of the needs. In other words, as we have seen above, the social and political context, particularly the social conflicts in the country and their international dimensions, permeate, affect, and shape the humanitarian access and its negotiations. All in all, the case of Afghanistan shows that failure to understand the multifaceted and multilevel nature of humanitarian negotiations makes humanitarian action in the country more difficult and, at times, even impossible. This understanding therefore invites further research to consider the multi-level and multi-dimensional nature of humanitarian negotiations and to consider how what is negotiated and decided is renegotiated and interpreted various times before it sees the light of day.

Note

1 Humanitarian clusters are groups of organisations that coordinate and collaborate to address specific needs in humanitarian emergencies across various sectors. The main clusters are: Camp Coordination/Management; Early Recovery; Education; Emergency Shelter and Non-Food-Items (NFI); Emergency Telecommunications; Food Security; Health; Logistics; Nutrition; Protection; Water Sanitation Hygiene (OCHA, 2019).

References

AFP and *Le Monde*. (2023). Taliban Prohibit Afghan Women from Working with United Nations. April 5. https://www.lemonde.fr/en/afghanistan/article/2023/04/05/taliban-bans-afghan-women-from-working-with-united-nations_6021768_218.html

Aparicio, J. R. (2015). *Rumores, residuos y estado en "la mejor esquina de sudamérica". Una cartografía de lo "humanitario" en Colombia*. Ediciones Uniandes-Universidad de los Andes.

Azadi, R. (2022). *Cash-strapped Taliban Uses Foreign Aid Intended for Starving Afghans to Pay State Employees*. RadioFreeEurope/RadioLiberty. January 25. https://www.rferl.org/a/taliban-foreign-aid-starving-afghans/31670691.html

Barfield, T. J. (2010). *Afghanistan: A Cultural and Political History*, 27–28. Princeton, NJ: Princeton University Press.

Barfield, T. (2022). *Afghanistan: A Cultural and Political History* (2nd ed.). Princeton, NJ: Princeton University Press.

Barnett, M. N. and Weiss, T. G. (eds.) (2008). *Humanitarianism in Question: Politics, Power, Ethics*. Ithaca, NY: Cornell University Press.

BBC News. (2022, January 19). Afghanistan Conflict: Taliban vow to End Fighting and Respect Women's Rights. https://www.bbc.com/news/world-asia-64090549

Bizhan, N. (2018). *Aid Paradoxes in Afghanistan: Building and Undermining the State*. London: Routledge.

Baitenmann, H. (1990). NGOs and the Afghan War: The Politicisation of Humanitarian Aid. *Third World Quarterly* 12(1), 62–85. https://doi.org/10.10 80/01436599008420215

Blinken, A. (2022). United States Announces Humanitarian Assistance for Afghanistan–United States Department of State. https://www.state.gov/united-states-announces-humanitarian-assistance-for-afghanistan/

Boersma, K., et al. (2016). *Humanitarian Response Coordination and Cooperation in Nepal*. http://keesboersma.com/wp-content/uploads/2014/09/White-Paper-Nepal-VU-Smart-Disaster-Governance.pdf

Byrd, W. (2022). U.S. to Move Afghanistan's Frozen Central Bank Reserves to New Swiss Fund. *United States Institute of Peace*. September 28. https://www.usip.org/publications/2022/09/us-move-afghanistans-frozen-central-bank-reserves-new-swiss-fund

De Cordier, B. (2009). The 'Humanitarian Frontline', Development and Relief, and Religion: What context, Which Threats and Which Opportunities? *Third World Quarterly* 30(4), 663–684.

Dijkzeul, D. and Hilhorst, D. (2016). Instrumentalisation of Aid in Humanitarian Crises, 54–71. In: Heins, V. M, Koddenbrock, K., and Unrau, C. (eds.). *Humanitarianism and Challenges of Cooperation*. London: Routledge.

Donini, A. (2007). The Taliban and Humanitarian Aid in Afghanistan: A Review of Issues. *Disasters* 31(1), S1–S23.

Donini, A. (2012a). Afghanistan. Back to the Future, 67–88. In: *The Golden Fleece: Manipulation and Independence in Humanitarian Action*. Boulder, CO: Kumarian Press.

Donini, A. (ed.). (2012b). *The Golden Fleece: Manipulation and Independence in Humanitarian Action*. Boulder, CO: Kumarian Press.

Euronews. (2021). *E.U. Announces €1 Billion in Humanitarian Aid for Afghanistan*. Euronews October 12. https://www.euronews.com/my-europe/2021/10/12/eu-announces-1-billion-in-humanitarian-aid-for-afghanistan

Glasius, M. (2018). What Authoritarianism Is … and Is Not: A Practice Perspective. *International Affairs* 94(3), 515–533.

Glasius, M. (2023). *Authoritarian Practices in a Global Age*. Oxford: Oxford University Press.

Gibbon, K. (2021). Understanding Pashtunwali: Implications for U.S. Strategic Communication. Defense Technical Information Center.

Grace, R. (2016). *Humanitarian Negotiation: Key Challenges and Lessons Learned in an Emerging Field* (White Paper Series). Cambridge, MA: Harvard Humanitarian Initiative. http://atha.se/presentations/negotiation/index.html

Hilhorst, D. (ed.). (2013). *Disaster, Conflict and Society in Crises: Everyday Politics of Crisis Response*. London: Routledge.

Hilhorst, D. and Mena, R. (2021). When Covid-19 Meets Conflict: Politics of the Pandemic Response in Fragile and Conflict-affected States. *Disasters* 45(S1), S174–S194.

Jackson, A. (2018). Life under the Taliban Shadow Government. Overseas Development Institute. https://www.odi.org/sites/odi.org.uk/files/resource-documents/12269.pdf

Jaspars, S. (2018). *Food Aid in Sudan: A History of Power, Politics and Profit*. London: Zed Books.

Jawad, M. (2023). UN Women Workers in Afghanistan will work from home. *BNN Breaking*. May 6. https://bnn.network/politics/un-women-workers-in-afghanistan-will-work-from-home/

Joint Statement of the Second Informal Meeting on Afghanistan between Foreign Ministers of China, Russia, Pakistan and Iran. Ministry of Foreign Affairs of China. (2023, April 14). https://www.fmprc.gov.cn/mfa_eng/wjdt_665385/2649_665393/202304/t20230414_11059063.html

Kelly, L. (2021). Lessons Learnt from Humanitarian Negotiations with the Taliban, 1996-2001. OpenDocs Home. September 17. https://opendocs.ids.ac.uk/opendocs/handle/20.500.12413/16858

Kugelman, M. (2019). Afghanistan's Ethnic Fault Lines: Understanding the Challenges to a Lasting Peace. Wilson Center. https://www.wilsoncenter.org/article/afghanistans-ethnic-fault-lines-understanding-challenges-lasting-peace

Magone, C., Neuman, M., and Weissman, F. (eds.) (2012). *Humanitarian Negotiations Revealed: The MSF Experience*. https://msf-crash.org/en/publications/humanitarian-negotiations-revealed-msf-experience

Mancini-Griffoli, D. and Picot, A. (2004). *Humanitarian Negotiation: A Handbook for Securing Access, Assistance and Protection for Civilians in Armed Conflict*. Centre for Humanitarian Dialogue. http://www.hdcentre.org/wp-content/uploads/2016/07/Humanitarian-Negotiationn-A-handbook-October-2004.pdf

Mehran, W. (2022). The Evolution in the Taliban's Media Strategy. Program on Extremism. August 18. https://extremism.gwu.edu/evolution-taliban-media-strategy#:~:text=1996%2D2001%3A%20Maximum%20Control,city%20fell%20to%20the%20Taliban.

Mena, R. and Hilhorst, D. (2022). Path Dependency When Prioritising Disaster and Humanitarian Response under High Levels of Conflict: A Qualitative Case Study in South Sudan. *Journal of International Humanitarian Action* 7(5).

News, A. (2022). President Ghani to Issue Legislative Decree on Recognising 'Sadat' as Ethnic Group. Ariana News. October 24. https://www.ariananews.af/president-ghani-to-issue-legislative-decree-on-recognizing-sadat-as-ethnic-group/

OCHA. (1999). Strategic Framework for Afghanistan Endorsed by UN Agencies. *ReliefWeb*. January 4. https://reliefweb.int/report/afghanistan/strategic-framework-afghanistan-endorsed-un-agencies

OCHA. (2019). What Is the Cluster Approach? *Humanitarian Response. Info*. https://www.humanitarianresponse.info/en/about-clusters/what-is-the-cluster-approach

OCHA. (2023). Afghanistan Humanitarian Needs Overview 2023. United Nations Office for the Coordination of Humanitarian Affairs (OCHA). https://www.unocha.org/afghanistan

OHCHR. (2023). Afghanistan: Systematic crackdown on Women's and Girls' Rights, UN Experts Say. Office of the United Nations High Commissioner for Human Rights (OHCHR). https://www.ohchr.org/en/statements/2023/05/afghanistan-systematic-crackdown-womens-and-girls-rights-un-experts-say

Panda, A. (2021). China's Afghanistan Calculus: Managing Terrorism, Engaging the Taliban. Carnegie Endowment for International Peace. https://carnegieendowment.org/2021/09/16/china-s-afghanistan-calculus-managing-terrorism-engaging-taliban-pub-85452

Pottier, J. (2006). Roadblock Ethnography: Negotiating Humanitarian Access in Ituri, Eastern Dr Congo, 1999–2004. *Africa* 76(02), 151–179.

Samarkand Declaration of the Fourth Meeting of Foreign Ministers of Afghanistan's Neighboring States. Samarkand (2023, April 14). http://se.china-embassy.gov.cn/eng/zgxw_0/202304/t20230414_11059110.htm

Sawe, B. E. (2019). The Ethnic Groups of Afghanistan. WorldAtlas. https://www.worldatlas.com/articles/ethnic-groups-of-afghanistan.html

Shah, S. F. (2021). The Taliban and China's Strategic Goals in Afghanistan. *Journal of Asian Security and International Affairs* 8(3), 298–317.

Suhrke, A. (2021). Relief Is Not Enough in Afghanistan. Centre for Policy Research, United Nations University. https://cpr.unu.edu/publications/articles/relief-is-not-enough-afghanistan.html

Thomas, C. (2021). Taliban Government in Afghanistan: Background and Issues for Congress. November 2. https://crsreports.congress.gov/product/pdf/R/R46955/3

UN. (2022). One UN Transitional Engagement Framework (TEF) Afghanistan. Retrieved from https://www.unocha.org/sites/unocha/files/TEF%20Afghanistan%20-%20February%

UN. (2023, March 8). Security Council Emphasizes that Punitive Restrictions on Women's Rights, Escalating Hunger, Insecurity Taking Devastating Toll in Afghanistan. https://press.un.org/en/2023/sc15222.doc.htm

UNAMA. (2023, January 11). Cash Shipments to the UN in Afghanistan – Info Sheet. UNAMA. https://unama.unmissions.org/cash-shipments-un-afghanistan-%E2%80%93-info-sheet

UNDP. (2021). Humanitarian Response Plan 2021. https://www.undp.org/content/undp/en/home/librarypage/crisis-prevention-and-recovery/humanitarian-response-plan-2021–afghanistan.html

UNICEF. (2022). Afghanistan: Demographics, Health & Infant Mortality. UNICEF DATA. https://data.unicef.org/country/afg/

UN News. (2023). Afghanistan Still a Grave Humanitarian Crisis, Senior Aid Official Says February 28. United Nations. https://news.un.org/en/story/2023/02/1134002

USAID. (2022, December 21). The United States Has Provided More than $1.1 billion to Respond to Humanitarian Crisis in Afghanistan since August 2021: Press release. U.S. Agency for International Development. https://www.usaid.gov/news-information/press-releases/sep-23-2022-united-states-provided-more-11-billion-humanitarian-assistance-afghanistan

Viken, T. M. and Kaplan, I. (2021). Aid and Conditionality in Afghanistan. Norwegian Afghanistan Committee (NAC). https://afghanistankomiteen.no/wp-content/uploads/2021/10/NAC-Discussion-note-Aid-and-conditionality.pdf

Watkins, A. (2022, August 17). One Year Later: Taliban Reprise Repressive Rule, but Struggle to Build a State. United States Institute of Peace. https://www.usip.org/publications/2022/08/one-year-later-taliban-reprise-repressive-rule-struggle-build-state

Wood, A. P., Apthorpe, R. J., and Borton, J. (eds.). (2001). *Evaluating International Humanitarian Action: Reflection from Practitioners.* London: Zed Books.

World Bank. (2021). Afghanistan. https://data.worldbank.org/country/afghanistan

Xinhua. (2021, December). Uzbekistan Provides 3,700 Tons of Humanitarian Aid to Afghanistan. https://english.news.cn/20211224/af0c32478fb244f3b3d2199b137f7e7a/c.html

Zakariya, S. (2022, August 14). *Overview: A year of Taliban rule in Afghanistan*. VOA. https://www.voanews.com/a/overview-a-year-of-taliban-rule-in-afghanistan-/6698682.html

Zhang, K. (2022, July 6). China Delivers Millions in Aid to Afghanistan, Fulfilling Promise to Taliban. *South China Morning Post*. https://www.scmp.com/news/china/diplomacy/article/3184316/china-delivers-us37-million-aid-afghanistan-fulfilling-promise

HUMANITARIAN AUTHORITARIAN
AUTHORITARIAN HUMANITARIAN

COMMENTARY

A brief critical reflection on Afghanistan

Mera Bakr

The chapter presents a great review of the state and humanitarian negotiations. It was quite helpful to see the different approaches used by aid organisations for their negotiations with states. Most importantly, a clear insistence is seen when it comes to a context-based approach, demonstrating that different regions and states, where aid organisations operate, require a contextual analysis for effective negotiations.

More work, however, is needed by the sector to develop a theoretical analysis to address the key fault lines that exist now in Afghanistan. In my view, it is an oversimplification to attribute the challenging situation in Afghanistan simply to the Taliban's pursuit of policies that are against women and that are violating human rights. No one should doubt how authoritarian, theocratic, and fundamentalist the Taliban are. Nonetheless, to my understanding, the fault line goes deeper, where there is a clash between a western liberal humanitarian intervention and the Taliban's insistence on sovereignty. The distrust and dilemmas run deep, which could be explained by the history of invasions of the countries, with the US invasion as the last one.

The Afghanistan case points again to how politicised humanitarian aid is. We spend insufficient time analysing how foreign aid shapes politics. In Afghanistan, such an analysis might allow us to understand why Taliban policies have been more in line with the protection of absolute sovereignty of the regime, fearing how foreign aid could be used as a means that they think is a threat to their authority. Also, it is of vital importance to mention that these analyses are not to defend Taliban but rather to understand the situation from their perspective, too.

We must do a better job of understanding and clearly presenting an analysis of the entire set of emerging Taliban policies, outside where the problems

DOI: 10.4324/9781003316541-13

revolve around human rights and women. These issues are fundamental; however, a deeper understanding of the situation and Taliban's policies needs better contextualisation before being deconstructed. Such an analysis could present helpful ways and opportunities for foreign aid and organisations for their negotiations with the regime.

7

ROMA STRUCTURAL DISCRIMINATION IN CONTEMPORARY RUSSIA

Institutions involved and measures (not) taken

Iana Vladimirova

Introduction

Due to the absence of legislative mechanisms for overcoming discrimination against individuals and groups in the Russian Federation, all problems related to discrimination are regulated in modern Russia through institutions of interethnic and ethno-cultural governance (Malakhov and Osipov, 2006, 533). The Russian state provides support to ethnic minorities, which is often declarative in nature and does not impose legally binding obligations on the state. For decades, it has neglected its obligations to the committees and conventions (Cviklova, 2015, 2149) and ignored ongoing human rights violations against the Roma people[1] (European Roma Rights Centre (ERRC) report, 2005, 10). In current Russian discourse, issues of structural discrimination against minorities are often overshadowed by discussions of interethnic conflicts and cultural politics, with more emphasis placed on 'equal opportunities in cultural development' (Osipov, 2013, 75).

In the late Soviet period, a cultural and intellectual elite among the Roma formed a number of public organisations, known as NPOs (non-profit organisations) or NCAs, which have had certain opportunities in reducing discrimination against Roma through representation in local and regional advisory bodies. However, it should be noted that some of these organisations exist only nominally and do not function, while others are led by informal leaders who conduct public activities without formal legal status. These organisations provide their leaders with political agency through representation on municipal, regional, and federal advisory councils. Despite this, there has been only minor effective action taken to address structural discrimination against Roma in Russia by state institutions or Roma organisations (Expert

DOI: 10.4324/9781003316541-14

Interview #2). Currently, the activities of these organisations are mainly limited to organising cultural festivals, roundtable discussions, and other events that do not address the pressing issues facing Roma in Russia (Smirnova-Seslavinskaya and Tsvetkov, 2011, 38).

Given these circumstances, the following questions arise that motivated this study. Why do Roma civil society organisations have almost no anti-discrimination measures in their agenda? What institutional limitations prevent organisations from anti-discriminatory activities? Who solves the problems of structural discrimination against Roma in the Russian Federation, and how is this done? How is communication structured between institutions involved in solving the problems of the Roma population in contemporary Russia?

The problem of structural discrimination against Roma and Roma activism as a response to such discrimination, particularly in the territories of the post-Communist states of Central and Eastern Europe, has been widely studied by foreign researchers in the framework of theories of ethnic mobilisation and political representation of minorities. There is a lack of comprehensive research on Russian Roma that goes beyond an ethnological approach. This paper attempts to fill the gap in research on the Russian context of the Roma social activity, the reasons for its cultural orientation, and the limitations of political agency of Roma activists and the organisations they lead.

In this study, I used two types of sources: primary (legislative acts, manifestos/charters, in-depth interviews with Roma leaders/experts) and secondary (studies on Russian ethno-cultural politics, Roma studies on culture/language, reports on structural discrimination). This chapter is reflective and empirical, focusing on the results of my initial research carried out in 2021. As the political environment in Russia changes rapidly, research data quickly become outdated. However, the processes described in this chapter and the events taking place in Russia today can be viewed retrospectively as consistent in the context of Russia's authoritarian practices.

In early studies of National Cultural Autonomy in Russia, A. G. Osipov adhered to the term 'organized hypocrisy' (Brunsson, 1989) for the 'gap between symbolic and instrumental politics, or rhetoric and actions of power' in post-Soviet Russia.[2] Further, V.S. Malakhov and A.G. Osipov (2021, 30), using the expression of Ó Beacháin and Kevlihan (2013), refer to this gap as 'strategic ambiguity'. For instance, this relates to the fact that the central government can simultaneously promote multinationalism while also acknowledging the unique role of ethnic Russians. V.S. Malakhov and A.G. Osipov pay special attention to 'unconsciousness' and the propensity of actors to opportunistic behaviour. Within P. Bourdieu's approach, habitus action only appears to be the product of a conscious 'cynical' or 'mercantile' strategy, but in reality, it is an objective but unconscious strategy.[3] Following this approach, I do not focus on the extent to which agents' interests, goals, and motivations are conscious and reflexive, and I assume their tendency to exaggerate their accomplishments in solving the problems of the Roma population in contemporary Russia.

The structure of the chapter is as follows. First, I discuss the state of the art considering problems of the Roma population in Russia since the 1990s and look closer at the opportunities open for domestic Roma public associations during that time. Further I examine how the changes in Russian foreign policy and Russian nationalistic turn in 2010s influenced the international aid and cooperation for Roma NPOs. Later, I focus on the communication gap between different instances that are involved in solving the problems of Roma population in the contemporary Russia and what anti-discriminatory actions can yet be taken by leaders of Roma organisations in light of these limitations.

Roma discrimination in Russia

Ethnic discrimination against Roma increased significantly in the 1990s. The media contributed to the ethnicisation of crime and the spread of notions of 'collective responsibility', as well as other ethnocentric narratives and essentialist characteristics entrenched in the public consciousness with respect to Roma. Roma are perceived as the ultimate 'other' and are characterised by marginality and exoticism, leading to the spread of anti-Roma racism and hindering their social adaptation and integration in post-Soviet Russia. The withdrawal of Russia from the Soviet socialist republics, which manifested itself in a dramatic change in the previous economic equilibrium, has greatly affected the Roma population of post-Soviet Russia through the establishment of a monopolistic-oligarchic order in the 1990s, when the political power was concentrated in the hands of economic elite (Acemoglu, 2008), the destruction of a large part of small traders, and the expulsion of Roma from 'established economic niches' (Smirnova-Seslavinskaya and Tsvetkov, 2011, 36). On the one hand, Roma could now openly conduct commercial activities, which were no longer illegal. Freedom of movement throughout the world, economic freedoms, and guarantees against religious oppression were extended to Roma; commerce was no longer prosecuted; and shortages of necessities were combined with opportunities for free enterprise (Demeter, et al., 2000, 215). However, the growing competition of professional entrepreneurs and the plight of small businesses in the 1990s left many Roma without jobs, access to medical and social assistance, and means of livelihood. Under conditions of ethnic discrimination, in particular by law enforcement agencies, and the lack of effective government measures in the 1990s to address socio-economic issues, inter-ethnic conflicts between Roma and the surrounding population arose. The low level of legal education of the general Roma population, combined with a fear of interacting with any state institutions, led to widespread neglect of the problem of re-registering housing and passports in the new state. The absence of personal documents confirming citizenship, the right to medical care, and rights to housing and property have become a widespread phenomenon for Roma in Russia (Demeter, 2018, 519, 520). Because legal and institutional means of support are inaccessible, informal networks of social and economic interaction, circumventing institutional rules and norms, have been the primary means of resolving any issues for discriminated Roma. The marginalisation of large segments of the Roma population occurred in parallel with the development of representatives of the more integrated ethnic subgroup of the Ruska Roma[4] into contemporary leaders of the Roma public organisations.

Institutional opportunities for organisations

During the 1990s, several Roma associations were established in Moscow whose activities were exclusively in the field of music and dance (Marushiakova and Popov, 2019, 207). The possibilities of Russian legislation[5] allowed Roma activists to institutionalise public associations and create NPOs and NCAs – public organisations at the local, regional, and federal levels. Since this period, a group of Roma activists, representatives of the late-Soviet Roma elite associated with NPO Romano Kher, have taken steps to form the Federal National Cultural Autonomy (FNCA). Since under Russian law an NCA at the federal level could only be formed as a pyramid, that is, through the existence of similar autonomies at the regional and local levels, there was a kind of 'race' for FNCA status among Roma activists of different groups. Due to the fragmentation of ethnic Roma groups and the persistence of communication networks, especially in the cultural sphere, the vast majority of organisations were created by representatives of the Ruska Roma. Representatives of this ethnic subgroup are much more integrated into the urban space and are usually well educated, including legally. The FNCA of Russian Roma was established in November 1999, registered in March 2000, and became one of the first NCAs at the federal level in the Russian Federation. Since there can only be one federal-level NCA in the Russian Federation for each nation, in the case of the Roma minority, it serves as an intermediary between all other Roma organisations (NPOs and NCAs) on the one hand and the government on the other. The FNCA gradually increased the number of branches; the emerging local and regional NCAs, however, were able to make independent decisions as separate organisations. The Roma movement in the Russian case was mainly formed 'top-down' (Marushiakova and Popov, 2019, 209), or, in my interpretation, from the centre to the periphery: from the creation of organisations in Moscow to their regional and local branches.

With the opening of borders after the collapse of the Soviet Union, the opportunity for Roma activists to travel abroad, and their first interactions with international Roma organisations and European Roma rights institutions, the leaders of the Roma movement have to some extent developed an understanding of the structure and purpose of Roma organisations in Russia. Russian Roma maintained close contacts with European organisations in the early period and shared common goals: countering structural discrimination and facilitating the adaptation and integration of Roma into their host society (Interview #2). Projects that received funding from abroad began to appear.

The legislative regulation of 'inter-ethnic relations' and the ethno-cultural sphere in Russia reveals a significant disconnect between symbolic and instrumental policies. The official rhetoric of 'multinationality', as embodied in the Federal Law 'On National Cultural Autonomy' (The NCA Law),[6] does not provide special status or officially established rights and powers for certain ethnic minorities (Torode, 2008, 190). In other words, the public expression of political encouragement for multi-ethnicity in contemporary Russia does not reflect this encouragement in actual socio-cultural practices. Constitutional provisions regarding minorities are too abstract and lack mechanisms for implementation and enforcement of state obligations.

The concept of national-cultural self-determination was first introduced in 1990, and the term 'cultural-national autonomy' was first used in 1992. The Russian Federation approved a non-binding conceptual plan in 1996, known as the Concept of National Policy, which emphasised the development of NCAs as a key component of the country's ethnic policy. The NCA Law was passed soon after, granting ethnic minorities the right to form NCAs for the purpose of preserving their identity, language, culture, and education. This law marked a turning point in the state's policy towards ethnic minorities, promoting their inclusion in the political arena through bureaucratic representation in advisory bodies. The registration of cultural autonomies by ethnic communities increased. However, following legislative amendments and court decisions, NCAs lost their significance and advantage over other ethnic associations and NPOs. The provisions of Articles 20 and 19, which included state funding for NCAs, were no longer in force,[7] and NCAs lack clearly defined and transparent conditions for state funding.

Ethnic activists' requests for state funding do not challenge the principles of the NCA as outlined by the government. A. Osipov (2010, 2013) explains the popularity of NCAs due to their symbolic status, which boosts the visibility of ethnic groups in social and political spheres despite their ineffectiveness. NCAs can symbolise equality among ethnic groups and create their systematics; at the same time, the government benefits from NCAs as they act as proof of support for ethnic cultures or to avoid responsibility in ethnocultural governance. The contradictory status of NCAs comes from the state's role as a 'gatekeeper' and its right to make final decisions on their use and recognition, which are often non-transparent and subjective, while successful ethnic leaders may use NCAs to boost their own status rather than to defend rights. The NCA Law and Russian electoral legislation state that NCAs and ethnic NPOs can't participate in elections or run for office, which sends a message of incompatibility between ethnicity and politics. Activists enter the public sphere through the status of the NCA, and through it, they enter the political field as agents within the political structure. The proclaimed 'apoliticism' of leaders is thus considered to be a rhetorical formula defined by the need to conform to a common political and public discourse. It does not represent a hypocritical position of leaders but an opportunistic one, emanating from their unstable subordinate position in the political structure. Practically, NCAs don't add any benefits that aren't already provided by legislation and instead create bureaucratic hurdles and restrictions for those who wish to organise and protect their ethnic identity. Other public associations of ethnic minorities exist and perform just as effectively as NCAs in achieving similar tasks.

Due to the lack of full-fledged political representation of Roma in Russia, the role of representing Roma is performed by the Chairman of the FNCA of Roma in the Council on Inter-Ethnic Relations under the President of the Russian Federation. Similarly, leaders of Roma organisations have bureaucratic representation at the regional and municipal level in advisory bodies under the Governors, but they do not have a say in decision-making on issues directly affecting the communities they represent; they can only ask questions and recommend certain measures to government representatives. The NCA institution has provided a unique opportunity for contact between representatives of organisations and government agencies at various levels and for direct dialogue between representatives of the Roma social movement and the authorities (Interview #3, #6). However, the restrictions on the principles and goals approved in the organisation's charter for NCA registration force Roma activists to undertake some projects ('off the books').

International cooperation

A retrospective evaluation of the efforts of international organisations that focus their activities on protecting the rights of Roma and the attempts made to develop the human rights ideas and practices of the Roma social movement in general shows the insignificance of such influence. However, it allows us to identify a 'boom' period in the emergence of Roma organisations in the Russian Federation in the early 2000s and to characterise this time as the period of the closest interaction with foreign institutions (Marushiakova and Popov, 2019, 210, 211). Organisations were able to conduct crowdfunding campaigns and receive grants and sponsorship from foreign foundations for human rights and educational projects. The specific nature of European organisations, namely, their focus on overcoming structural discrimination against Roma in the Russian Federation, was expressed in significant financial support for initiatives by Russian Roma and their organisations that conform to the principles of integration prevalent in Europe.

The ERRC, the leading European Roma rights organisation, made certain efforts in the 2000s to support the Roma movement in the initial post-Soviet political institution, the Commonwealth of Independent States (CIS), which was one of the factors behind the growth of Roma NCAs/NPOs in Russia. The Roma International Union of the Baltic States and the CIS, 'Amaro Drom', which was established in 2003, was a source of hope for the Roma movement. The creation of this union was supported and endorsed by the ERRC director, who expressed confidence that this organisation would become a starting point for the development of the human rights movement in the CIS and the Baltic states and called for making protection of human rights one of the main priorities in the work of this organisation. However, the ideas of protection of human rights and specifically of the Roma ethnic minority were not even mentioned in the statutory documents of the Union, and the following goals were declared: preservation of ethnic specificity, promotion of the Roma language, education, and culture, and raising the social status and economic well-being of Roma. The ERRC's hopes that 'Amaro Drom' would become a centre and a catalyst of the struggle for Roma rights in Russia did not materialise; in fact, no Roma organisation, whose main activities were in the field of struggle for the rights of the Roma population, has ever emerged. Subsequently, the ERRC supported the independent human rights organisation Anti-Discrimination Centre (ADC) Memorial[8] to a greater extent, whose activities in the early period of its existence were limited solely to the implementation of projects to overcome structural discrimination against Russian Roma (Expert Interview #2).

In the 2000s, Roma organisations cooperated with the Ministry of Foreign Affairs of the Russian Federation and, through its mediation, sought opportunities for dialogue with international organisations such as the United Nations, Organisation for Security and Co-operation in Europe, and the Council of Europe on issues of human and minority rights protection. Roma activists themselves considered this interaction important and effective, but, in fact, it was nominal: an appeal to the Council of Europe, drafted by Romano Kher and supported by the Foreign Ministry, containing a programme of assistance to Roma, resulted in several visits to Russia by a representative of the Council of Europe to monitor the situation of Roma in Russia. As a result of these visits, several roundtables were held to discuss ways to address discrimination against Roma and violations of their rights,[9] but the outcomes of these discussions were not implemented in practice (Expert Interview #2).

Russia's nationalistic turn in 2010s

Since the early 2010s, the Russian Federation's internal ethno-cultural policy has started to turn towards nationalisation, which became enshrined in legislation. Thus, in 2012, the 'Amendments to the Legislative Acts of the Russian Federation Regulating the Activities of Non-Commercial Organisations Performing the Functions of Foreign Agents' (the so-called 'Foreign Agents Law') came into force. This law significantly narrowed the opportunities for NCAs and NPOs to be funded by foreign organisations and sponsors and led to the restriction of activities and the closure of a number of organisations. In 2014, the law 'On National Cultural Autonomy' was amended to formulate the principles and goals of NCAs aimed at strengthening 'the unity of the Russian nation, harmonisation of interethnic relations, promotion of inter-religious dialogue', as well as activities aimed at the social and cultural adaptation and integration of migrants. A number of other adopted laws and normative acts emphasise the role of the Russian people, language, and culture as systemic factors of Russian statehood.

This turn towards nationalisation in domestic politics occurred in parallel and was associated with changes in the state's foreign policy. The confrontation with the West, which had been escalating since the mid-2000s and intensified in 2014 after the annexation of Crimea and the beginning of the armed conflict in eastern Ukraine, was accompanied by aggressive official rhetoric opposing the idea of national unity to the hostile environment. In March 2014, in his speech on the occasion of the annexation of Crimea, V.V. Putin referred to the 'Russian people' in an explicitly ethnic sense and called Russians a 'divided people'. Thus, an important shift occurred in the official discourse at the federal level: for the first time, the image of the Russian people as victims of an external force appeared (Malakhov and Osipov, 2021). The concepts of the 'Russian world' and the 'divided people' who find themselves in the position of victims have helped to strengthen the ethnocentric perspective of the perception of domestic and foreign policy processes in the public and political spheres. The centralisation of power and the increase in administrative space inevitably affected the educational sphere, language policy, and the media, which in practice meant cultural homogenisation.

At this point, 'multiethnicity' still receives some form of state support, such as educational and cultural institutions that support the languages and cultures of non-Russian peoples, festivals and events, and ethnic organisations at various levels that are financed and maintained. However, this support is not legislated and imposes certain obligations, limiting the activities of movements and organisations to 'the development of folklore or the promotion of all-Russian national unity' (Malakhov and Osipov, 2021, 31, 32).

In terms of international cooperation, there has been a shift from imitative actions in the past to a complete disregard for implementing UN provisions or fulfilling the requirements of the Convention on the Elimination of All Forms of Racial Discrimination (CERD)[10] (Cviklova, 2015, 2149–2153). The state bodies of the Russian Federation have practically ceased to take into account the opinion of the international community, regardless of the nature of the issues raised (Marushiakova and Popov, 2019, 217). During this period, the majority of independent Roma organisations and foundations either stopped their activities or were dissolved. The remaining organisations are extremely cautious about accepting foreign funding, as it may jeopardise their legal status. Since the law of 'foreign agents' was first adopted, many organisations, including those which specialise on human rights issues, had to shut down due to the burden of complying with the law's labelling and reporting requirements, as well as the hefty fines imposed for non-compliance or to avoid being labelled as such. The risk of being classified as 'foreign agents' has greatly reduced the activities of these organisations and the possibility of implementing projects related to protecting the rights of Roma and educating the Roma minority, as well as working with representatives of the authorities and law enforcement agencies in their interactions with the Roma population.[11] As a result, the Russian state has become the sole financial sponsor of Roma organisations, making them entirely dependent on it. These changes did not provoke widespread protests from ethnic leaders, and in fact, some Roma activists welcomed them.

Communication gap

The following are the levels of institutions that are involved in solving the problems of Roma population in Russia. The constructive communication in regard to what measures and by whom should be implemented with respect to Roma appears particularly problematic or almost totally lacking.

- International UN institutions: Committee on the Elimination of Racial Discrimination, Framework Convention for the Protection of the Rights of National Minorities
- International Roma rights organisations (ERRC, OSI, and IRU)
- Legislative branch of the Russian Federation
- Executive power (Federal Agency for Nationalities (Agency) as a body that forms 'Comprehensive Plans' since 2015 and reporting, which is based on data from local and regional self-government bodies)
- Independent charity and human rights organisations
- FNCA of Russian Roma and its branches (which can also be considered separately)
- Other regional and local Roma NGOs and their leaders

Keeping in mind the 'gap in rhetoric and actions' in the ethnocultural politics of post-Soviet Russia, I will focus on how interaction between them is organised in carrying out specific measures, in particular the approval and implementation of the 'Comprehensive Plans for the Socio-Economic and Ethno-Cultural Development of Roma in the Russian Federation'. Expert informants believe that comprehensive plans are drawn up primarily to present Russia's participation in regulating the situation of national minorities and racial discrimination in the international arena (Expert Interviews #1, #2, and #3).

On the one hand, actions by the Russian Federation related to international obligations and agreements appear to be mostly formalistic and without any real influence on the situation of Roma in the Russian Federation. Thus, following the recommendations of the UN Committee on the Elimination of Racial Discrimination, elaborated at a session in the autumn of 2008, the Interagency Working Group on Inter-Ethnic Relations in the Russian Federation approved the Comprehensive Plan of Action for the Socio-Economic and Ethnocultural Development of Roma in the Russian Federation for 2013–2014. However, as ADC Memorial notes, the development and approval of the plan took place only in 2012, just a few months before another report on the Russian authorities' compliance with the CERD was due to be submitted to the UN. The text of the plan itself was not published during the discussion or even after its adoption. In response to ADC Memorial's request for the text of the plan, the Ministry of Regional Development sent a document consisting of a list of 20 'measures' to improve the lives of Roma, a brief description of the conditions and deadlines for their implementation, those responsible, and the sources of funding. The form and content of the document and the set and order of the listed measures create the impression of a chaotic set of answers from the developers of the plan related more to their own ideas about the problems of the Roma in Russia. Some of the points are formal, so the first point was stated verbatim: 'Implementation of the Council of Europe program for the training of mediators (intermediaries) on issues of cooperation between Roma communities and executive authorities of all levels in the areas of education, healthcare, employment, etc'.[12] The document does not contain a more detailed plan or programme for this point but rather vaguely indicates the timeframe for implementation, sources of funding, and responsible executors – the executive agencies of a number of subjects of the Russian Federation, which, to all appearances, should act according to their own ideas on this issue, assuming that the document was in principle intended for implementation in practice.

It is also important to note that the second notion was the 'development and approval of a set of preventive measures to combat illicit drug trafficking among Roma'. This measure reflected and reinforced the exact opposite of the idea the document was intended to reflect: 'raids' and 'anti-Roma campaigns' against the Roma population, regularly practised by Russian law enforcement agencies, were a vivid example of discrimination and oppression of

Roma. The FNCA also pointed to the absence in the final version of the Plan of measures recommended by Roma representatives, including a pre-school education programme and paragraphs concerning measures to develop infrastructure, improve areas of compact Roma residence, bring schools closer to them, access to medical and ambulance services, and public transportation. The character of the publication is interesting: gratitude and appreciation to the Russian state that is the exact opposite of the indignation of human rights activists: 'We understand that it is not easy to immediately solve all the problems that have accumulated for so many years of inaction, and we very much hope that the next step will be the creation by the Government of the Russian Federation of a federal target programme for the economic, social, and ethnocultural development of Russian Roma in order to achieve a balance between the interests of the state and those of the Roma community'.

Within the framework of the Presidential Council on Inter-Ethnic Relations, the Federal Agency on Nationalities (FAN) was created in 2015 as the main body responsible for ethno-cultural policy and minority issues. Further 'Comprehensive Plans' were drafted by the FAN's experts. Recent reports from the agency contain contradictory data. Reports on the implementation of such plans are formed on the basis of inquiries to the administrations of municipalities and regions. Administrations may not have sufficient information on the situation of Roma or initiatives directed towards them in the region they serve. In addition, the reports may contain information about activities carried out by administrative agencies as part of the implementation of the comprehensive plan that in reality were carried out by independent organisations (for example, ADC Memorial) (Expert Interviews #1 and #3).

There is a tendency that in each new Comprehensive Plan, the provisions to be implemented come closer and closer to the actual problems of the Roma minority (Expert Interview #1). The Comprehensive Plans themselves may serve as additional leverage for Roma activists in communicating with representatives of the authorities at the local or regional level since they imply, albeit abstractly formulated, legally stated support for certain measures. The data for one of the Agency's reports indicate that settling inter-ethnic conflicts is often difficult 'due to the absence of public institutions representing the interests of the Roma population that are in dialogue with the authorities and local self-administration'. But according to our data, the leaders of the organisations (and there are approximately 30 in various regions and municipal districts) work closely with the respective administrations (Interview #5). This contradiction may speak to the narrow spread of the reach of Roma public organisations throughout Russia's regions.

The updated text of the latest Comprehensive Plan (2022) is not available online, but it already has a provision for tracking educational processes.[13] This is a major improvement that the problem has become recognised at the federal level, but it remains unclear exactly how the state wants to solve it:

what measures the state is going to apply to this issue and who is supposed to implement them (Expert Interview #4).

The leader of the FNCA supports the ethno-cultural policies of modern Russia and negatively evaluates the experience of European integration programmes, which objectively have not achieved their goals with great funding and public attention to the Roma problem (Interview #6). Since 2014, the connection between the Russian and international dimensions of the Roma social movement has been weakening as part of the general trend of the Russian Federation towards cultural isolation. The general trend of Russia's national policy towards cultural homogenisation and the strengthening of the state control apparatus, the provisions of the 'Strategy', focused on the preservation of traditions and culture and the identity of peoples and limited the level of acceptable activity for ethnic minority organisations, in particular the Roma NGO sector. After being recognised as a 'foreign agent', ADC Memorial, a human rights organisation whose main area of expertise is discrimination against Roma minorities in the post-Soviet space, closed its registration in Russia. The organisation was subsequently re-registered outside the Russian Federation and continued to provide legal assistance to Russian Roma to some extent and to present a variety of reports and analytical reports at the international level. After the beginning of Russia's full-scale invasion in Ukraine, the only way ADC Memorial can address the issues of structural discrimination against the Roma minority in Russia is through mechanisms of international advocacy. As Russia was excluded from the Council of Europe as a consequence of its aggression towards Ukraine,[14] the main work of ADC in relation to the rights of Roma is still focused on the influence of UN structures, which remains at the level of tracking and monitoring the current state of affairs. Even with human rights activists watching from the outside to see how Russia fulfils its obligations, without careful monitoring from the inside, much of the recommendations get lost in the communication between the instances of power.

The functioning of the Comprehensive Plans, according to the gathered data, follows the following scenario. The Russian Federation does not fully comply with its obligations to UN committees and international conventions. The Russian state, through the Agency, creates Comprehensive Plans to promote the social and economic integration of Roma, often with the help of Roma experts, whose proposals may be ignored. Reports on the implementation of the Plan are based on data from local and regional authorities, who may not have up-to-date information on the real situation of Roma in the territory under their care or a clear understanding of how to implement the 'Plan's recommendations due to its vague wording. Reports on the implementation of the provisions of the Comprehensive Plan are then provided to international bodies as proof of Russia's fulfilment of its international obligations. The Russian state shifts responsibility for interethnic conflicts and the implementation of ethno-cultural programmes to regional and local governments. According to the expert, the Agency's position on the ineffectiveness of the Plan is expressed in the fact that, on the ground, no one wants to implement its provisions (Expert Interview #1). An expert associated with the human rights movement argues that if the Russian state really wanted to implement the provisions of the Plan, 'it would definitely follow up on their implementation' (Expert Interview #2). Human rights reports emphasise that structural discrimination against Roma cannot be overcome without direct government intervention.[15]

An alternative viewpoint assumes that state institutions cannot facilitate the adaptation of certain groups in a situation where these groups are not willing to trust state agencies, including law enforcement agencies, for various reasons. A necessary measure to overcome structural discrimination in this optic is the existence of a strong independent NGO sector that will not be bound by political/bureaucratic constraints. At the same time, such NGOs should not be organised only by the Roma themselves; on the contrary, it is through interaction with a variety of non-state, independent intermediaries that the trust of disadvantaged groups can be nurtured.

Informal action of the leaders

In the absence of full-fledged political representation and independent intermediary organisations, the role of mediators is assumed by leaders of Roma organisations, who address pressing issues of Roma individuals and groups at the local and personal level outside of their NCA/NGO head status. They interact with local state structures and the host community through their informal connections, bypassing institutional norms. In addition to issues related to interactions with state authorities, they may be involved in issues of pre-trial conflict resolution, both within the Roma community and in clashes with the surrounding population. The agents I studied generally self-identified as Ruska Roma, and some respondents were trained in mediation in Strasbourg as part of UN programmes. They have high social capital and connections in cultural and business circles, and in one way or another, they may be integrated into state structures or have fairly close informal ties with them, which they use to address various pressing issues concerning Roma communities with varying degrees of effectiveness. In a number of cases, informal leaders also occupy official positions in registered (but not necessarily carrying out any real activity) Roma organisations. That is, the phenomenon is common when an organisation exists nominally, but its head, being both an informal actor and a leader of the Roma community, uses his status to advocate informally for certain issues of the represented community in interaction with local institutional structures.

As a rule, the leaders make great efforts to help Roma communities out of sincere motives and often on altruistic grounds, but the vulnerable side of their position remains their 'self-appointedness'. In most cases, leaders are separated from the local Roma community on whose behalf they act, often identifying themselves with the broader concept of Roma (often including all Roma in the nominally trusted territory). They use a special way of accumulating social capital, bypassing the forms traditionally accepted in Roma communities, the leaders do not compare themselves to a '*Rom baro*' or a '*zam/baro*' (the local names for the heads/leaders of ethnic Roma communities), nor do they attempt to become one. Due to this fact, not all Roma communities treat such leaders with trust, even after years of acquaintance. In some cases, the leader is perceived by the groups whose interests he or she intends to represent with a certain amount of scepticism. As 'a person from the administration'. The authority of leaders extends more to the clan environment, often delineated by ethnic group boundaries. Even people from other ethnic groups living nearby will, in practice, only turn to the leader of a local or regional organisation for help in a critical situation. This is especially true of the Kotliar communities, which are the most marginalised and vulnerable and need help more than others, but which are more closed and recognise the authority of the representatives of the Ruska Roma group to a lesser extent. Nevertheless, since informal channels of communication are familiar to the general population and are often the only channels available to discriminated segregated groups, representatives of various Roma ethnic groups may be forced to turn to such leaders for assistance.

The question arises: to what extent do informal leaders have legitimate reasons to speak on behalf of broader groups that may not be interested in such representation? Valiente (2003, 242), drawing on N. Fraser's theory, argues that for a discriminated group to be fully integrated into the broader community, it needs a representative of its interests, even if he is not a member of that community. Mediated bureaucratic representation may be the only chance for many Roma communities to have any representation of their interests since members of groups subject to structural discrimination themselves do not have sufficient resources for independent political participation. At the same time, there have been precedents in which the right to representation of the Roma community has been challenged by official structures. For example, a representative of the regional administration questioned the legitimacy of the position of the leader of the Roma NCA due to his low authority within the regional Roma community. This limitation was acknowledged by the NCA leader himself: the existence of an institutional position in a public association does not provide guarantees or grounds for the authority of the leadership position of the heads of organisations. In most cases, over time, the issue of representation and mandate becomes less relevant for all parties involved as the utilitarian application of the enthusiasm of informal leaders becomes more and more in line with the real needs of individuals and groups. Although organisational leaders do not have direct influence on decision-making processes concerning the Roma communities they represent within advisory boards, all informants emphasised that they have extremely trusting relationships with local and regional administrations, which are critical to mediating regularly occurring interethnic conflicts.

Thus, the following roles/functions of Roma leaders are intertwined: (1) an informal leader with authority within Roma communities; (2) a representative of Roma communities at the administrative level (in advisory bodies), expressing the interests/opinions of the communities he serves; (3) a mediator in communication between state institutions (such as the local administration) and representatives of Roma communities. Each of the roles/functions seems to be highly unstable, subject to any external influences, and can be changed or eliminated at any time.

Conclusion

In this chapter, I have given different types of restrictions for different types of public associations acting in the interests of the Roma population in the Russian Federation – domestic and international: (1) The 'organised hypocrisy' or the 'gap between rhetoric and action' of the authorities, the eclecticism and vagueness of the language of the legislation – have led to a lack of constructive communication between the authorities at different levels involved in solving the problems of the Roma minority; (2) Increasing cultural homogenisation combined with the dominant ideology of national unity form a common political and public discourse in which the ability to express the political intent of agents is limited; (3) The Law on Foreign Agents limited the possibility of international funding of projects and made the NGO sector almost completely dependent on the state apparatus; and (4) The inconsistency of the Law on NCAs, which gives the leaders of Roma NCAs political agency through the possibility of consultative representation, while limiting the possibility of its realisation through the ethnocultural orientation of the goals of this type of public association enshrined in the Law. Under these constraints, leaders of organisations cannot fully exercise their political agency.

On a broader level, only representatives of international human rights organisations can speak about Roma issues in the Russian Federation, although it's important to note the limited usefulness of instruments of international influence. At the federal level, the problems of discrimination against Roma are not discussed openly, and the instruments of international pressure are no longer given great weight in the implementation of measures within the

Russian Federation. Since the formal anti-discriminatory activities of the leaders of Roma public associations are no longer possible, most work with vulnerable groups is conducted invisibly and informally. This entails solving the problems of the Roma communities and individuals concerning housing, documentation, and access to education on a personal and informal level. It happens through bypassing institutional forms and through informal practices and institutions that are customary and widespread in the post-Soviet space, allowing them to avoid formal rules or adapt them to individual current needs. This research suggests that the lower the level of communication among civic activists, the more can be achieved in support of vulnerable groups without attracting the unwanted attention of governmental agencies. A deeper examination of the informal actions taken by various actors involved in assisting the Roma population is necessary in light of the evolving forms of civic activism and the increasing authoritarian control in modern-day Russia.

Acknowledgements

The initial version of this research was presented as an MA Thesis in Moscow School of Social and Economic Sciences and University of Manchester (2021). I am very grateful to my research supervisor, Mr. M. Simon, for his keen guidance, and to Mr. A. Gumenskiy, Prof. V.S. Malakhov, and Dr. A. Cunningham for their comments and notes.

Notes

1 The expression 'Roma' (or 'Romani') is used in this study to briefly refer to various social and ethnic groups in the Russian Federation who self-identify as, and are perceived by others, as Roma.
2 N. Brunsson, The Organisation of Hypocrisy. Talk, Decisions and Actions in Organisations. Chinchester, NY: John Wiley & Sons. 1989. Cit. by Malakhov V., Osipov A., 2006. See also Osipov A. G. Natsional'no-kul'turnaya avtonomiya: idei, resheniya, instituty. SPb.: Tsentr nezavisimykh sotsiologicheskikh issledovanij, 2004. Osipov A. G. Avtonomiya, men'shinstva i mul'tikul'turalizm: v chem smysl «upravleniya mnogoobraziem»? // Mir Rossii. 2008. T. 17. № 1. S. 102–121.
3 See for example, Bourdieu, P. In Other Words: Essays toward a Reflexive Sociology, Stanford University Press, Stanford, CA, 1990: Bourdieu, P. The Logic of Practice, Polity Press, Cambridge, MA. 1990.
4 During the Soviet period, the Romani literature and education that were allowed were based on the language of Ruska Roma. This allowed more integrated urban Roma to improve their social and cultural standing as representatives of the 'titular' variation of Romani culture and language. However, the cultural and linguistic developments, as well as the activism of the Roma, had only a minimal impact on the various ethnic subgroups within the larger Roma population of the USSR. Due to the fragmentation of the ethnic Roma subgroups and the persistence of communication networks within them, particularly in the cultural realm, the vast majority of organisations were established by Ruska Roma. As a result, the marginalisation of the wider Roma population occurred in parallel with the rise of representatives of the more integrated Ruska Roma ethnic subgroup as the current leaders of Roma civil society organisations.

5 Federal Law No. 82-FZ "On Public Associations" of May 19, 1995; Federal Law No. 7-FZ "On Non-Commercial Organisations" of January 12, 1996.
6 Federal Law No. 74-FZ "On National Cultural Autonomy" of June 17, 1996.
7 The Article 20 "Basic conditions for the provision of State financial support to National Cultural Autonomies" was abolished in 2003. The Article 19 "Financial Support of National Cultural Autonomies by the State and Local Government" was repealed in 2009. The provisions of the articles have not been transferred to other articles of the Federal Law.
8 In 2007, the Human Rights Anti-Discrimination Centre "Memorial" was registered as an independent organisation, which in the early 2000s acted on behalf of the St. Petersburg Memorial as part of the programme "North-West Centre for Social and Legal Protection of Roma". The focus of the organisation was advocacy and lobbying on behalf of the Roma minority in order to counteract structural discrimination. Activities included human rights outreach programmes, seminars, educational projects, social monitoring, field work with the population, legal and psychological assistance, litigation, etc. They presented various human rights reports to UN committees (the Committee on the Elimination of Racial Discrimination, the UN Committee on Socio-Economic and Cultural Rights) and engaged in dialogue with state authorities and local self-government bodies. https://adcmemorial.org/en/. As a part of the International Memorial, the organisation was among 2022 Nobel Prize laureates.
9 Moscow Roma Cultural and Educational Society "Romano Kher. 'Vozvrashchayas' k istokam".http://цыганероссии.рф/services-details/романо-кхэр/.
10 The Committee on the Elimination of Racial Discrimination (CERD) is a group of unbiased specialists responsible for overseeing the enforcement of the Convention on the Elimination of All Forms of Racial Discrimination by its member nations. https://www.ohchr.org/en/treaty-bodies/cerd.
11 See for example Human Rights Watch article on the changes to the Foreign Agent Law in Russia. New Restrictions for 'Foreign Agents'. Foreign Influence Would Now Suffice for Toxic Designation https://www.hrw.org/news/2022/12/01/russia-new-restrictions-foreign-agents, December 1, 2022.
12 Texts containing the content of 'comprehensive plans' for the socio-economic and ethnocultural development of Roma are not freely available, but information is available on the implementation of such plans. The latest such document with current edits is available on the official FAN website.
13 See, for example: FAN updates plan for socio-cultural development of Roma https://tass.ru/obschestvo/16181027, October 28, 2022.
14 After discussing with the Parliamentary Assembly on 25 February 2022, the Committee of Ministers chose to activate the procedure outlined in Article 8 of the Statute to suspend the Russian Federation from their representation rights in the Council of Europe, adhering to the applicable Resolution regarding the legal and financial outcomes of the suspension. The decision was made with unanimous agreement on 15 March 2022. At the same day, the Government of the Russian Federation informed the Secretary General of its withdrawal from the Council of Europe in accordance with the Statute of the Council of Europe and of its intention to denounce the European Convention on Human Rights. https://search.coe.int/cm/pages/result_details.aspx?objectid=0900001680a5d7d9, https://www.coe.int/en/web/portal/-/the-russian-federation-is-excluded-from-the-council-of-europe.
15 Strukturnaya diskriminaciya Roma v Vostochnoj Evrope i Central'noj Azii. Report on Structural discrimination of Roma in Eastern Europe and Central Asia. ADC «Memorial». 2018. P.5.

References

Acemoglu, D. (2008). Oligarchic Versus Democratic Societies. *Journal of the European Economic Association* 6(1), 1–44.

Bowring B. (2013) Russian Legislation in the Area of Minority Rights, 15–36. In: Protsyk O. and Harzl, B. (eds.). *Managing Ethnic Diversity in Russia.* Routledge.

Brunsson, N. (1989). *The Organisation of Hypocrisy. Talk, Decisions and Actions in Organisations.* Chinchester, NY: John Wiley & Sons.

Comprehensive plan of measures for socio-economic and ethno-cultural development of Roma in the Russian Federation for 2013-2014 // Federal National Cultural Autonomy of Russian Roma. Official site. 29.11.2018. http://цыганероссии.рф/2018/11/29/комплексный-план-мероприятий-по-соци/.

Cviklova, L. (2015). Direct and Indirect Racial Discrimination of Roma People in Bulgaria, the Czech Republic and the Russian Federation. *Ethnic and Racial Studies* 38(12), 2140–2155.

Demeter, N. G., Bessonov, N. V., and Kutenkov, V. K. Istoriya cygan – Novyj vzglyad. Voronezh, IEA. 2000.

Demeter, N. G. (2018). Cygane na postsovetskom prostranstve. Cygane. Pod red. N. G. Demeter, A. Chernykh. M.: *Nauka*, 519–536.

Expert interview # 1, April 22, 2021 // author's archive.

Expert interview #2, April 26, 2021 // author's archive.

Expert interview #3, April 29, 2021 // author's archive.

Expert interview #4 of January 22, 2023.

Information on the implementation of a comprehensive plan of action for the socio-economic and ethnocultural development of Roma in the Russian Federation in the second half of the year 2020. https://fadn.gov.ru/documents/prochee/9102-informatsiya-o-realizatsii-kompleksnogo-plana-meropriyatiy-po-sotsialno-ekonomicheskomu-i-etnokulturnomu-razvitiyu-tsygan-v-rossiyskoy-federatsii-vo-ii-polugodii-2020-goda

Interview #2, April 1, 2021 // author's archive.

Interview #3, April 04, 2021 // author's archive.

Interview #4, April 13, 2021 // author's archive.

Interview #5 April 19, 2021 // author's archive.

Interview #6 with the leader of the FNCA of Russian Roma, April 20, 2021 // author's archive.

Interview #7, April 20, 2021 // author's archive.

Malakhov, V. and Osipov, A. (2006). The Category of Minorities in the Russian Federation: A Reflection on Uses and Misuses. International Obligations and National Debates: Minorities around the Baltic Sea/Ed. S.S. Åkermark. Mariehamn: Åland Islands Peace Institute, 495–542.

Malakhov, V. S. and Osipov, A. G. (2021). Dinamika etnokul'turnoj politiki v Rossii, Kazahstane i Ukraine: otlozhennaya «nacionalizaciya»? *Mir Rossii* 30(2), 26–47.

Marushiakova, E. and Popov, V. (2019). Between Two Epochs: Gypsy/Roma Movement in the Soviet Union and in the Post-Soviet Space, 202–234. In: Slavkova, M., Maeva, M., Erolova, Y., and Popov, R. (eds.). *Between the Worlds: People, Spaces and Rituals.* Sofia: IEFSEM – BAS & Paradigma.

Materials for the report of the Deputy Head of the Federal Agency for Nationalities S. A. Bedkin at the meeting of the board of the Federal Agency for Nationalities

"On the results of the implementation of the comprehensive plan of measures for the socio-economic and ethno-cultural development of Roma in the Russian Federation" September 18, 2020.

Ó Beacháin, D. and Kevlihan, R. (2013). Threading a Needle: Kazakhstan between Civic and Ethno- nationalist State-building. *Nations and Nationalism* 19(2), 337–356.

Official website of the All-Russian public organisation "Federal National and Cultural Autonomy of Russian Roma". http://цыганероссии.рф.

Osipov, A. (2010). National Cultural Autonomy in Russia: A Case of Symbolic Law. *Review of Central and East European Law* 35(1), 27–57.

Osipov, A. (2013). National-Cultural Autonomy in Russia: A Matter of Legal Regulation or the Symbolic Construction of an Ethnic Mosaic? 62–84. In: Protsyk O. O. and Harzl, B (eds.). *Managing Ethnic Diversity in Russia*. London: Routledge.

Smirnova-Seslavinskaya M. V. and Tsvetkov G. N. (2011). *Antropologiya sotsiokul'turnogo razvitiya tsyganskogo naseleniya Rossii*. M. Moscow: Federal'nyj institut razvitiya obrazovaniya.

Structural Discrimination against Roma in Eastern Europe and Central Asia. ADC Memorial report. 2018.

The Ministry of Regional Development "planned" the development of Roma in Russia. ADC 'Memorial'. 06.03.2013. https://adcmemorial.org/novosti/ministerstvo-regionalnogo-razvitiya-zaplanirovalo-razvitie-tsyigan-v-rossii/.

The project Supporting Roma NGOs through the Introduction of New Practices helps the socialization of Roma // "ALL OF WE ARE RUSSIA!" Information Portal on the Friendship of Peoples. 28.09.2020. https://www.samddn.ru/novosti/novosti/proekt-podderzhka-tsyganskikh-nko-posredstvom-vnedreniya-novykh-praktik-pomogaet-sotsializatsii-tsyg/?type=original.

Torode, N. (2008). National Cultural Autonomy in the Russian Federation: Implementation and Impact. *International Journal on Minority and Group Rights* 15(2–3), 179–193.

V poiskah schastlivyh tsygan. (2005). Presledovanie otverzhennyh men'shinstv v Rossii. ERRC Report on Roma Right Violations in Russia. № 14.

Valiente, C. (2003). Mobilizing for Recognition and Redistribution on Behalf of Others? The Case of Mothers against Drugs in Spain, 239–259. In: Hobson, B. (ed.). *Recognition Struggles and Social Movements*. Cambridge: Cambridge University Press.

HUMANITARIAN AUTHORITARIAN
AUTHORITARIAN HUMANITARIAN

COMMENTARY

Different types, different responses

Andrew J Cunningham

This book focuses on how authoritarian practices impact humanitarian ne-gotiations. Much can be learned, however, by examining the experiences of other types of civil society organisations that bear the brunt of authoritarian practices. This chapter by Iana Vladimirova researches an authoritarian re-gime which implements restrictions against a variety of civil society organisa-tions. In this case study, the civil society actor is one which is set up to protect the rights of a specific minority group in the Russian Federation. In this case, the administrative framework dictates the form of assembly, constraining the content of action. Contemporary Russia is a good case study for how civil society organisations respond to an environment of authoritarian as well as illiberal practices.

International humanitarian non-governmental organisations (INGOs) typically respond to a crisis referencing humanitarian principles (humanity, impartiality, independence, and neutrality). These organisations are external actors, working in sensitive internal political dynamics. Being external actors they may strive to stay present and operational in a context or, however re-luctantly, decide to leave. Barring being forced out by a government, it is for the INGO to calculate the level of their acceptance by the state and society and their level of tolerance of the working conditions.

Local humanitarian organisations are in a different situation. They are from and fully embedded in the context and do not have the choice to leave (although they can stop action). The pressing nature of their work in respond-ing to a crisis and the sense by the government that they are more controllable may give them some leeway with the government. Even more different from international NGOs are human rights organisations. These work on issues which are very sensitive to any government, more so with governments with

DOI: 10.4324/9781003316541-15

authoritarian tendencies. Organisations that have some sort of official mandate linked to upholding the rights of a particular ethnic group are yet in a
different category, as described in Vladimirova's chapter.

One way we can use to analysis the difference between the social, political,
and regulatory environments within which these different types of organisations work is by conceptualising the overlap between illiberal practices (e.g.,
human rights abuses directed at vulnerable portions of the population) and
authoritarian practices (e.g., limitations on civic space). How do local civil
society organisations react to these two sets of practices? In Vladimirova's
chapter, we see how a local organisation responds to limitations on the work
of civil society organisations but it as well looks at the human rights situation of the population for which the organisation is meant to advocate. There
is an overlap between the group, the organisation, and the practices. These
organisations do not have the ability to leave but must stay and find ways in
which to productively work.

International humanitarian organisations respond to the impetus of the
crisis – usually illiberal practices, often equating to human rights abuses.
But the focus of negotiations is on humanitarian needs and the space within
which the organisation has to constructively respond. In this situation, the
point of humanitarian principles is to give comfort to the government that
the organisation is not taking a political stand in opposition to the policies
of the government, but rather impartially responding to the consequences of
the crisis.

In the 2000s, during the conflict in Chechnya as international humanitarian aid workers we tried to negotiate with the government to find the space
in which to provide assistance without becoming politically involved. This is
obviously easier said than done in such a situation when we were confronted
daily with evidence of egregious human rights abuses. But the imperative to
find ways to assist people prevails. Fears of compromising too much, of complicity, and of doing more harm than good preoccupied us, and we used our
principles to help guide our action. But in the end, we knew that we could,
however reluctantly, depart.

The organisations Vladimirova describe so elegantly are in a different situation, as there is no space between authoritarian and illiberal practices in the
environment within which they work. The very nature of the organisations,
why their existence is necessary, and the contested space within which they
seek to work overlap completely. Studying this difference in situation between international humanitarian actors and local civil society organisations
helps us, as international actors, to isolate where the space for negotiations
lies.

To compare with other contexts, a good example is Afghanistan, where
such an overlap of practices also exists for humanitarian INGOs. In many
contexts, from an international NGO perspective, authoritarian practices

are limitations on access which are designed to limit the scope of civil society action and external engagement with the population. Illiberal practices are more related to the conditions within which the population lives – the very human rights abuses which help create the humanitarian crisis in the first place. In the Afghanistan context, illiberal practices would be related to human rights abuses of certain populations, such as women. Authoritarian practices would be limits placed on the work on international actors. But isn't the issue that the edict on not employing women is both? The difference and potential overlap are very important; what are we actually concerned about? There is a big space between policy and practice – how much do we care about policy?

Thus, the issue to be explored here is whether this overlap between authoritarian practices – those that limit us as an organisation – and illiberal practices – those that do harm to a segment of the population and constitute a human rights abuse – helps explain why Afghanistan has become such a hot topic for debate in the humanitarian world. It seems as if the perception (or reality) is that aid organisations are not only being constrained by the edicts of the Taliban but are being made part of the implementing apparatus of the edicts, and thus aid organisations are not only impacted but fundamentally made complicit. It is a similar set of questions concerning INGO work in contemporary Russia.

It behoves humanitarian organisations to closely study local civil society actors and actions, particularly those working with the most vulnerable groups. Vladimirova's chapter is a brilliant case study of Roma organisations in Russia and the overlapping formal and informal administrative barriers to true action. In comparing how such organisations work, how the state responds to them, and the civic space they inhabit, it informs how INGOs manage their work and space.

8

HUMANITARIAN APPARATUS OF SILENCE

Authoritarian denial and aid assemblage in Venezuela

Fernando Garlin Politis

Introduction

From the popularity of the 'Bolivarian Revolution' to its economic collapse and recent transformations, the case of Venezuela continues to distinguish by the perpetuation of its multiple crises and the political polarisation around humanitarian aid. In recent years, the Venezuelan regime has conducted a process of 'authoritarian upgrade' (Hall and Ambrosio, 2017; Heydemann and Leenders, 2011) to maintain its grip on power and the status quo, with three distinctive features: first, the opening and informal dollarisation of the economy,[1] allowing the entry of an increasing number of actors and resources into the country; second, the decline or withdrawal of government 'humanitarian public action' (Fassin and Vasquez, 2005; Vásquez Lezama, 2011, 2014), brought about by the collapse of the oil rentier model (Bull and Rosales, 2020; Peters, 2019), while maintaining civic-military oversight of community structures; and third, the censorship or banning of data as well as information around the meaning of 'crisis' or 'humanitarian aid'.

The government's official denial to recognise the crises in the country has not prevented the deployment of two 'humanitarian apparatuses' (Agamben, 2009; Dodier and Barbot, 2016; Naepels, 2019), rearranged around the regime's humanitarian policy. On the one hand, the 'humanitarian public action' (Fassin and Vasquez, 2005; Vasquez Lezama, 2011, 2014), organised in a civic-military alliance and represented by the structures of the communal councils, and, on the other hand, the interventions of international 'humanitarian aid' agencies (Atlani-Duault, 2011; De Lauri, 2016). However, the denial of the crisis would have impacted the activities of the latter apparatus, which has to conduct its activities informally and through ad hoc agreements. In this chapter, I explain how the articulation of the two humanitarian

DOI: 10.4324/9781003316541-16

apparatuses is only possible in this particular context precisely because of the silence (Puccio-Den, 2017, 2019). The proximity and complementarity of humanitarian actors to the authoritarian regime play an ambivalent role. Sometimes it legitimises the silences, and sometimes it makes visible the human rights violations. Here, there is an ambiguity that international organisations continually confront: what is the right balance between containing authoritarianism and preserving its humanitarian policies?

Thus, I seek in this text to question how the practices of denial of an authoritarian regime influence humanitarian negotiation in Venezuela and to analyse the arrangements of the two principal humanitarian actors. To support my argument, the following text is divided into three parts: the first is an exploration of the main actors around the 'humanitarian crisis' and the functioning of the politics of denial; the second is an analysis of the 'humanitarian apparatus of silence', considering their frictions as well as their contestations; and finally, the third is an explanation of the two functions of this aid assemblage.

Since 2018, I have analysed NGO reports, media, and academic literature, and conducted over 50 interviews with international humanitarian officials, local NGO officials and directors, activists, legal and opposition party officials, as well as former government officials. Between 2020 and 2022, I made several trips to the Colombia-Venezuela border, where I researched the dynamics of humanitarian aid at the margins of the state. The advantage of moving along the Colombian-Venezuelan border was that I avoided the risk of a lengthy investigation on a censored subject in Venezuela. This positioning also allowed me access to interviews with government officials, military, and former military personnel. All persons, testimonies, and organisations have been anonymised or modified for protection.

An authoritarian policy of denial in the face of crises

Venezuela's recent economic, institutional, and social collapse has been the subject of multiple studies that have attempted to capture the particularity of this 'crisis'. In particular, this notion appears to describe the maintenance and strengthening of an authoritarian regime (Acosta, 2018; Azkoul, et al., 2019; Martínez and Andréani, 2020) and to explain the failure of an oil rentier model (Bull and Rosales, 2020; Peters, 2019; Van Roekel and De Theije, 2020). These uses of the word 'crisis' are part of an effort to reveal what is hidden, latent, and virtual within society. 'The fundamental antagonisms, the subterranean seismic ruptures, the occult path of new realities' (Morin, 2012). Outside of the Venezuelan case, other research has explored the kind of work that the term 'crisis' does in the construction of narrative forms (Roitman, 2014) and how it is an affect-generating idiom, mobilising radical endangerment to foment collective attention and action (Masco, 2017).

In Venezuela, the term 'complex humanitarian crisis'[2] has emerged as the preferred formula for describing a national socioeconomic collapse that did not originate in a natural disaster or war. This notion is initially mobilised with distinct interests between two factions[3]: on the one side, by the alliance of opposition parties, and on the other hand, by the grouping of some local NGOs. The first, in 2019, sought to denounce the country's crisis through a 'humanitarian media'[4] to mobilise Venezuelan society and the army against the regime. To this end, the alliance of opposition parties has seized on the term 'humanitarian crisis' to justify the urgency of a change of government. This humanitarian politicisation culminated in the holding of two humanitarian concerts, 'Live Aid' and 'Hands Off Venezuela', on the Colombian-Venezuelan border, in which the governments of Colombia, Chile, and the United States, as well as some Venezuelan NGOs, participated to denounce 'the dictatorship that has ruined the country'. Despite all this support, the staging of the humanitarian crisis has not succeeded in producing political transformations but rather the exacerbation of a confrontation between two elites through so-called humanitarian interventions.[5] After the 'concert battles', a possible negotiation between the government and the opposition regarding crisis management was significantly reduced. Finally, the opposition parties anchored themselves in two actions outside the humanitarian field. First, the search for international legitimacy as an interim government, gaining recognition from many countries[6]; and second, the maintenance or increase of economic sanctions.[7] Nevertheless, considering the harmful consequences of the latter, the Venezuelan political opposition has called for relief from economic sanctions.[8]

The second faction concerns local associations that, since 2016, have been carrying out joint action at the international level to prove that there is indeed a crisis in Venezuela. According to the NGO leaders interviewed, the UN agencies were ideologically close to the government. They underestimated the magnitude of the Venezuelan crisis, agreeing to use figures that were not in line with the socio-economic deterioration of the country. In the end, local associations obtained, first, the appointment of new UN officials in the country and, second, an increase in dialogue on the representation of the crisis. This joint action would have updated the role of local NGOs in collecting data (on people, events, conflicts, or disasters) for two purposes: either to argue that a humanitarian situation exists or to obtain funding. However, these organisations' efforts face government censorship regarding the country's meaning and the dimension of crises.

For several years, the Venezuelan regime has implemented denial propaganda to counter studies, analyses, or reports dealing with the different crises. According to Cohen (2001), denial can be defined as 'assertions that something did not happen, does not exist, is not true, or is not known about'. Indeed, when it comes to a financial crisis, the regime blames the US economic war (Chinea and Pons, 2016); the hospital crisis was qualified as the effect of a 'hospital mafia' (Delgado, 2022); and the rejection of investigations into the violation of human rights or crimes against humanity was pointed out by the regime as 'lies' invented by 'governments subservient to Washington' (BBC News, 2020). We could classify these denial schemes and sabotage of information in the country as the primary expression of authoritarian practices. Following Glasius (2018), the latter is 'a pattern of actions, embedded in an organised context, sabotaging accountability to people ('the forum') over whom a political actor exerts control, or their representatives, by disabling their access to information and/or disabling their voice'.

Even if this authoritarian policy does not seek to block the arrival of humanitarian aid,[9] we observe that it affects the legitimacy of the humanitarian response, both internationally and locally. In the first case, at the international level, the government officially contradicts the country's mass migration, sometimes treating it as 'fake news' (France 24, 2018) and sometimes as a campaign against the state (El Comercio, 2018). In the second case, at the national level, the regime's representatives have implicitly disavowed the magnitude of the crises. This type of denial is characterised by the absence of an attempt to 'deny either the facts or their conventional interpretation [...] what is denied or minimised are the psychological, political, or moral implications that arise from them' (Cohen, 2001). We can highlight two illustrative situations. The first, in 2013, when the shortage of many foods and necessities became widespread, the chancellor questioned in an official party rally, 'Do you prefer a nation or toilet paper?'[10] This type of statement downplayed the importance of an economic crisis compared to the defence of a more noble cause. The second was during an interview between the country's president, Nicolas Maduro, and a CNN reporter. The reporter asked Maduro about the government's denial of human rights abuses during protests and the country's food shortage and supply problem, showing him images of Venezuelans eating out of garbage cans. During the interview, Maduro stood up and ordered to confiscate the recording and expel the journalists from Venezuela.

These organised deceits show how denial is an ideological façade of the state to manage situations for which it is not capable of taking responsibility. By actively disrupting or sabotaging accountability (Glasius, 2018), Maduro's government achieves to impose the official narrative of denial. Based these circumstances raises another question: How can these practices affect the humanitarian response in the country?

A humanitarian intervention to the measure of denial?

Although most international aid agencies have stayed out of the humanitarian politicisation in the country, the regime's ideology has constantly stigmatised their activity as an instrument of North American interference. For years, the government did not support humanitarian aid from the United States and Europe because it could compete with the regime's social welfare systems for the most vulnerable (food stamps, distribution of medicines …). If we consider that the political exploitation of aid is its main condition of existence (Magone, et al., 2011), humanitarian aid in Venezuela depends mainly on its capacity to integrate into the government's humanitarian management networks. Thus, we notice two forms of control in this incorporation: first, through the conditioning of numbers, and second, through *ad hoc* and informal agreements.

Some interviewees point to the conditioning of numbers as a consequence of prioritising humanitarian access 'at all costs' in order to gain access to negotiations with the state over the humanitarian crisis. For many interviewees, this meant leaving state recognition of a humanitarian emergency, as information gathered by international organisations came from secondary sources supporting the government. For example, in the first diagnosis, carried out in 2018, the humanitarian needs amounted to 7 million, a report that the government vetoed. For 2019, the government refuses to release the second plan, where several NGOs indicate that the number of people in need of assistance is 9 million. In the end, the figure of 7 million people was tacitly accepted. For the third humanitarian plan, for 2020–2021, the exact figure of 7 million people is maintained, despite the impact of the COVID-19 pandemic. Currently, this figure is estimated to be around 13 million people, according to local NGOs surveys.[11] Despite this considerable gap, the priority of multilateral agencies has not been to verify, debate, or make these numbers visible. Thus, the work of counting – and we add: but also not doing so – becomes a means of stabilising an existing condition (Masco, 2017). This question problematises the priority given to numbers during a 'humanitarian crisis' in an authoritarian context: is it always the numerical magnitude that counts or rather the place of truth?

The informal and ad hoc agreements between the humanitarian teams in Venezuela and the government are the consequence of the interruption or rupture of the formal agreements. In Venezuela, the United Nations Development Assistance Plan (UNDAP) got suspended in 2019. As a result, ad hoc deals prevail between the United Nations and the government in the presence of a humanitarian team. This operation is parallel to the existing regulations and allows for the arbitrary use of both tools. According to the organisations, the government has created a registration platform for international agencies, but they have yet to receive this certificate, nor have they received a visa to stay. For this reason, many aid workers reside on tourist visas and must leave the country every three months to renew them. To extend the metaphor, this 'tourist' status in the relationship between international cooperation and the government favours the official narrative since the humanitarian teams operate without officially recognising their activity or the crisis. In other words, both are 'virtual' because they exist in the state of mere possibility.

This lack of formal recognition has two implications: on the side of the humanitarian agencies, the plans developed do not come out until six months after data collection due to the time it takes to negotiate the figures with the government, which has an impact on the effectiveness of the response. Local NGOs explain that international cooperation often must subcontract complex tasks and spend available funds quickly with concise implementation times. A local organisation official mentions the example of an offer they received: 'We needed to set up a canteen, so they told me: "We have $2,000, and we have to deliver food to 5,000 people"'.

The constant dispute between data use and the functioning of relationships and resources raises some questions about humanitarian logic: what actions are privileged and based on what kind of protocol? Should universal humanitarian norms be adapted to local power negotiations, where the arenas for negotiation are informal and ad hoc?

Humanitarian apparatus of silence

Generally, for humanitarian organisations to obtain funding, they must show and demonstrate that a humanitarian emergency exists. Two processes, emotional *mobilisation* and *media coverage*, make a crisis visible and prove to donors the impact capacity of organisations or institutions. In this section, I analyse how two humanitarian apparatuses were deployed in Venezuela through silence, evoking two opposite processes: imitating dominant practices and reproducing bureaucratic opacity and informality. At the same time, local NGOs' responses to these dynamics must modulate between their capacity to denounce and their capacity to act.

The government's official denial to recognise the crises in the country has not prevented the deployment of two 'humanitarian apparatuses' (Agamben, 2009; Dodier and Barbot, 2016; Naepels, 2019), rearranged around the government's redistributive networks. Following Naepels (2019), the notion of apparatus seems helpful in describing the institutional ecology of loosely coordinated organisations, each with its agenda. The first apparatus is 'humanitarian public action' (Fassin and Vasquez, 2005; Vasquez Lezama, 2011, 2014), represented by the structures of the communal councils organised in a civic-military alliance. We consider the current social policy of the Venezuelan government as an extension of 'humanitarian public action' (Vásquez Lezama, 2011). In other words, the government's social action is closer to a humanitarian policy than a social policy. We justify this choice by taking into account that it is carried out outside an institutional framework, greatly weakened, which cannot carry out such actions (D'Elia, 2006), failing to cope with humanitarian crises (Vásquez Lezama, 2014), and is poorly prioritised and insufficiently linked to real social management in the face of a declining economy (Aponte Blank, 2017a, 2017b). Indeed, this humanitarian public action has failed to create a new public institution necessary to increase its effectiveness and has reinforced the military authorities as 'new social managers' (Alvarado, 2004).

Because of these characteristics, this first humanitarian mechanism fulfils both a redistributive and a monitoring role. The latter is manifested mainly through exemplary sanctions against individuals or organisations that 'make much noise' and cannot protest or challenge these actions. For example, international agencies have been expelled from hospitals without the event being reported in the press, which would mean being permanently banned from their activities. Three forms of state repression against humanitarian organisations – local or international – can be identified throughout: (i) arrest warrants, as in the case of organisations on the border that published reports on paramilitary violence and whose leaders were subsequently imprisoned; (ii) defamation suits against people who publish reports analysing the number of massacres and state violence in popular neighbourhoods; and (iii) the arbitrary promotion of registries and laws to control or block humanitarian provisions or visas. In the previous section, we mentioned the registration form for humanitarian organisations as well as the obtaining of humanitarian visas. In addition, we can add the proposed 'cooperation laws'. This type of law has been proposed for approval in the General Assembly on at least four occasions (2005, 2006, 2010, and 2015). This tool has served as a constant threat[12] to organisations, as it includes arbitrary restrictions and sanctions. In 2022, this proposal returned to the debate, stating that:

> In the context of the multiform aggression to which the Republic has been subjected, it is understood that within the framework of the principle of co-responsibility that concerns Venezuelan men and women and natural and juridical persons in the security of the Nation, it may be submitted to evaluation for its prohibition, suspension, restriction or definitive elimination the existing cooperation of civil associations in Venezuela with other associations, governments or international organisations that participate in the application, directly or indirectly, of unilateral coercive measures, due to the fact that they are involved in the application of unilateral coercive measures, restriction or definitive elimination of the existing cooperation of civil associations in Venezuela with other associations, governments or international organisations that participate in the application, directly or indirectly, of the application of unilateral coercive measures inasmuch as they attempt against the integral development of the Nation (12)

These proposals were continually interrupted by the second apparatus, the international 'humanitarian aid' agencies (Atlani-Duault and Vidal, 2009;

de Lauri, 2016; Pandolfi and Corbet, 2011). Their work falls into one of the three dimensions we identified in this arrangement. First, the constant negotiation with the government on access to the population through informal and ad hoc agreements; second, the provision of technical assistance and support to local governments, schools, and hospitals; and third, the collection of data through the delegation of tasks to local NGOs, which oppose the government.

This 'in-between' position of international cooperation forces it to make choices about its discourse, codes, and practices on the ground. We identify that articulating these activities is only possible through a regime of 'silence' (Puccio-Den, 2017, 2019) that allows the two humanitarian apparatuses to articulate under a particular regime of action, interlocution, and interaction between actors, resources, and discourses. As Puccio-Den (2019) suggests, 'Silence cannot exist either ontologically or socially without leaving traces'. In our case, we analysed the 'crumbs' of interview information. As mentioned earlier, the rapprochement between the regime and humanitarian actors has guaranteed the latter unprecedented access to new spaces and data. Indeed, this is the case of isolated indigenous territories in the country's east, where HIV resources are beginning to address significant epidemics.

Nevertheless, the authoritarian regime does not publish and prohibits official publication on humanitarian needs, which circulates only privately between aid agencies and government officials. These arrangements with the government also include protecting or omitting state controls so that humanitarian actions can be carried on. The informal deals are critical because most humanitarian organisations that import medicines, food, or other resources may be subject to unannounced checks, unfounded paperwork, and extortion. However, these agreements of silence have also had implications for the logic of action of international organisations.

Specifically, we observe two practical implications. The first is the mimicry of language and institutional silence. According to interviewees, it is imperative never to mention that there is a 'complex humanitarian crisis' or even an 'emergency', which would be tantamount to using the language of political opposition. Indeed, humanitarians try to avoid any language that could be considered oppositional or political. According to a leader of an international organisation:

> We have done so much rhetoric exercise to say what we want that we no longer know what to say. I have erased the word 'problem' or 'crisis' from my vocabulary, and we have blurred the language to say things without saying anything

As a risk reduction measure, the humanitarian agencies engaged former government officials in the humanitarian aid negotiations, which has been particularly effective, as one interviewee points out: 'You have to know what issues can paralyse ... we were close to reaching an agreement in the negotiation spaces, but if the word "humanitarian crisis" was written somewhere, there was no agreement'.

The second feature is the reproduction of regime opacity and bureaucratic informality. At the local level, these relationships are conditioned by the following principle: 'If you are a friend of ... you are my friend'. The closeness principle involves a series of informal agreements with the heads of the communal councils, typically the person who also manages the distribution of humanitarian aid from the state, mainly in the form of CLAP (The Local Committees for Supply and Production) food bags. At the national level, obtaining a series of permits and informal agreements with the regime is necessary to enter or transport humanitarian goods legally. Finally, a third characteristic is the lack of interaction between the local and national levels. As interviewees point out, it is possible to have contacts and approvals at the national level, but more is needed to guarantee access to town halls or communities.

For this reason, many organisations mention a 'double negotiation' process where agreements with a ministry do not imply implementing a programme in a territory. The disconnection between the two levels is both a weakness of the state and an opportunity for international cooperation, which remarks the success of establishing humanitarian roundtables with different pro-regime governorates without the approval of national bodies. However, this dynamic has some limitations, as organisations mention that they must play a secondary role and collaborate with local authorities, or else they face the risk of expulsion without any complaints possible. This configuration shows that the interlocutions take place in a fragmented and isolated way, ensuring that the regime maintains control – at least rhetorical – of the actions at different scales.

Silence has thus become the basis for the deployment of the two humanitarian actors under strong mistrust. For the regime, the provision of humanitarian aid is seen as a constant threat, as it could represent the failure of social policies and crisis management in the country. In this sense, the official narrative explains that US economic sanctions drive the crisis. For many regime officials, the problem in hospitals and supplies is a direct consequence of these sanctions. As a result, they consider the arrival of humanitarians as a means of pressure from North American imperialism. In this context, humanitarian action can easily conflict with the legitimacy and power structures of the regime. For example, government distribution of CLAP food bags can constantly vary in time and quality of products, while international organisations can deliver good quality food without asking for anything in return from the people receiving it. The slow pace of international food programs is a way to avoid politicising government humanitarian aid, allowing the government to maintain its clientelist structures. For international cooperation, conversely, silence has a more pragmatic function: First, it is a form of negotiation in areas where laws change or are applied discretely; second, it allows a minimal presence in the field. Based on informal and ad hoc arrangements, this strategy must continuously reassure the complementarity of the two aid apparatuses on the belief that humanitarian actions could be extended and benefit a larger population if they demonstrate their effectiveness and agreement.

However, there are several instabilities in silence-based deals. First, due to the constant rotation of regime officials, many organisations argue that this is a highly volatile strategy, as compatibilities and synergies with a minister, mayor, or community council member can change rapidly. Second, the NGOs interviewed indicate that silence works against the visibility needed to raise awareness of the humanitarian emergency, which is ultimately obscured by the regime, passing off the humanitarian agenda as the authoritarian agenda. In this sense, the mere exposure of a specific situation of vulnerability in some locality could be seen as a threat; 'too much exposure is countering', says a former government official. Third, the associations point out that the responsibility to collect information, report, and denounce the degradation of rights or precarious conditions is neglected by international cooperation. Currently, the primary providers of data and information are local NGOs, with very few resources, who assume the risks of collecting and publishing data in an authoritarian context.

These forms of interlocution between organisations and government need to be understood within a new conceptual and theoretical framework that escapes the logic or framework of polarisation or denunciation to consider actions beyond these silences. We then ask what kind of assemblages these apparatuses produce and what policy responses are possible. The following section examines how these two apparatuses are articulated and continually contested in an 'aid assemblage'.

The aid assemblage

In this final section, I examine how silence apparatus is part of the local and global connections that allow this functioning. Indeed, if we want to understand how an aid assemblage works, we do not ask what its essence is but rather what it can do (Nail, 2017). The relationships between activists, humanitarians, and state actors have created a specific aid assemblage characterised by two functions that exhibit 'stability over time and normative consistency' (Díaz Lizé, 2022): Fragmentation in negotiations and the duality of humanitarianism, both of which have a significant influence by practices of silence.

The term 'assemblage' is particularly relevant because it is 'constructed through very specific historical processes, in which language plays an important but not constitutive role' (De Landa, 2016). Looking at its origins, the notion of 'assemblage' comes from philosophy (Deleuze, et al., 1980) and has been taken up in different types of anthropological research[13] to understand complex social situations that have evolved from relationships of power, time, and control (Yu, 2013). Based on the existing literature, we retain Ong and Collier's (2007) definition of assemblage as 'alignments of technical and administrative practices extract and give intelligibility to new spaces by decoding and encoding environments'. We might also note three salient features: assemblage is characterised by both 'strategic necessity' (Foucault, 1994) and 'unintentional coordination' (Naepels, 2019) between different actors seeking to deploy their discourses, actions, and resources. In this vein, Delanda (2016) views assemblages as 'contingently obligatory rather than logically necessary'. Thus, Olds and Thrift (2005) argue that we should not think of 'these computing centres as homogeneous, welded structures, or even as a loosely constrained constitution, but rather as "functions" that involve particular populations, territories, affects, events – "with"'.

Moreover, the assemblage underlines the importance of heterogeneity. This trait allows us to understand the 'singular' aspect of social or political phenomena as 'a unity that retains its multiplicity of heterogeneous elements and brings them together into a common vector while modifying but not eliminating their diverse properties' (Rabinow, 2011). As a result, it generates persistent conundrums about 'process' and 'relationship' instead of leading to systematic understandings of these *topos* of classical social theory and the everyday discourse it has shaped (Marcus and Saka, 2006). Finally, this approach allows us to analyse 'an object with the materiality and stability of classical metaphors of structure, but the intent in its aesthetic uses is precisely to undermine these ideas of structure' (ibid., 2006).

Fragmentation in the negotiations

In this section, we seek to analyse how the 'in-betweenness' among humanitarian actors in the field shapes or distorts exchange practices. How do they coordinate, and what are the limits of the forms of engagement between them? During the interviews, each organisation emphasised the importance of a 'careful distance' between civil society, international cooperation, and the government. This separation does not aim for the actors' autonomy but instead results from the confusion and suspicion of the 'arbitrary', 'disjointed', or 'inorganic' functioning attributed to the state, its institutions, as well as its allies, including international cooperation.

To begin, dispersion refers to both the distribution of information and actors' strategies. The collection of information is more important than how to quantify and qualify a crisis, as we saw in the first section. On this point, the actors who collect information about the crisis cannot distribute it, nor do they have access to spaces where the state can legitimise it. As the director of an NGO working in a precarious community in Caracas points out, 'In a hostile environment, the important thing is not to negotiate, but to access'. However, how to use the testimonies and evidence obtained once on the ground? International organisations follow government protocols, which we have described as silencing apparatus, to obtain certain agreements, while local organisations ignore or reject these processes. Thus, there is a gap between international and local organisations in managing norms and codes, in which the institutional capacities of international cooperation ultimately prevail, 'overstating the degree to which bureaucratic practices can create order' (Dunn, 2012). This configuration affects how political phenomena are defined and mobilised, as summarised by a director of a local association: 'Currently, if you talk about peace, it's because you're taking advantage of the government's simulation; if you talk about negotiation, you're from the government; if you talk about human rights, you're in frustration'. Such perceptions show how the inability to negotiate can turn into an unwillingness to do so. Finally, the decrease in interactions also reduces the capacity for political action, providing an open field for international cooperation to manage humanitarian issues as they seem more appropriate.

On the other hand, strategic dispersion is a term used by local NGOs in their sporadic approach to government and to describe the coordination between international cooperation and local NGOs. In both situations, there is a gap that we wish to highlight. First, local associations have tried to group to improve the dialogues and demands that they inevitably must present to the government when other options have been exhausted. For this purpose, a group is considered more 'diplomatic' and another more 'denunciatory'. The former is led by a manager of an organisation for the treatment of chronic diseases and malnutrition, who explains that discussions with the government have been used for concrete actions: Reactivating electricity services in hospitals, recovering treatments seized by the military, or protecting a humanitarian facility that violates the procedures of the law in the event of a police requisition, among others. These actions, considered minimal by local associations, demonstrate that the 'exceptional' interactions are agreements that have not been formalised. Second, the international cooperation decided to set up training and discussion meetings to continue progressing in the field. According to the interviewees, these meetings positively impact the perception of the role of international cooperation, as they show its complementarity with the communities and local authorities. However, national authorities can interrupt their presence if reports are published on the functioning of these roundtables. Local NGOs need more access to these spaces, as the government has promoted its civil society to be included in the discussions, questioning the role of local humanitarian organisations. Finally, some international cooperation agencies question the identity of local associations as humanitarians. This issue has led to a questioning of their presence at political tables, creating confusion about the role they should play and further dispersing their activities depending on the usefulness or legitimacy they can offer in each situation.

According to the interviews, the main consequence of fragmentation is the prevalence of individual interests over morality based on certain humanitarian or collective principles. In a way, this form of dispersed action, in the name of neutrality and access to the field, privileges inconsistent and quantifiable results (distribution of stocks, food, cash, and medicine) rather than the expansion of negotiations with actors from different factions to reach a broader social scope.

Duality of humanitarianism

Complementing the work of Cullen Dunn (2012), who points out that 'new regimes based on humanitarianism are much more limited in scope than their ambitions suggest', we found that the scope of humanitarian practices in Venezuelan shows a duality between (i) the extent of its engagement and (ii) its capacities for action. I will use these two points as coordinates to position the circumstances of constant evolution between the practices of the Venezuelan authoritarian regime and the expectations of local organisations.

First, in international sanctions contexts, Bala Akal (2022) examines the cases of Nairobi, Syria, and Afghanistan to propose 'tacit local engagement' as a practical, unform form 'that takes place at the local level without any formal guidance or direction from the top leadership'. Indeed, in our study, we also did not observe any formal directives to guide the effectiveness or appropriateness of meetings, discussions, or joint actions between international cooperation and the government. In these cases, it is problematic to define the role of neutrality, as, in practice, some actors define it as 'how compatible one can be with regime officials'. I have met humanitarian officials who are former government officials and have become the best mediators. However, they are also the ones who follow the (written) rules the least, as everyday practices and gestures of silence orient them towards, for example, recognition, gratitude, and solidarity with the regime and its power structures. On another level, local associations point out that the arrival of international cooperation in Venezuela has not increased the impact or involvement of their actions in the field. In response, the head of an international organisation explains: 'We do not arrive to fulfil the agenda of the needs of the community-based organisations, but to try to do humanitarian work according to the permits and agreements we manage to obtain'. These testimonies allow us to establish that the engagement of international humanitarian actors in the field is extremely limited by international norms of humanitarian bureaucracy, which do not provide specific guidelines in relations with the authorities of an autocratic regime. However, the 'spillovers' from the norms are numerous. They include the lack of a diverse political agenda in informal negotiations, the deficiency of empowering local organisations, or the creation of a collective agenda. At the same time, we also observe that humanitarian commitment has evolved as the capacity of international organisations to act has grown, which brings us to the second point.

International and local organisation officials report that their engagement and complementarity with the regime can reduce or expand their capacity to act. This informal 'indicator' allows for measuring the balance between humanitarian and government offers. Considering that humanitarian aid raises several suspicions within the regime, as many officials still see it as a form of opposition to revolutionary policies, humanitarians need to show how bank transfers do not compete with government 'bonuses'. To this end, organisations highlight a few precautionary measures; not using the same payment platforms as those used by opposition parties, not working in territories where there are no regime programmes, and having an ongoing dialogue with local community leaders, who are the ones who ultimately decide whether a programmes is maintained or discontinued, regardless of its impact on the community.

Despite these restrictions or modes of action, international humanitarian aid remains the primary actor that contains the abuses of authoritarian power, according to a large majority of local organisations. First, the presence of international organisations generates greater visibility of repressive actions, which, according to the interviewees, reduces the intensity of aggression, even if the threats remain latent. In this sense, the proximity and complementarity of humanitarian actors to the authoritarian regime play an ambivalent role. Sometimes it legitimises the silences, and sometimes it makes visible the human rights violations. The unanswered question is whether the well being of the minimum will serve to build actions that will reduce the vulnerability of those with the mandate to respond to the maximum. Here, there is an ambiguity that local organisations continually confront: what is the right balance between containing authoritarianism and preserving its humanitarian policies?

Notes

1 Since 2019, a de facto dollarisation process can be observed that, while the regime has deregulated it, it is not yet formalised. See Luján (2022a, 2022b).
2 Although all humanitarian crises are complex, the *Encyclopaedia Brittanica* defines it as a 'type of disaster event that is caused by and results in a complicated set of social, medical, and often political circumstances, usually leading to great human suffering and death and requiring external assistance and aid. Complex humanitarian emergencies (CHEs) are associated with various factors, such as war, poverty, overpopulation, human-caused environmental destruction and change, and natural disasters. The United Nations (UN) considers a CHE to be a crisis involving multiple causes and requiring a broad and integrated response with long-term political and peacekeeping efforts' (Pakes, 2019).
3 One could also name other groups that have mobilised the notion of 'humanitarian crisis', such as the church or diplomatic corps. However, we do not focus on these other groups because they have not been active in advocating, defending, or challenging the humanitarian crisis in the country, although some people from the Church have maintained an individual commitment to certain territorial issues, especially regarding the violence in the country.

4 Some studies have shown how humanitarianism is inextricably linked to media reporting of disaster and suffering, advancing the idea of 'mediatisation' and 'commodification' of the aid and development sector (Benthall, 1993; Vestergaard, 2008, 2011). Indeed, in today's mediated world, visual images play a central role in determining which violence is 'redeemed' or acknowledged (Tester, 2001). According to Paulmann (2019), this is why the media plays a crucial role in setting public agendas, stirring up emotions, and fanning public debate. The central role of emotion and sympathy allows Boltanski (1993) to introduce the notion of the 'politics of pity' and the 'crisis of pity', showing that the urgency of action to end suffering always prevails over considerations of justice. Extending this reflection, Chouliaraki (2006, 2013) analyses the ethical role of the media and how certain scenes of suffering are interpreted on television as 'strategic moral discourses capable of eliciting viewers' emotions. In addition, Cottle and Nolan (2007) point out that aid agencies are increasingly entangled with media predilections, and their organisational integrity may be compromised. As summarised by Vestergaard (2011), humanitarian organisations are caught in a tension between commercial strategies for visibility and public skepticism toward a mediated morality, which is referred to as 'compassion fatigue' (Vestergaard, 2011). Finally, de Genova (2013) analyses how spectacularity can also aim to exclude those who are displayed on stage.

5 See Garlin Politis (2021).

6 Morales (2022) explains that this is a strategy that counts on the support of the Organisation of American States and the belligerence of its secretary general, Luis Almagro, to show the world 'the nature of the government of Nicolás Maduro'. See BBC News (2019).

7 For the repertoire and impacts of U.S. economic sanctions imposed on Venezuela, see Montenegro (2021). While economic sanctions on Venezuela have been in place since 2014, in 2018 they are generalised and prohibit transactions or financing related to the purchase of any debt owed to the Government of Venezuela, as well as the sale, transfer, assignment, or pledge of collateral of the Government of Venezuela and any equity interest in any entity in which the Government of Venezuela has a 50% or greater ownership interest (Montenegro, 2021). These sanctions inevitably impact on humanitarian organisations working with schools, hospitals, or public structures owned by the state, further affecting conditions, provisioning, and access to resources.

8 See La informacion (2019) and Reuters (2021).

9 Although in 1999, former President Hugo Chávez rejected the US government's offer to rebuild the coastal strip of Caracas devastated by the Vargas landslide, and Chávez feared that the US Marines would 'invade' the country. In this text, we do not address the denial of access to humanitarian aid but rather the denial of the crisis and its consequences on the functioning of humanitarian aid. On the former topic, see Labonte and Edgerton (2013).

10 See Infobae (2013).

11 Based on a total of 28.7 million people in Venezuela by 2021, the results of Hum-Venezuela's measurement (2022) show that multidimensional poverty affects 68.7% of the population and, on average, for more than 50% of the population, humanitarian needs present high levels of severity: 65.7% in food, 56% in health, 55.5% in water and sanitation and 54.8% in education. More specifically, the increase of people with humanitarian needs reaches 19.1 million in health, water, and sanitation, 18.7 million in food, and 6.2 million children and adolescents with severe difficulties receiving primary education or are out of the education system. Of these people, 55%, on average, have severe humanitarian needs: 65.7% in food, 56% in health, 55.5% in water and sanitation, and 54.8% in education.

12 See OEA (2022).
13 Ong and Collier (2009) published a collective work entitled 'Global Assemblages' which defines these assemblages as 'domains in which the forms and values of individual and collective existence are problematised or at stake, in the sense that they are subject to technological, political, and ethical reflection and intervention'. Anna Tsing (2017) uses the term assemblages as a global supply chain of contaminated diversity, indeterminacy, and precariousness. More recently, Díaz Lizé (2022) uses the term 'place-assemblage of death' to understand the arrangement of heterogeneous entities composed of different apparatuses of political and economic sovereignty, properties and appropriations of land, subsoil, roads, and people, which function together, without necessarily having organic connections.

References

Acosta, Y. (2018). Sufrimiento psicosocial del siglo XXI: Venezuela y la Revolución. *Revista de Investigacion Psicologica* 19, 111–134.

Agamben, G. (2009). *'What Is an Apparatus?' and other Essays*. Stanford, CA: Stanford University Press.

Alvarado, N. (2004). Gestión social, pobreza y exclusión en Venezuela a la luz de las misiones sociales. Balance y perspectivas (2003–2004). *Revista Venezolana de Análisis de Coyuntura*, X(2), 25–56.

Aponte Blank, C. (2017a). La política social durante la gestión de Maduro (2013–2016). *SIC* 794, 176–180.

Aponte Blank, C. (2017b). La política social formulada durante las gestiones presidenciales de Hugo Chávez : 1999–2012. *Espacios Publicos* 45, 67–95.

Atlani-Duault, L. (2011). Introduction. Les figures de l'aide internationale. *Ethnologie Française*, 41(3), 389. https://doi.org/10.3917/ethn.113.0389

Azkoul, J., Salas, A., and Gómez-Pérez, R. (2019). Emergencia Humanitaria Compleja En Venezuela. Realismo Mágico De Alto Nivel. *Revista Venezolana de Endocrinología y Metabolismo* 17(2), 55–60.

Bala Akal, A. (2022). *Tacit Engagement as a Form of Remote Management. Risk Aversity in the Face of Sanctions Regimes*. NCHS PAPER 7. Peace Research Institute Oslo. https://www.humanitarianstudies.no/wp-content/uploads/NCHS-paper-07-June-2022-Tacit-engagement-as-a-form-of-remote-management-Risk-aversity-in-the-face-of-sanctions-regimes.pdf

BBC News. (2019). *Crisis en Venezuela : Países europeos reconocen a Juan Guaidó como « presidente encargado » y crece la tensión internacional*. https://www.bbc.com/mundo/noticias-america-latina-47115699

BBC News. (2020). *Crisis en Venezuela : Una investigación de la ONU acusa a Maduro de crímenes de lesa humanidad y su canciller dice que son « falsedades » de « gobiernos subordinados a Washington »*. https://www.bbc.com/mundo/noticias-america-latina-54176459

Benthall, J. (1993). *Disasters, Relief and the Media*. London: I.B. Tauris.

Boltanski, L. (1993). *La Souffrance à distance. Morale humanitaire, médias et politique*. Éditions Métailié; Cairn.info. https://www.cairn.info/la-souffrance-a-distance--9782864241641.htm

Bull, B., and Rosales, A. (2020). The Crisis in Venezuela : Drivers, Transitions, and Pathways. *European Review of Latin American and Caribbean Studies* 0(109), 1.

Chinea, E. and Pons, C. (2016). *Maduro decreta estado de emergencia en Venezuela por « catastrófico » desempeño económico.* https://www.reuters.com/article/economia-venezuela-emergencia-idLTAKCN0UT26X

Chouliaraki, L. (2006). *The Spectatorship of Suffering.* London: SAGE Publications.

Chouliaraki, L. (2013). *The Ironic Spectator : Solidarity in the Age of Post-humanitarianism.* Cambridge: Polity Press.

Cohen, S. (2001). *States of Denial : Knowing about Atrocities and Suffering.* Cambridge: Polity; Hoboken, NJ: Blackwell Publishers.

Cottle, S. and Nolan, D. (2007). Global Humanitarianism and the Changing Aid-media field. *Journalism Studies* 8(6), 862–878.

De Genova, N. (2013). Spectacles of Migrant 'Illegality' : The Scene of Exclusion, the Obscene of Inclusion. *Ethnic and Racial Studies* 36(7), 1180–1198.

De Landa, M. (2016). *Assemblage Theory.* Edinburgh: Edinburgh University Press.

De Lauri, A. (ed.). (2016). *The Politics of Humanitarianism : Power, Ideology and Aid.* London: I.B. Tauris.

Deleuze, G., Guattari, F., and Deleuze, G. (1980). *Mille plateaux.* Paris: Éditions de minuit.

Delgado, M. I. (2022). *Maduro culpa a los médicos por la crisis en los hospitales públicos.* https://www.perfil.com/noticias/internacional/maduro-culpa-a-los-medicos-por-la-crisis-en-los-hospitales-publicos.phtml

D'Elia, Y. (2006). *Las misiones sociales en Venezuela : Una aproximación a su comprensión y análisis.* https://elibro.net/ereader/elibrodemo/76202

Díaz Lizé. (2022). D'Atacama au Sonora : Assemblages d'une inquiétante étrangeté. *Condition humaine / Conditions politiques*, 3. http://revues.mshparisnord.fr/chcp/index.php?id=760

Dodier, N. and Barbot, J. (2016). La force des dispositifs. *Annales. Histoire, Sciences Sociales*, 71e année(2), 421–450. Cairn.info.

Dunn, E. C. (2012). The Chaos of Humanitarian Aid : Adhocracy in the Republic of Georgia. *Humanity: An International Journal of Human Rights, Humanitarianism, and Development* 3(1), 1–23.

El Comercio. (2018). *Cabello dice que migración venezolana es una campaña contra Maduro.* https://elcomercio.pe/mundo/latinoamerica/diosdado-cabello-dice-migracion-venezolanos-campana-nicolas-maduro-noticia-550549-noticia/

Fassin, D. and Vasquez, P. (2005). Humanitarian Exception as the Rule : The Political Theology of the 1999 Tragedia in Venezuela. *American Ethnologist* 32(3), 389–405.

Foucault, M. (1994). *Dits et écrits, 1954-1988. IV. 1980-1988.* Paris: Gallimard.

FRANCE24. (2018). *Venezuela niega la crisis migratoria que desborda a América Latina.* https://www.france24.com/es/20180829-venezuela-niega-la-crisis-migratoria-que-desborda-america-latina

Garlin Politis, F. G. (2021). Chacun sa fête : Désaccords humanitaires et confrontations politiques : Les concerts Venezuela Live Aid et Hands Off Venezuela, 85–106. In: Atlani-Duault, L. & Velasco-Pufleau, L. (éds.). *Lieux de mémoire sonore: Des sons pour survivre, des sons pour tuer.* Éditions de la Maison des sciences de l'homme. http://books.openedition.org/editionsmsh/29045

Glasius, M. (2018). What Authoritarianism Is ... and Is Not: A Practice Perspective. *International Affairs* 94(3), 515–533.

Hall, S. G. F. and Ambrosio, T. (2017). Authoritarian Learning : A Conceptual Overview. *East European Politics* 33(2), 143–161.

Heydemann, S. and Leenders, R. (2011). Authoritarian Learning and Authoritarian Resilience: Regime Responses to the 'Arab Awakening'. *Globalizations* 8(5), 647–653.

HumVenezuela. (2022). *Informe de seguimiento a los impactos de la Emergencia Humanitaria Compleja en Venezuela tras el confinamiento por la pandemia de COVID.* HumVenezuela.

Infobae. (2013). Canciller venezolano : « ¿Ustedes quieren patria o papel higiénico? » *Infobae.* https://www.infobae.com/2013/06/24/716863-canciller-venezolano-ustedes-quieren-patria-o-papel-higienico/

Lainformacion.(2019). *Guaidó pide a la UE y España sanciones contra Maduro para forzar su salida.* https://www.lainformacion.com/mundo/guaido-pide-ue-mas-sanciones-gobierno-de-maduro/6501068/

Labonte, M. T. and Edgerton, A. C. (2013). Towards a Typology of Humanitarian Access Denial. *Third World Quarterly* 34(1), 39–57.

Luján, R. (2022a). *La dolarización en Venezuela y su informalidad, más allá de la narrativa chavista.* https://www.bloomberglinea.com/2022/04/21/la-dolarizacion-en-venezuela-y-su-informalidad-mas-alla-de-la-narrativa-chavista/

Luján, R. (2022b). *¿Por qué no se oficializa la dolarización en Venezuela?* https://www.bloomberglinea.com/2022/05/26/por-que-no-se-oficializa-la-dolarizacion-en-venezuela/

Magone, C., Neuman, M., and Weissman, F. (eds.). (2011). *Humanitarian Negotiations Revealed: The MSF Experience.* London: Hurst & Co.

Marcus, G. E. and Saka, E. (2006). Assemblage. *Theory, Culture & Society* 23(2–3), 101–106.

Martínez, J. and Andréani, F. (2020). Radiographie du commandantisme vénézuélien: Du « chavisme » au « madurisme ». *Multitudes n°81*(4), 183. https://doi.org/10.3917/mult.081.0183

Masco, J. (2017). The Crisis in Crisis. *Current Anthropology* 58(S15), S65–S76.

Montenegro, Y. A. (2021). Sanciones impuestas por Estados Unidos a Venezuela : Consecuencias regionales. *Revista de Relaciones Internacionales, Estrategia y Seguridad 16*(2), 121–140.

Morales, M. (2022). Reconocimiento internacional de Juan Guaidó y su gobierno encargado luego de tres años : ¿evolución o involución? *Cronica Uno.* https://cronica.uno/reconocimiento-internacional-juan-guaido-gobierno-encargado-tres-anos-evolucion-involucion/

Morin, E. (2012). Pour une crisologie. *Communications* 91(2), 135.

Naepels, M. (2019). *Dans la détresse : Une anthropologie de la vulnérabilité.* Éditions EHESS.

Nail, T. (2017). What is an Assemblage? *SubStance* 46(1), 21–37. https://doi.org/10.1353/sub.2017.0001

OEA. (2022). *La CIDH y la RELE urgen a Venezuela no aprobar el anteproyecto de « Ley de Cooperación Internacional ».* Comunicado de prensa. https://www.oas.org/es/CIDH/jsForm/?File=/es/cidh/prensa/comunicados/2022/130.asp

Olds, K. and Thrift, N. (2005). Cultures on the Brink : Reengineering the Soul of Capitalism—On a Global Scale, 270–290. In: Ong, A. and Collier, S. J. (eds.).

Global Assemblages: Technology, Politics, and Ethics as Anthropological Problems. Hoboken, NJ: Blackwell.

Ong, A. and Collier, S. J. (eds.) (2007). *Global Assemblages.* Hoboken, NJ: Blackwell Publishing Ltd.

Pakes, B. (2019). Complex Humanitarian Emergency. In: *Britannica.* https://www.britannica.com/topic/complex-humanitarian-emergency

Paulmann, J. (ed.) (2019). *Humanitarianism & Media : 1900 to the Present.* New York: Berghahn Books.

Peters, S. (2019). Sociedades rentistas : Claves para entender la crisis venezolana. *European Review of Latin American and Caribbean Studies, 108,* Art. 108.

Puccio-Den, D. (2017). De l'honneur à la responsabilité : Les métamorphoses du sujet mafieux. *L'Homme* 223–224, 63–99.

Puccio-Den, D. (2019). Mafiacraft : How to Do Things with Silence. *HAU: Journal of Ethnographic Theory* 9(3), 599–618.

Rabinow, P. (2011). *The Accompaniment : Assembling the Contemporary.* Chicago, IL: University of Chicago Press.

Reuters. (2021). *Líder opositor de Venezuela Guaidó pide levantamiento progresivo de sanciones de EEUU.* https://www.reuters.com/article/venezuela-politica-guaido-idLTAKBN2CS2AW

Roitman, J. L. (2014). *Anti-crisis.* Durham, NC: Duke University Press.

Tester, K. (2001). *Compassion, Morality, and the Media.* Open University.

Tsing, A. L. (2017). *Le champignon de la fin du monde : Sur la possibilité de vivre dans les ruines du capitalisme.* les Empêcheurs de penser en rond-la Découverte.

Van Roekel, E. and De Theije, M. (2020). Hunger in the Land of Plenty : The Complex Humanitarian Crisis in Venezuela. *Anthropology Today* 36(2), 8–12.

Vásquez Lezama, P. (2011). L'action publique humanitaire : La militarisation de la prise en charge des sinistrés de La Tragedia (Venezuela). *Ethnologie Française* 41(3), 473.

Vásquez Lezama, P. (2014). *Le chavisme: Un militarisme compassionnel.* Éditions de la Maison des sciences de l'homme.

Vestergaard, A. (2008). Humanitarian Branding and the Media: The Case of Amnesty International. *Journal of Language and Politics* 7(3), 471–493.

Vestergaard, A. (2011). *Distance and Suffering: Humanitarian Discourse in the Age of Mediatization.*

Yu, J. E. (2013). The use of Deleuze's Theory of Assemblage for Process-oriented Methodology. *Historical Social Research* 38(2), 196–217.

COMMENTARY

Between instrumentalisation, depoliticisation, and legitimation of humanitarian action in Venezuela

Rodrigo Mena

Focusing on Venezuela, this chapter by Garlin Politis is a good example of how humanitarian action can be understood as an *arena*, as depicted by Hilhorst and Jansen (2010), in which multiple actors shape the everyday realities of aid by negotiating, contesting, and using its outcomes to further their interests. The political scenario in Venezuela shapes these interactions in particular ways. Here I would like to highlight two processes suggested in Garlin Politis' chapter: the instrumentalisation and depoliticisation of aid.

The instrumentalisation of aid is as old as aid itself (Barnett, 2012). In the humanitarian arena, it is common to see actors instrumentalising the outcomes of aid for their own agendas and interests (Donini, 2012). Alongside describing this reality, Garlin Politis' chapter also shows how the alliance of opposition parties, the Government of Venezuela, and multiple non-government organisations (NGOs) also instrumentalised the very idea of the existence of a humanitarian crisis. This is important, as declaring a humanitarian crisis is a political act that involves a range of messages that many actors contest, exploit, or remain silent about (Hilhorst and Mena, 2021). The messages can include statements indicating that the government in power is not capable of responding to the needs of the people, the recognition that there is an ongoing socio-economic predicament in the country, or the need to involve actors (many times external) in the implementation of public policy and in the delivery of goods and social services. Each of these three messages has been contested in Venezuela, as depicted in Garlin Politis' chapter.

A reading group discussion on humanitarian action in Latin America (see Mena, et al., 2022) and my ongoing research on the topic in the region suggested the idea that declaring or neglecting a humanitarian crisis is a sensitive topic for Latin-American states. Many countries see accepting the

DOI: 10.4324/9781003316541-17

presence of a humanitarian crisis as a problem of legitimacy, in which the government can be portrayed as failing in its duties. Moreover, humanitarian crises open the door to international aid, which is feared in the region due to possible interventionism from foreign powers. Last but not least, in Latin America, humanitarian crises are associated with images of problems happening elsewhere, such as famines in Africa or war-related conflicts in the Middle East. Governments therefore tend to reject the idea of crises for fear of being associated with such upheavals. In many authoritarian spaces, moreover, the idea of a conflict or large-scale disasters in their territories is usually vetoed, as the regimes themselves often come to power claiming they will solve ongoing crises.

The instrumentalisation of the crises and outcomes of aid, moreover, has resulted in the creation of spaces for collaboration whilst at the same time hindering humanitarian action in Venezuela, a not uncommon paradox in the humanitarian arena (Barnett, 2012; Hilhorst and Jansen, 2010). On the one hand, such instrumentalisation has forced collaboration between governmental actors, NGOs, and civil servants for the provision of aid. These collaborations, however, have introduced multiple dilemmas for the aid actors mentioned in Garlin Politis' chapter, ranging from the limits of humanitarian principles to the possibilities to be seen as legitimising the Government and human rights violations. On the other hand, the chapter indicates that actions such as the 'humanitarian concerts', instead of mobilising and facilitating aid intervention, actually hindered possible negotiations between the Government and opposition groups. Humanitarian actors are also seen as an instruments of political interference and therefore need to be contained. Thus, the instrumentalisation of aid in the case of Venezuela shows how humanitarian organisations can be seen as 'a prize to capture or a threat to neutralise' (DeMars, 2005, in Dijkzeul and Hilhorst, 2016).

Regarding the depoliticisation of aid, the chapter depicts well the tensions behind the historical assumption that humanitarian action can be separated from politics (Donini, 2012; Kleinfeld, 2007). It first illustrates how aid agencies and even opposition groups seek to 'humanitarianise' their actions and so dress them up as ethical and non-political, concealing 'their intended or unintended political roles' (Hilhorst and Jansen, 2010, 1119). Secondly, in Venezuela, the depoliticisation of aid can be seen as a strategy to defuse political sensitivities of 'collaborating with those who would otherwise be considered enemies (strategic depoliticisation) and of remaining safe (coerced depoliticisation)', as described by Desportes and Moyo-Nyoni (2022, 1115), referring to other authoritarian cases.

The depoliticisation of aid, nevertheless, needs to be seen as a political act, particularly when aid becomes part of the delivery of public services and is entangled with government actions and actors at the local level, as the chapter shows. As such, the depoliticisation of aid in Venezuela unveils two key characteristics of a humanitarian arena: the outcomes of aid result from ongoing negotiations between multiple actors, but not every actor is equally powerful in that process. While aid organisations see such collaborations as the only way to survive and use depoliticisation strategies to overcome the tensions and dilemmas of doing so, the Government has the power to impose these collaborations and by so doing ensures that its actions are labelled humanitarian and less political. The (de)politicisation of aid then becomes a legitimation strategy for different actors to interact and respond to the threat that each sees in the other.

As illustrated by these instrumentalisation and depoliticisation processes, Garlin Politis' chapter clearly indicates that humanitarian action is not only driven by the need to aid others and by humanitarian actors' relationship with those affected. It is also driven by those actors' interaction with other actors and by the context in which they operate, with authoritarian and conflict-affected spaces being a particular example (Mena and Hilhorst, 2022). Although these spaces are usually seen as restrictive with little space for an actor's agency, Galin Politis' chapter goes beyond that idea and shows the multiple and dynamic negotiations and actions that actors display to manoeuvre in these contexts. In fact, it seems at moments that these authoritarian spaces, due to their lack of legitimacy, can be more malleable that those more 'democratic' ones with the legitimacy to impose regulations, policies, laws, and frameworks.

While Garlin Politis describes the difficulties of conducting research in Venezuela, the chapter would have benefitted from somehow including the voice of those affected by and receiving humanitarian assistance. In a humanitarian arena, all actors have agency, including those affected, who often claim legitimacy in the system for being the ones in need and the victims of the crises – 'victimcy', as coined by Utas (2005), to represent the agency of self-representing as victim.

The humanitarian arena of Venezuela thus shows how authoritarian and conflict-affected scenarios in Latin America relate with humanitarian practices in particular ways as a result of the specificities of the region in terms of how humanitarian action is conceived and perceived, including the region's history of interventionism and the legitimisation strategies of its countries. More specifically, the chapter by Galin Politis manages to illustrate the everyday realities of aid in an authoritarian scenario: its contestation, depoliticisation and instrumentalisation mechanisms, and how these are negotiated by multiple actors to further their own interests and be able to build an aid *assemblage*.

References

Barnett, M. (2012). The Golden Fleece: Manipulation and Independence in Humanitarian Action, Donini, A. (ed.). *International Review of the Red Cross* 94(887), 1169–1172.

Desportes, I. and Moyo-Nyoni, N. (2022). Depoliticising Disaster Response in a Politically Saturated Context: The Case of the 2016–19 Droughts in Zimbabwe. *Disasters* 46(4), 1098–1120.

Dijkzeul, D. and Hilhorst, D. (2016). Instrumentalisation of Aid in humanitarian Crises, 54–71. In: Heins, V. M., Koddenbrock, K., and Unrau, C. (eds.). *Humanitarianism and Challenges of Cooperation*. London: Routledge. https://doi.org/10.4324/9781315658827

Donini, A. (ed.). (2012). *The Golden Fleece: Manipulation and Independence in Humanitarian Action*. Boulder, CO: Kumarian Press.

Hilhorst, D. and Jansen, B. J. (2010). Humanitarian Space as Arena: A Perspective on the Everyday Politics of Aid. *Development and Change* 41(6), 1117–1139.

Hilhorst, D. and Mena, R. (2021). When Covid-19 Meets Conflict: Politics of the Pandemic Response in Fragile and Conflict-affected States. *Disasters* 45(S1), S174–S194.

Kleinfeld, M. (2007). Misreading the Post-tsunami Political Landscape in Sri Lanka: The Myth of Humanitarian Space. *Space and Polity* 11(2), 169–184.

Mena, R., Aparicio, J. R., and Villacis, G. (2022, December 16). Humanitarian Action in Latin America: Same but Different? Facultad de Ciencias Sociales, Uniandes. Observatorio Humanitario de América Latina y el Caribe. https://cienciassociales.uniandes.edu.co/observatorio-humanitario-de-america-latina/humanitarian-action-in-latin-america-same-but-different/

Mena, R. and Hilhorst, D. (2022). Path Dependency When Prioritising Disaster and Humanitarian Response under High Levels of Conflict: A Qualitative Case Study in South Sudan. *Journal of International Humanitarian Action* 7(1), 5.

Utas, M. (2005). Victimcy, Girlfriending, Soldiering: Tactic Agency in a Young Woman's Social Navigation of the Liberian War Zone. *Anthropological Quarterly* 78(2), 403–430.

9

MOPPING UP, KEEPING DOWN, AND PROPPING UP

Ethical dilemmas in humanitarian negotiations with authoritarian regimes

Kristoffer Lidén and Kristina Roepstorff[1]

Introduction

From the level of formal negotiations with governments to ad hoc negotiations at the frontlines of operations, humanitarian agencies face hard ethical choices on a daily basis: between whom to help and whom to let die, between ensuring the safety of staff and the safety of others, and between principled action and pragmatic compromises. When confronted with partisan demands from political authorities for serving their interests, favouring their supporters or keeping silent about atrocities, they are left with the question of where to draw their red lines beyond which they can no longer justify a deal.

Forced to choose between uncomfortable compromises and inaction, this often leaves agencies operating in normative grey zones. In addition to instrumental concerns of how to achieve one's objectives and legal concerns of how to do so in a lawful manner, these choices raise the ethical question of what is morally right and wrong to do, independent of whether it serves the interests of the agency. When forced to choose between two options that both seem ethically required but that cannot possibly be combined – like assisting victims of atrocities, on the one hand, and rejecting to compensate the perpetrators for access to the victims, on the other – it is an ethical dilemma. In these types of settings, 'doing no harm' (Anderson, 1999) may be easier said than done and turn into questions of the lesser evil when trying to do something morally good.

As seen from the preceding chapters of this book, these tough decisions are further aggravated when faced with authoritarian political actors and institutions (also ALNAP, 2022, 37, 38). Caught in a web of 'authoritarian practices' that actively undermine the accountability of authorities to their

DOI: 10.4324/9781003316541-18

citizens (Glasius, 2018, 525), humanitarian actors risk becoming political instruments for authoritarian rulers:

> The difficult balancing act for an agency operating in such a context is defining at what point compliance turns into complicity. Humanitarian agencies are forced to balance pragmatism against principles in their relation with state power, and accept compromises set by sovereign states, including restrictions on geographic access, programmatic options, and modalities of work.
>
> *(del Valle and Healy, 2013, 198)*

Or in the words of Fernando Politis in this book: 'What is the right balance between containing authoritarianism and preserving its humanitarian policies?' (Chapter 8). In effect, humanitarian agencies face an 'authoritarian dilemma' of either accepting a role as a prolonged arm of authoritarian rulers or withdrawing their helping hand from people under the rulers' control. With the necessity of oversimplification, we suggest distinguishing this dilemma into three general types, where *helping people in dire need requires*: (1) *mopping up* after authorities that cause humanitarian problems; (2) *keeping down* minorities or political opposition; and (3) *propping up* the authorities by becoming an ad hoc part of the governance apparatus.[2] These may occur in isolation but usually appear in various combinations.

While the ultimate question for humanitarians is whether to withdraw under these circumstances, the dilemmas are reflected in pervasive questions of which tasks to take on and how to carry them out (del Valle and Healy, 2013; Walton, 2015). In practice, the authoritarian dilemma thus sets the stage for negotiations on compromises and alternatives at various levels, from international forums and government offices to local councils and roadblocks. Given a reliance on harmonising with the political interests of states, international humanitarian law (IHL) and humanitarian organisations have always had to balance between humanitarian ideals and the art of the possible (Barnett, 2011, 33). This has entailed continuous critiques of resorting to 'band aid' where more radical political solutions are needed (e.g., Keen, 2008; Rieff, 2002; Terry, 2002). The advantage of bringing ethical analysis into this equation is not so much to answer the 'Hamlet question' of 'to be or not to be' in a given setting but to help thinking about what exactly the ethical problems are and how they can be addressed in pursuit of humanitarian objectives.

As the previous chapters have also shown, humanitarians have little clout for changing the policies of authoritarian counterparts. It is nonetheless expected that they do whatever they can to uphold the humanitarian principles of humanity, impartiality, neutrality and independence and that they reduce their contribution to harm. As Healy and Cunningham argue in Chapter 1, this is nearly impossible when relying on the collaboration of authorities wittingly committing atrocities and limiting access to their victims. Under such circumstances, compromising on one's principles and lending the authorities a hand in order to alleviate suffering does not automatically translate into moral blameworthiness, however. Exactly the fact that the authorities may have caused the harm in any case and that the agencies have no options but to strike 'dirty deals' in order to assist the victims can make their role ethically justified. As Healy and Cunningham also argue, authoritarian regulation of humanitarian work nonetheless comes on a spectrum from such egregious cases to situations where the authorities act upon reasonable security concerns or even justified resentments with humanitarian agencies. Handling the ethics of the humanitarian's authoritarian dilemmas thus requires considering them in concrete settings and distinguishing between their various components. The purpose of this chapter is to lay the foundation for such analysis. As such, we do not say much about the very negotiations with authoritarian regimes but about the ethical problems that international humanitarian agencies are confronted within these situations (be they nongovernmental like MSF and Oxfam or governmental like the UN).

For this purpose, we begin this chapter by relating the authoritarian dilemmas to more general ethical problems in humanitarian action and to the problem of moral complicity in particular. We then introduce a set of ethical positions that place these ethical problems in different perspectives. These are *deontology*, concentrating on moral duties; *consequentialism*, focusing on effects rather than motives; *pluralism*, subjecting international ethics to the principle of state sovereignty; and *solidarism*, seeing state sovereignty as secondary to universal moral standards. Against this theoretical backdrop, we turn to the three types of authoritarian dilemmas identified above. First, we introduce them and relate them to prominent examples from the literature and to the preceding chapters of this book. Second, we analyse examples from the chapters on Venezuela, Syria and Ethiopia, respectively, regarding the question of moral complicity. Third, we discuss whether such complicity would be ethically justified by applying the four ethical positions.

Ethical problems in humanitarian action

Quoting a humanitarian negotiator par excellence, Jan Egeland: 'If you are there to help the victims from the depths of hell, you have to speak to the devil' (Hoge, 2004). As such, humanitarian negotiations exemplify what has elsewhere been discussed as moral dilemmas, tragic choices, 'dirty hands' problems, emergency ethics and non-ideal theory (Slim, 2015, 163–167). Recurrent dilemmas that were identified in a survey by the Centre of Competence on Humanitarian Negotiation (CCHN) in 2017 included: security rules vs. proximity to beneficiaries; denunciation/advocacy vs. silent cooperation;

impartial assistance vs. conditional assistance; how much to compromise on international humanitarian law and human rights; and whether to engage with 'controversial' stakeholders in the first place, putting one's reputation at risk (CCHN, 2019, 11). All these dilemmas are relevant to negotiations with authoritarian rulers and when working under their rule. They reflect the familiar ethical quandary of how to do good without doing too much harm (Ahmad and Smith, 2018; Anderson, 1999; Slim, 1997). Meanwhile, international humanitarian organisations are themselves subject to ethical critique and soul-searching. Common themes include Western political dependencies, cultural biases and lacking impact, entailing calls for localising and decolonising aid and enhancing trust in humanitarian agencies (Lidén, 2019; Roepstorff, 2020).

Dilemmas like that of accepting political demands from oppressive regimes in order to gain access to people in desperate need are commonly experienced by humanitarian workers as truly ethical dilemmas (Broussard, et al., 2019; Grace, 2020). Indeed, the purposes of humanitarian organisations and the moral engagement of their staff may be closely intertwined (Malkki, 2015), meaning that it is often hard to distinguish instrumental calculations of operations from ethical arguments.[3] Although being closely interconnected, these are nonetheless different types of questions: where instrumental reasoning is about what it takes to reach a particular goal, while ethical/moral reasoning is about whether this goal and the means to harmonise with fundamental values (cf. Korsgaard, 1997; Wolff, 2020, 10).[4]

In *Humanitarian Ethics* (2015, 183–230), Hugo Slim has provided a comprehensive overview of persistent ethical problems in humanitarian action that are helpful for analysing the authoritarian dilemmas that are discussed in this chapter. These general problems include risks of association with political and military representatives who are pursuing inhumane policies; risks of complicity by cooperating with perpetrators of wrongdoing in order to alleviate the effects of their wrongs; and the risk of silence about atrocities in order to assist the victims when one should rather have spoken out to alert the outside world to the need for concerted action. Classic examples include the collaboration of the Red Cross with Nazi authorities in concentration camps during the Second World War (Favez, 1999). Few doubt that such collaboration was the morally right thing to do if it genuinely helped a significant number of people without entailing too high political costs by lending the Nazis a hand (complicity) and a humanitarian touch of legitimacy (association). Yet, the question remains how they should have worked within these confines – a question that entailed substantial soul searching and resulted in the eventual codification of what is now known as the humanitarian principles. Indeed, the decision of the ICRC not to alert the world to early evidence of the Holocaust (silence) in order to maintain the trust of the authorities has been much criticised (Barnett, 2011, 157).

In *Complicity and Compromise* (2013), Chiara Lepora and Robert E. Goodin criticise the common conflation of phenomena like connivance, contiguity, collusion, collaboration, condoning, consortium, conspiring and full joint wrongdoing into the general label of complicity. They show how complicity – contributing to wrongs done by others – comes on a sliding scale where these various meanings have distinct roles:

> At one end of the scale (indeed, 'off the scale': more than 'complicit' on our view) are people who act in unison. We call them 'co-principals'. They are full partners in the wrongdoing. [...] At the other end of the scale are people whose actions are not at all causally connected to the wrongdoing, or people who had no way of knowing that what they were doing could have contributed to the wrongdoing of others. In between are various gradations of causal distance, knowledge, and contribution, and hence complicity.
>
> *(Lepora and Goodin, 2013, 8)*

As we see from this quote, the degree of complicity relies on a range of factors: how bad the wrongdoing is, whether the actor *knows* about the wrongdoing and of their contribution to it, whether they act voluntarily, the extent of their causal contribution, and whether they share the purpose of the principal wrongdoer (Lepora and Goodin, 2013, 102–110). While legal complicity tends to concentrate on the most unison types where all these criteria are fulfilled, moral complicity concerns the whole spectrum. Although Slim's distinction between association, complicity and silence is helpful in highlighting the element of causal contribution in 'complicity', the moral problems of 'association' and 'silence' also relate to their place in this broader scheme of moral complicity.

The reason why complicity is such a central concern and 'a source of significant moral unease' for humanitarian actors is evidently that they work in settings of extensive harm (Buth, et al., 2018, 299). When operating under the control of authoritarian regimes that neglect, repress and exploit their population, the problem is reinforced. Then the humanitarian agencies may not only get entangled in the responsibility of the authorities for the humanitarian problems but may be accused of contributing to their general wrongdoing as a harmful regime. This is where the distinction between the elements of mopping up, keeping down and propping up comes in – where the former relates to the reproduction of the humanitarian problem, while the latter two concern two aspects of the broader political effects of humanitarian action. With the above 'complicity formula', the extent to which this is morally problematic relies on how bad the regimes are, the significance of the agencies' contribution, their awareness of the wrongs and of their contribution to it, the extent to which they have a choice to act otherwise, and whether they actually share the political purpose of the regimes. The latter may be rare, but even without in any way endorsing the aims of the wrongdoing, humanitarians may 'have to do things that they recognize will have the effect of furthering the aims of the bad in order to do any good' (Lepora and Goodin, 2013, 9). In practice, authoritarian regimes may do whatever they can to preclude the knowledge of humanitarians thereof and snaring them into such situations of 'moral entrapment' where all options entail harmful effects for which they cannot be blamed (Slim, 2015, p. 206). Along these lines, Julian C. Sheather and colleagues characterise the designation of unwitting and unwilling contributions to harm as 'complicity' as an unhelpful form of 'moral narcissism' (Buth, et al., 2018). Moreover, it may well be that moral complicity is outweighed by the good that humanitarian agencies do. In addition to establishing whether and to what extent they are morally complicit, it is therefore necessary to consider whether such complicity is justified, all things considered.

Lepora and Goodin argue that even though certain compromises will often be ethically justified all things considered, it is still important to recognise that they do something partially ('*pro tanto*') wrong and that they seek to address this problem. Again, this is where negotiations come in as a central measure for reducing the harmful effects of potentially justifiable complicity. It is therefore not just a question of whether the complicity was justified but also whether it could have been reduced and what agencies do to address its consequences. As Fiona Terry writes in the context of refugee camps in Zaire discussed below:

> [T]here are often steps that could be taken to mitigate the badness of complicity when it is a necessary evil. Complicity can be minimised by careful planning and reflection. The separation of military and civilian populations from the outset in establishing the camps, for example, would have achieved that. But there might have been other ways even after that crucial error had been made. For example: through concerted action on the part of the international community consistently blocking arms-dealing and thus the rearmament of the FAR; through involvement of the civilian population in designing a safer return to their own country; and above all through faster and more equitable political processes in re-establishing security in the area.
>
> *(Terry, 2002, 149)*

Moral complicity is a much-debated problem that pervades the humanitarian enterprise, but it has not been systematically studied in negotiation settings. By taking these settings into account, it becomes easier to determine exactly what the options in the hands of humanitarians actually were. As argued by Lepora and Goodin, moral complicity requires that the contribution to harm could be anticipated: 'The question is not "how much, in the end, the act contributed", but rather how much, in prospect, it could have been expected to contribute' (2013, 106). This makes retrospection on historical cases no less significant, however. Although the involved agencies could not necessarily anticipate what we now see as a pattern of contributions to harm, agencies have a moral responsibility for learning from these lessons when operating in 'non-ideal' settings like manipulative authoritarian regimes.

Dasandi and Erez (2019) point to a distinction between complicity, 'double effect' and 'dirty hands' that may help us understand why many would see certain cases where humanitarians contribute to harm as more problematic than others, even when they end up with the same 'score' in Lepora and Goodin's scheme (see also Chapter 4 in Rubenstein, 2015). They define complicity as limited to action that has the *side-effect* of contributing to wrongdoing committed by others and where the wrongdoing would happen nonetheless, although potentially not to the same extent. *Double effect* is also about negative side effects but involves a situation where these are caused by the humanitarian actor. For instance, to grant legitimacy to an oppressive political regime through association is something that would not happen without the presence of the humanitarian agency. Third, they define *dirty hands* as a situation where an actor wittingly causes a negative effect in order to achieve a higher good. Suppose that an agency actively offers guarantees of non-disclosure of atrocities they might witness in order to gain the trust and cooperation of an armed group. Then, this is not a side effect of the deal they reach but an intended means to a higher end. While people who concentrate on the effects only would see these distinctions as insignificant, those who think about ethics in terms of norms and duties for moral behaviour might see the latter two types as more blameworthy than the former.

In his overview of ethical problems, Slim also brings up a range of problems that are not caused by harmful counterparts but by humanitarian agencies themselves. These are no less important to consider given the direct responsibility involved. The list is long and includes: humanitarian cruelty and disregard when aid workers treat people in inhumane ways; the risk of pity and paternalism by not seeing the problems from the perspectives of the persons they assist; and systemic moral risks of humanitarian power when taking disproportionate responsibility for governing people's lives. Related problems include a negative footprint on communities (e.g., by disrupting local economies), hierarchies between international and local staff or between international and local partners, bureaucratisation that distances decision-making processes from the assisted populations, and excess of zeal when organisations pursue redundant 'humanitarian solutions' to humanitarian problems. As such, international organisations also face internally driven 'authoritarian dilemmas' of lacking representation and accountability when turning into large professional apparatuses of humanitarian governance (Rubenstein, 2015; Stroup and Wong, 2017).

Hence, when considering the ethical justification of humanitarian action 'all things considered', it is insufficient to weigh problems of association, complicity and silence against the benefits. It is also necessary to include harms caused by the humanitarians themselves in the scale of the 'moral costs'. When considering a compromise with an authoritarian regime it is thus equally important to ask whether the ensuing operations would involve paternalism, cultural biases or excessive humanitarian governance. Might other political options be more feasible and consequential in the long run?

Any answer to these ethical questions nonetheless relies on a set of underlying assumptions about the nature and justification of humanitarian action. Instead of taking a position on these descriptive and normative presuppositions and jumping to conclusions, we thus wish to highlight their role in moral reasoning on the authoritarian dilemmas. In this way, you are invited to make up your mind as a reader and apply the framework to analyses of normative debates and concrete cases of your own. The multiplicity of such underlying assumptions evades any neat categorisation, but it is still helpful to introduce some basic distinctions, resulting in a set of 'ideal-typical' positions from which the ethical problems are seen in different perspectives.

Ethical positions

A distinction is commonly made between 'Dunantist' and 'Wilsonian' or 'traditional' and 'new' approaches to humanitarian action (e.g., Gordon and Donini, 2015; Salomons, 2014). The Dunantist traditionalists insist on political neutrality, impartiality and independence, while the Wilsonians see humanitarianism as integral to a larger political picture to which these principles must adapt. In a more recent iteration, the 'new' alternatives to Dunantist approaches have emphasised 'resilience' through local capacities and ownership as a political priority rather than the Wilsonian integration in a global liberal political community (Hilhorst, et al., 2019). In his history of humanitarian action, Michael Barnett describes the gist of the Dunantist and Wilsonian positions as 'emergency' and 'alchemist' forms of humanitarianism. He writes: 'Humanitarianism comes in many shapes and forms, but a critical difference is between a humanitarianism that largely limits itself to saving lives at risk – emergency humanitarianism – and a humanitarianism that adds a desire to remove the causes of suffering—alchemical humanitarianism' (Barnett, 2011, 32). In order to gain access to victims and the cooperation of all parties, emergency humanitarians take no political stance. The alchemist, on the contrary, starts from a political analysis of the situation (be it in a religious or secular sense). Alchemists might still commit to political neutrality as a means for access and source of legitimacy, but the understanding of the problem and its solutions – including the role of humanitarian action therein – remains explicitly political (although not necessarily openly formulated or justified as such).

Instead of juxtaposing these approaches as mutually exclusive, however, we propose to situate them along two dimensions of humanitarian ethics: *professional ethics* isolating humanitarian action from politics while drawing on aspects of medical ethics, social work ethics etc., and *political ethics* seeing humanitarian action as part of a larger political picture. While theories and policies may emphasise one dimension or the other, we would suggest that any humanitarian practice involves a combination of both (cf. Slim, 2015, 112, 113). This also means that designating the dimension of professional ethics as non-political or apolitical is misleading. It would be more precise to call it 'extra-political' in the sense of portraying itself as being 'outside of' normal politics and thereby becoming 'extra political' by turning humanitarian action into a political field of its own. In comparison, *political* humanitarian ethics may be characterised as 'intra-political' in integrating humanitarian action into more general political outlooks.

Rather than explaining the difference between emergency and alchemist practices with the distinction between apolitical and political, we thus see them as the result of more or less conflicting variations within each of these dimensions. Focusing on opposites within each dimension, the extra-political dimension of professional humanitarian ethics may be divided into *deontological* (duty oriented) and *consequentialist* (goal oriented) approaches, where deontologists see adherence to the humanitarian principles as an aim in itself while consequentialists see them as a means to producing humanitarian effects (saving lives and reducing suffering) (Baron, et al., 1997; Slim, 1997). In practice, most approaches involve a combination of these two forms of moral reasoning, but it is still helpful to highlight the difference.

The (intra-)political dimension, with its multitude of political strands, invites a series of distinctions, like between political realists, liberalists, socialists, conservatives, Islamists, Confucians and other strands of political thought. However, in this chapter, we suggest to distinguish all these into *pluralist* and *solidarist* variations, relating to the fundamental question of state sovereignty and international norms (Brown, 1992; Buzan, 2004; Lidén, 2019; Roepstorff, 2013; Wheeler and Dunne, 1996). Pluralists see politics as a largely internal affair of states where the task for international politics is to support self-determined government and uphold an international order of sovereign states (e.g., Jackson, 2000). This is because they see norms and values as relative to bounded political communities, usually defined as states or nations, meaning that there is little moral scope for external political interference. Solidarists, to the contrary, subject political communities to universal norms and ideals, like human rights or material equality (cf. Clark, 2007; Cohen, 2012). As exemplified in the next sections, the solidarist prescriptions

TABLE 9.1 Positions in the Ethics of Humanitarian Action

	Professional Ethics		Political Ethics	
	Deontological	Consequentialist	Pluralist	Solidarist
Contribution to authoritarian rule	Justified if humanitarian principles are upheld	Justified if the benefits outweigh the costs	Justified if the regime is the lawful sovereign authority	Depending on an ethical assessment of the regime

for humanitarian operations in a country will thus rely on their assessment of the political order in question and the prospects for influencing it through humanitarian action. We have summarised these positions in Table 9.1.

The distinction between pluralist and solidarist approaches is for instance key for understanding the origins of the MSF, distancing itself from the ICRC's pluralist commitment to state sovereignty. As recounted by Barnett, MSF combined an ICRC-like (deontological) pledge to apolitical medical ethics with a (solidarist) critique of *raison d'etat* and commitment to human rights (Barnett, 2011, 166, 167). OXFAM, with its emphasis on justice, equality and international solidarity, shared this solidarism but in a more consequentialist development oriented variation (Barnett, 2011, 164).

In practice, pluralist and solidarist positions thus come in deontological and consequentialist variations, and vice versa. As with the latter, they are rarely held in their purest 'ideal-typical' forms but may be conceived as opposites on a continuum that intersects with the continuum between deontological and consequentialist positions. In the following, however, we will isolate the four positions that define the opposites of the continuums in order to develop a framework for a more nuanced analysis. We do so by applying them to the three general authoritarian dilemmas of: (1) *mopping up* after authorities that cause humanitarian problems; (2) *keeping down* minorities or political opposition; and (3) *propping up* the authorities by becoming an ad hoc part of the governance apparatus.

Mopping up

Authoritarian rulers that are responsible for humanitarian problems might not only remain unaffected by humanitarian responses but also benefit from and strategically calculate with them. If keeping a war going or keeping their people in disarray secures their grip on power, then humanitarian agencies may thus paradoxically contribute to prolonging the problem they set out to resolve when 'mopping up' after them. In *Condemned to Repeat*, Fiona Terry identifies four ways in which refugee camps may not only make warfare less costly but provide incentives for its continuation: by providing protection to combatants and affiliated civilians (sanctuary and the provision of food and other necessities); by contributing to the economy (through taxation, trade, aid to public services, subcontracting, employment, black market economy, bribes and being subject to looting); by lending legitimacy to armed groups and political leaders (through collaboration and access to international organisations); and as in instrument for population control (through the steering of migration and the distribution of aid to certain groups and regions) (Terry, 2002, 27–51).

These four dimensions are also relevant when analysing the uses of humanitarian action to authoritarian rulers more broadly. If they can steer the security, revenues, legitimacy and population control that result from humanitarian governance, then their incentives for ending the emergency may at least be weakened. In *The Neutrality Trap* (2021, 90–99), for instance, Carsten Wieland documents how the Assad regime has manipulated humanitarian aid to support its war economy and strategic interests. And in Chapter 1 of this book, Healy and Cunningham recount how the MSF criticised the authoritarian Ethiopian Derg government in 1984 for using famine and the resultant relief efforts as a deliberate war-fighting strategy. The strategic uses by governments of famine against own citizens in settings of civil conflict have been systematically documented, and authors like Alex de Waal, Mark Duffield, David Rieff and David Keen have demonstrated how relief sometimes becomes an integral part of the problem (de Waal, 1997, 2015, 2017; Duffield, 2014; Keen, 2008; Rieff, 2002). As they all recognise, however, the extent to which this is the case remains an empirical question to be considered on a case-by-case basis, and as Slim (2015) emphasises, the causal contribution of humanitarians to war or famine can easily be exaggerated. Moreover, it often appears in these debates like if any causal contribution by humanitarians to harm translates into moral blameworthiness and a reason for withdrawal (Buth, et al., 2018). However, as we have seen, causal contribution alone does not entail complicity, and complicity does not necessarily entail blameworthiness. A more nuanced analysis of their contribution, knowledge and will is therefore required, combined with a consideration of the alternatives and the overall nature and effects of their engagement.

In this book, we have seen several traces of the problem of mopping up. In addition to the above mentioned example of the Ethiopian Derg government, the chapter on MSF experiences with authoritarian regimes includes the story of collaboration of humanitarian agencies with the Sri Lankan authorities when defeating the LTTE. Although the government was democratically elected, its co-optation of international agencies in a military strategy that involved serious war crimes clearly qualifies as 'authoritarian practices' (see also ICG, 2010; Weissman in Magone, et al., 2011). As mentioned, the case of Syria, discussed in Chapter 3, might be the most egregious example of 'mopping up' from recent history – forcing humanitarians into an asset in inhumane warfare by the regime that caused the problem in the first place. This case, however, ticks all the boxes of the authoritarian dilemmas, and we will discuss it in the next section on 'keeping down'.

The recent history of international humanitarian engagement in Afghanistan, both under the Taliban and the Western backed regimes in between, also involves elements of mopping up. Currently, international agencies mop up after the mess since the Taliban regained control of a state reliant on international budget support. When this support stopped and the banking system was sanctioned, millions of Afghans were left in disarray. Humanitarian aid has been the tool for international donors to alleviate the worst human costs of these policies. The Taliban, on its side, has not been willing to accept the political conditions of donors in order to save its people from this humanitarian crisis. Again, the humanitarian assistance may further reduce its incentives for giving in. But does this make the assistance complicit to harm? During the NATO operations in the country, international agencies were co-opted into a role of relieving suffering in support for a counterinsurgency strategy with high civilian costs (Donini, 2012). Again, the agencies may also be accused of keeping down political opposition and propping up the regimes by providing essential social services. In distinction from these, the question of mopping up is concerned with their contribution to policies causing humanitarian problems. Indeed, these three elements may be intricately linked, but evaluating their ethical significance requires that each problem is considered in its own right.

The example we will concentrate on here in this respect is the account by Politis in Chapter 8 of humanitarian operations in Venezuela under the Maduro regime since 2018. In line with the authoritarian playbook of 'sabotaging accountability', the regime denies the existence of a humanitarian crisis in spite of massive migration into neighbouring countries and an estimate of 7–13 million with humanitarian needs. Politis describes how international agencies have to adjust to the regime's priorities and refrain from referring to the situation as a crisis. Provided that the emergency does not result from war or natural disaster but the policies of the regime and the international responses thereto, the collaboration of the agencies with the regime has the effect of not only propping it up but thereby reinforcing humanitarian problem. Indeed, the regime and its supporters would deny that they are to blame and point to the international sanctions as the cause of the problems. While the sanctions have reinforced the economic collapse, the regime's unwillingness to acknowledge it as a crisis and take the necessary measures to address it is nonetheless testament to its authoritarian disregard for the suffering of its people for a higher political cause.

Are international agencies to blame for their subservient collaboration in this situation? Regarding the nature of their contribution, they are both reducing the costs for the regime in continuing its harmful policies and letting the regime take the credits for their efforts by not voicing their disagreement. In addition to these problems of association and silence, this implies a causal contribution to the regime's wrongdoing. One might expect that the agencies are fully aware of this problem and that they may experience it as a problem of (justified) complicity themselves. They are not forced by the regime to engage, so while they do not share in the purpose of the regime as 'co-principals' they can not claim it was not of their choosing. The question nonetheless remains of whether this partial complicity is outweighed by the moral benefits of their engagement. This is where the different ethical positions that were introduced in the former section enter the picture. There is simply no theoretically neutral answer to the question of its ethical justification all things considered, as different professional and political ethical perspectives render these things differently.

According to the deontological perspective, the agencies are justified in mopping up if they can do so without compromising the humanitarian principles. Keeping silent about the crisis and the wrongdoings of the regime is acceptable from this perspective if required for gaining unhindered access to the victims and treating them impartially. Indeed, the classical case of treating victims of war on the battlefield is literally a matter of 'mopping up', becoming an integral component of the war machinery. To Dunantists, this will always be an acceptable cost compared to letting wounded soldiers die in order to potentially reduce future warfare. However, to the extent that the Maduro regime interferes with their work in order to serve its own political interests, it collides with the principles of neutrality and independence. Irrespective of the effects of their work, this would make their work unjustified, all things considered.

Humanitarian consequentialists would rather focus on the overall effects of the engagement: Do the agencies reduce more humanitarian problems than they cause? In this spirit, Terry questions the argument (ascribed to Mary Anderson) that abstaining from alleviating harm will never be an option to humanitarians. If producing more harm than it alleviates, then alleviating the harm is actually harmful (Terry, 2002, 25). That said, consequentialists are even less sceptical than deontologists to compromising with wrongdoers and mopping up after them if necessary for reducing the suffering of their victims. They may also see a longer-term benefit in doing so in order to influence future decisions of the perpetrators on humanitarian matters and maintain a presence in the country in case of future emergencies. On the other hand, consequentialists may also see the humanitarian principles as key to achieving humanitarian outcomes. Without conceiving the principles as moral duties to be respected in their own right, they may therefore see their violation by the Maduro regime as a significant negative effect to be reckoned with in the larger calculus.

As pluralists do not see it as a task for international humanitarian agencies to judge the actions of regimes, they would see the subjection of assistance to the sovereign dictates of the Maduro government as a necessary condition. As such, they are still committed to the principle of neutrality, but in a different reading than that of solidarists. However, they would also not want the agencies to make a qualitative difference to the internal distribution of power in a country – meaning that there is a limit to how much the Maduro regime could benefit from humanitarian assistance. This is more relevant to the problems of keeping down and propping up however – both of which are also at play in this case of Venezuela.

The solidarist position on this matter relies on the political type of solidarism involved. If we are speaking of a liberal orientation opposed to the authoritarianism of Maduro's regime, then mopping up after it is highly problematic. Mopping up after efforts to pressure the Maduro regime in a liberal direction through international sanctions, however, might be justified in this view. As such, a liberal solidarist might also support efforts by international humanitarian agencies to join forces with the Venezuelan opposition instead of either mopping up after the regime or withdrawing. Such engagement may come in the form of subversive 'resistance humanitarianism' working under the radar or outside the reach of a regime, or it may entail support of coercive international 'humanitarian intervention'. A solidarist supporting the political ideology of the Maduro regime would evidently reach the opposite conclusion.

From this analysis, we see that different ethical positions do not only assess the problem of complicity differently but that they also render the 'internal' problems of humanitarian action in different light. From a pluralist perspective, any resemblance of 'humanitarian governance' beyond the control of sovereign authorities will be looked upon with suspicion, while solidarists might want *more* governance of particular sorts. Indeed, the combination of consequentialism and solidarism opens for the most activist forms of 'new humanitarianism', while any resemblance thereof is morally problematic to deontological pluralists.

Keeping down

Humanitarian agencies are expected to align with the laws and regulations of the countries in which they operate. When these are designed to keep marginalised groups and political opposition down, the humanitarian agencies become entangled in repressive political strategies. This is most evident in settings of civil war where the authorities restrict aid to opposition controlled territories, like in the formative example of the Biafra war (Barnett, 2011, 153).

However, authoritarian regimes also use humanitarian assistance as a tool for upholding hierarchies, rewarding their followers and punishing opponents in times of peace, making it equally relevant to settings of natural disaster and 'low-intensity conflict'. In Chapter 1, this was highlighted by Healy and Cunningham as one of the key difficulties for the MSF when dealing with authoritarian regimes:

> [T]he difficulty of negotiating with a government on the terms for access to particular population groups that a government considers to be 'enemy' or at least suspect in some way. This might mean areas outright controlled by armed opposition groups (such as in Darfur, Sudan) or simply the home of discriminated-against communities (such as in Rakhine, Myanmar, the Tamils in the north of Sr Lanka, or the Chechens in Chechnya).
>
> *[page 30]*

In their study of disaster governance in Ethiopia, Myanmar and Zimbabwe, Isabelle Desportes and Dorothea Hilhorst (2020) document how political interests of state authorities, rather than humanitarian needs assessments, tend to steer who and what will be protected from disaster impacts in such authoritarian settings of 'low-intensity conflict'. Having analysed how this is done through a combination of bureaucratic restrictions, monopolising data and instilling uncertainty and fear, they argue that ethical questions are raised when 'gaining acceptance' [by state authorities] takes precedence over acting in accordance with humanitarian principles' (Desportes and Hilhorst, 2020, 351). Likewise, Duffield has analysed how the international humanitarian management of Dinka 'IDPs' in Sudan was manipulated by the regime in Khartoum, allowing for their systematic repression and exploitation (Duffield, 2014, 248). Cunningham (2018) has similarly explored how regimes may compromise humanitarian action in accordance with a logic (or discourse) of security rather than necessarily seeing it as a matter of ignoring needs or repressing the opposition. The effect may nonetheless be the same, and the contribution of humanitarians thereto warrants ethical consideration as another type of complicity.

In this book, dynamics of authoritarian repression have been well documented, including in Russia and China where humanitarian agencies are not welcome. The chapter on MSF experience (Chapter 1) mentions the disruptions by the Ethiopian authorities on aid to the Tigray region during the recent war, including attacks on aid workers. In the case of Venezuela discussed above, appeals of the opposition to seeing the situation as a humanitarian crisis in 2019 further politicised the regime's response– making sure that it did not in any way align with opposition interests. The most evident example of 'keeping down', however, is the barring by the Assad regime and accomplices of aid to opposition controlled territories in Syria. As described by

Bertamini in Chapter 3, this was reflected in UN Security Council debates on cross-border assistance in areas outside regime control. With first hand expertise on how assistance could be manipulated to support the war effort, the regime had good political reasons to prevent their enemies from this asset, but this does not justify their position from an ethical perspective. Worse still, withholding aid was integral to a regime strategy of laying sieges to opposition strongholds while allowing aid to neighbouring districts and promising access to aid in return for capitulation (Whittall, 2021, 153).

The cooperation of UN agencies and international NGOs with the Assad regime for the provision of humanitarian assistance under these conditions remains highly controversial. Indeed, the combination of supporting the regime's war economy, mopping up after its atrocities and keeping down the opposition by withholding humanitarian aid implies a massive case for complicity. In spite of continuous negotiations with the regime for access and protection, this may hardly be characterised as a compromise at all. At least since the high-profile report *Taking Sides: The United Nations' Loss Of Impartiality, Independence And Neutrality In Syria* (2016) by The Syria Campaign, the humanitarian community could be expected to be aware not only of the wrongdoing of the regime but also of their potential role therein. It is nonetheless hard to see what the alternatives for the agencies were. There was no other 'space' for humanitarians to occupy in government-controlled areas, although they could carve out 'micro-spaces' where they could operate more or less outside regime interference (Kool, et al., 2021). The alternative was to withdraw to opposition-controlled areas without the regime's blessing. In spite of opposition from the regime, this option became lawful under international law with the mandate carved out by UNSC Resolution 2165 in 2014 – the mandate that was eventually shrunken regarding cross-border aid. In terms of other alternatives in regime-controlled areas, Wieland (2021, 132–136) suggests the combination of concerted diplomatic pressure and united red lines among international agencies as a way in which their complicity could have been reduced. Still, this is clearly a case in which at least the humanitarian NGOs were 'morally entrapped' against their will in a contributory role, and where they presumably did what they could to mitigate it provided the Assad regime's manifest atrociousness. The question, then, is whether this is enough to tip the scale of ethical justification in their favour, all things considered.

The deontological position is put to the test in this setting, given the regime's blatant violations of the humanitarian principles. With the suffering of millions of Syrians in government-controlled areas in the balance and the clear responsibility of the regime for the violations, only the most extreme deontologist would insist that humanitarians should withdraw from such a scene. The question, then, is whether the agencies did enough to resist the violations by forming a concerted alliance and mitigating the effects of their complicity. According to Wieland and other critics, they did not, while others insist that they did what they could and strategically balanced between official compliance and unofficial resistance (Lidén, et al., 2023). In distinction from consequentialism, intentions or motives are key to deontologists, and if the intentions to uphold the principles in any way possible remain pure, adjusting to such 'non-ideal' circumstances may be excused. While the case of Venezuela also constituted a serious humanitarian crisis, the Maduro regime and local communities still had a capacity for responding to some of the most immediate needs, as described by Garlin Politis in Chapter 8. The choice to compromise in Syria was not really a choice if the principle of humanity was not to be fundamentally forfeited.

The consequentialist approach apparently has a much easier time in this setting. It just needs to calculate the costs of keeping the opposition down against the benefits and other costs of the aid. Presumably, the partial and politicised provision of assistance to communities in desperate need is better than withholding the aid from a consequentialist perspective, even if there are others who need it even more. Yet, this calculation gets more complicated when thinking of the longer-term effects of allowing a regime to manipulate assistance for openly political purposes in this way. How will such acceptance of keeping down opposition affect the ability to produce humanitarian outcomes elsewhere? In addition to actively withholding assistance, it undermined the legitimacy of humanitarians in the eyes of the opposition, with similar repercussions as when humanitarians colluded with NATO forces in their fight against the Taliban. Perhaps this larger calculus would make some consequentialists more, not less, open for drawing a thick red line in the face of the Assad regime's violations in spite of the significant immediate humanitarian costs. In a less profiled situation where the principles could be violated without much notice, consequentialists would have no quandaries with accepting it, however. That said, it seems like the public opinion in Western donor countries understood that the humanitarians were not to blame for the violations and that the Assad regime rather than unprincipled aid was the problem.

Provided that pluralists require humanitarian action to adjust to the laws and decrees of the sovereign authorities, this is also a hard case for pluralists to stomach. Indeed, the regulation by the Assad regime of the aid was rooted in well-established rules and bureaucratic procedures that generally preceded the war. To the extent that keeping down the opposition by humanitarian means thus reflected the established political order, it has the support of pluralist humanitarians. The problem, however, arises if the dynamics of the war turns the humanitarian assistance into a political weapon that tips this established order in favour of the regime. Then the assistance should be limited to activities that avoid such political interference. In Bertamini's chapter (Chapter 3), we see how these nuances are reflected in different stances on the principle of sovereignty. Where some pluralists (here used in a different meaning than Bertamini's notion of legal pluralism) would see all forms of 'keeping down' as acceptable as long as the regime remains the legally recognised ('de jure') authorities of Syria, others would see any international contribution to affecting the actual ('de facto') sovereignty of the regime as problematic. Pluralists will be divided on this matter.

Like with the question of mopping up, solidarists who are opposed to the Assad regime will be opposed to assistance that keeps more legitimate opposition down. If it is impossible to avoid this effect and it outweighs the humanitarian benefits in their view (be it based on deontological or consequentialist reasoning), then international agencies should have halted their operations and left with a call for political intervention. Presumably, consequentialist solidarists would thus have supported a military humanitarian intervention if it was expected to solve the problem, which was clearly not the case. In the absence thereof, solidarists have been left searching for lessons from Syria for future situations where authoritarian regimes tie their hands to partisan political and military objectives.

Propping up

The problem of propping up political authorities is closely related to the concerns of mopping up and keeping down, but it is still of a different kind. In the case of Syria discussed above, humanitarian agencies have not only contributed to the warfare and withheld aid from communities but also helped the regime carry out essential governmental services like the provision of food, housing, health care and education. Moreover, agencies have been required to buy all commercial services from domestic companies within the regime's fold, and they have paid taxes on their operations, among several other ways in which their presence has strengthened the economy of the regime. Although Western countries that are opposed to the regime have drawn a line at 'humanitarianism plus' and 'early recovery' to distinguish it from 'development aid' and 'reconstruction', the Assad regime still relies on foreign assistance for keeping a resemblance of responsive government (Wieland, 2021, 111–119). When The Syria Campaign (2016) criticised the UN and its associates for compromising on the humanitarian principles, its ultimate concern was not the persistence of the humanitarian crisis but how these activities were keeping the regime in power.

While the dilemma of propping up authoritarian regimes thus typically occurs together with the dilemmas of mopping up and keeping down, there are also examples where it occurs alone. As Healy and Cunningham write in Chapter 1, there are times when 'authoritarian regimes' have engaged in 'non-authoritarian' practices and been open, welcoming and facilitative towards humanitarian INGOs when it suits their perceived needs for their nations. They mention longstanding MSF operations in Russia, Sri Lanka and Belarus as examples and write that:

> When interests between MSF and these governments have coincided, such as when these governments have wanted MSF's medical capacities to meet a particular public health need (for example in Belarus), then successful programmes have resulted. While the eye might be drawn to those moments when MSF publicly spoke of matters of grand humanitarian principle, the daily reality has been a much more pragmatic one.

[page 31]

This is by no means exclusive for the MSF but a well-known feature of contemporary humanitarian action (e.g., Keen, 2008; Rubenstein, 2015). The extent to which it amounts to the propping up of authoritarian regimes at the expense of political change has nonetheless received less attention, not to speak of its ethical implications. Throughout this book, we have seen numerous examples of how this is done: by withholding official approvals, introduce laws and decrees to regulate their work and interfere directly with their operations (see also Kahn and Cunningham, 2013). As Healy and Cunningham write, this happens not only at the level of formal requests for state consent to operations, 'but at the level of practice, as in hundreds of different, daily ways, humanitarians need the cooperation of government officials – for customs clearance, tax matters, travel permissions, visas, work permits, registration, international bank transfers and so on'. This is not limited to authoritarian states, however, but when done to align operations with partisan political agendas to tighten a regime's grip on power, it becomes an ethical problem of complicity.

The account by Imri Schattner-Ornan (Chapter 5) of how these dynamics played out in a refugee camp in Western Ethiopia is a case in point. He shows how the authorities kept tight control of the operations of international NGOs through a combination of formal MoUs with agencies, permits for individual staff and continuous negotiations with local authorities and camp management. In the 2009 Charities and Societies Proclamation, the regime had tightened its control of NGOs, assuring that their work would align with their priorities and be a partner of the government (see also Cunningham, 2018, 113). Being challenged by opposition parties, the ruling Ethiopian People's Revolutionary Democratic Front (EPRDF) saw the recent upsurge of international agencies advocating for human rights as a political problem and demanded that they forfeited such political aims. Kendra Dupuy et al., (2015) document how most international agencies adapted to these conditions and stayed on because they wanted to keep addressing the humanitarian needs of the Ethiopian people. Meanwhile, the authorities exercised tight control on what they could do and say about the situation through the continuous threat of withholding permits or withdrawing agreements that Schattner-Ornan describes in detail. In effect, this turned international agencies into the type of support function that defines the ethical problem of 'propping up' authoritarian regimes.

Let us see this problem from the perspective of the agency that Schattner-Ornan describes in Chapter 5. It can hardly be argued that this agency alone contributed to the repressive rule and human rights violations of the regime in any significant way. Indeed, he commends the regime for its refugee policies, and being part of the implementation of these in refugee camps thus seems unproblematic. Yet, by accepting the dictates of the regime as part of a tightly controlled apparatus of international NGOs, testing their neutrality and independence, lending the regime legitimacy and ignoring the regime's abuses elsewhere, one may still argue that the agency contributed to keeping the regime in power. With extensive attention to the challenges for international agencies in Ethiopia since they entered the scene in the 1980s, it could also be expected that they were aware of the regime's authoritarian character and the problem of complicity that follows. In the absence of an instant emergency, they also do not have the excuse of being there against their will in the name of humanity. The engagement was clearly one of pragmatic engagement, testing out the chances for operating with sufficient autonomy for making an expanded presence in Ethiopian camps justifiable for the agency.

Provided that the agency could make a substantial difference under these circumstances, the verdict of the deontological position relies on whether the interference by the authorities qualifies as a violation of the principles of neutrality and independence. It seems from Schattner-Ornan's account that the agency shared the general humanitarian objectives of the refugee authority that it dealt with and that the problem was one of operating effectively rather than of being compromised politically. If this is the case, then the eventual contribution to propping up the regime is acceptable from the deontological perspective. It belongs to the type of political concerns that humanitarians should not concern themselves with. The same goes for the consequentialist perspective, as long as propping up the regime does not entail reproducing the humanitarian problem. If so, it would fall within the category of 'mopping up' instead.

Propping up authoritarian regimes is also not a problem for the pluralist position, as long as it does not radically eschew the domestic political order in the regime's favour. The agency's work in an Ethiopian refugee camp would thus be unproblematic from this perspective. There are pluralists who would see any foreign presence with political effects as ethically problematic, but here we are thinking of pluralists who accept the need for humanitarian assistance in troubled countries. As we have seen, adding the problems of giving in and mopping up to this equation does not necessarily change their position.

This is thus where the solidarist position stands out most starkly. Propping up regimes that are perceived as illegitimate is a serious ethical problem for solidarists that requires substantial humanitarian gains for being justified. To liberal solidarists, this goes for all authoritarian regimes, although the degree of their illegitimacy will still vary between semi-democracies and totalitarian states. The worldwide subjection of humanitarian agencies to the dictates of dictators thus amounts to a significant political problem. To socialist or Islamist solidarists, it is not the authoritarianism itself that would be the problem but the propping up of any state that conflicts with their ideologies, be it authoritarian or not.

The solidarist alternative of withholding aid to people in dire need for political reasons is evidently highly controversial, as seen in the debates on halting aid to Afghanistan, Syria, Ethiopia, Yemen or Myanmar. If doing so would likely result in the replacement of an illegitimate regime with a more legitimate government, then at least some solidarist consequentialists would see the sacrifice of people in immediate need as worthwhile. In practice, however, it is hard to imagine a situation where such withholding of aid could be decisive for generating a political transition. On the other hand, one might question the terminology of 'abstaining' and 'withholding' aid. Does the principle of humanity imply that humanitarian aid should be provided under all political circumstances, or is it more coherent to combine a professional and political perspective when deciding on where and how to use the limited resources available? Indeed, the solidarist position seems to harmonise with widespread demands for humanitarians to consider the wider political effects of their work. As such, the ethics of humanitarian action in authoritarian regimes actualises a major tension between pluralist and solidarist approaches that may have been mistaken as a tension between 'apolitical' and 'political' humanitarianism.

Conclusion

In this chapter, we have examined the ethical problems that humanitarian agencies are confronted with when working under authoritarian rule. These were categorised as:

- *Mopping up* after the humanitarian problems caused by regimes, reducing the costs of their policies, and facilitating their continuation
- *Keeping down* marginalised groups and political opposition by distributing aid in line with partial dictates from the authorities
- *Propping up* the authorities by aligning with their general political interests and strategies (beyond mopping up or keeping down) and thereby undermining the prospects for political change

These problems entail ethical dilemmas in humanitarian negotiations to the extent that they present humanitarian agencies with a choice between the principled concerns of avoiding moral complicity and failing to assist people in dire need. In practice, however, we have seen how these dilemmas set the stage for compromises and alternatives at multiple levels, from the UN Security Council to the office of a local camp manager.

In the literature on humanitarian action, discussions on the problem of complicity have tended to assume that as long as a causal contribution to authoritarian governance can be documented empirically it involves an ethical problem. We also often get the impression that as long as responsibility for an ethical problem can be established, the agencies are doing something fundamentally wrong. We have nonetheless demonstrated that (1) the presence of the authoritarian dilemmas does not necessarily involve complicity, (2) that complicity does not always entail moral blameworthiness, and (3) that such moral blameworthiness may be ethically justified all things considered. Meanwhile, the question of complicity must be seen in connection with potential wrongs committed by humanitarian agencies themselves (beyond their contribution to the wrongs of others), including problems of paternalism, hierarchy and excessive interference.

In effect, we applied this framework of analysis to the three ethical problems and discussed examples of mopping up after the Maduro regime in Venezuela, keeping down political opposition in Syria and propping up the EPRDF regime in Ethiopia. In all cases, we started out by applying the 'complicity formula' of Lepora and Goodin, analysing the badness of the wrongdoing committed by a regime, the nature of the causal contribution of the humanitarian agency, the extent to which the agency could know about the wrongdoing and their causal contribution, and whether the contribution was voluntary or even based on a shared purpose with the wrongdoer. We did not include a proper consideration of their own potential wrongdoing, but took the first steps towards such a comprehensive ethical analysis.

We then demonstrated how the assessment of moral complicity and its ethical justification relies on one's ethical perspective. Having distinguished between professional and political dimensions of humanitarian ethics, we constructed a field stretched out between four positions: deontological and consequentialist professional ethics and pluralist and solidarist political ethics. These are not the only relevant positions to these questions, but proved relevant to disentangle the prescriptive debate between Dunantist and Wilsonian approaches. In addition to exemplifying the application of the positions to the authoritarian dilemmas, we showed how they may lead to different prescriptions in different types of cases.

While the distinction between the three authoritarian dilemmas proposed here may be new, the associated problems are familiar from critical literatures on humanitarian action. The ways in which they represent ethical problems at various levels of humanitarian action, from international forums and government offices to the frontlines, nonetheless remain to be systematically studied. Provided that they confront agencies with the question of ethical red lines and grey zones to be settled through negotiations with authoritarian counterparts, this also serves as a contribution to an exploration of the ethics of humanitarian negotiations in general.

Acknowledgements

Thanks to Ayse Bala Akal for research assistance for this chapter, as well as to fellow members of the research project Red Lines and Grey Zones: Exploring the Ethics of Humanitarian Negotiations. We also thank the editor, Andrew Cunningham, and fellow contributors to this volume for feedback and discussions. The chapter draws on funding by the Research Council of Norway, grant no. 325238.

Notes

1 Lidén is first author and wrote the text based on joint research and discussions with Roepstorff and her eventual comments and suggestions.
2 These labels were partly suggested to us by Hugo Slim.
3 There are multiple definitions of ethics and morality in the literature, and the two concepts are often used interchangeably. In this chapter we use 'morality/moral' for convictions about what is right and wrong, good and bad, according to fundamental values, and 'ethics/ethical' about the consideration of such convictions.
4 In *The Good Project* (2014), for instance, Monika Krause shows how humanitarian efforts that are motivated by ethical objectives tend to end up in instrumental organisational and market logics that divert them from these objectives (see also Barnett and Finnemore, 2004).

References

Ahmad, A. and Smith, J. (eds.). (2018). *Humanitarian Action and Ethics*. London: Zed Books.
ALNAP. (2022). *The State of the Humanitarian System (SOHS)*. ALNAP/ODI. https://sohs.alnap.org/help-library/2022-the-state-of-the-humanitarian-system-sohs-%E2%80%93-full-report-0
Anderson, M. B. (1999). *Do no Harm: How Aid Can Support Peace—Or War*. Boulder, CO: Lynne Rienner.
Barnett, M. (2011). *Empire of Humanity: A History of Humanitarianism*. Ithaca, NY: Cornell University Press.
Barnett, M. and Finnemore, M. (2004). *Rules for the World: International Organizations in Global Politics*. Ithaca, NY: Cornell University Press.
Baron, M. W., Pettit, P., and Slote, M. (1997). *Three Methods of Ethics: A Debate*. Hoboken, NJ: Wiley-Blackwell.
Broussard, G., Rubenstein, L. S., Robinson, C., Maziak, W., Gilbert, S. Z., and De-Camp, M. (2019). Challenges to Ethical Obligations and Humanitarian Principles in Conflict Settings: A Systematic Review. *Journal of International Humanitarian Action* 4(1), 15.

Brown, C. (1992). *International Relations Theory: New Normative Approaches*. Birmingham: Harvester Wheatshef.

Buth, P., et al. (2018). 'He Who Helps the Guilty, Shares the Crime'? INGOs, Moral Narcissism and Complicity in Wrongdoing. *Journal of Medical Ethics* 44(5), 299–304.

Buzan, B. (2004). *From International to World Society? English School Theory and the Social Structure of Globalisation*. Cambridge: Cambridge UP.

CCHN. (2019). *CCHN Facilitator Handbook*. Center of Competence on Humanitarian Negotiation.

Clark, I. (2007). *International Legitimacy and World Society*. Oxford: Oxford University Press.

Cohen, J. (2012). *Globalization and Sovereignty: Rethinking Legality, Legitimacy, and Constitutionalism*. Cambridge: Cambridge University Press.

Cunningham, A. J. (2018). *International Humanitarian NGOs and State Relations: Politics, Principles and Identity*. London: Routledge.

Dasandi, N. and Erez, L. (2019). The Donor's Dilemma: International Aid and Human Rights Violations. *British Journal of Political Science* 49(4), 1431–1452.

de Waal, A. (1997). *Famine Crimes: Politics & the Disaster Relief Industry in Africa*. African Rights & the International African Institute in association with James Currey, Oxford & Indiana University Press, Bloomington.

de Waal, A. (2015). *The Real Politics of the Horn of Africa: Money, War and the Business of Power*. Cambridge: Polity Press.

de Waal, A. (2017, June 14). The Nazis Used It, We Use It. *London Review of Books* 39(12). https://www.lrb.co.uk/the-paper/v39/n12/alex-de-waal/the-nazis-used-it-we-use-it

del Valle, H. and Healy, S. (2013). Humanitarian Agencies and Authoritarian States: A Symbiotic Relationship? *Disasters* 37, S188–S201.

Desportes, I., and Hilhorst, D. (2020). Disaster Governance in Conflict-Affected Authoritarian Contexts: The Cases of Ethiopia, Myanmar, and Zimbabwe. *Politics and Governance* 8(4), 343–354.

Donini, A. (2012). Afghanistan: Back to the Future. In *The Golden Fleece: Manipulation and Independence in Humanitarian Action*. Boulder, CO: Kumarian Press.

Duffield, M. (2014). *Global Governance and the New Wars: The Merging of Development and Security*. London: Zed Books.

Dupuy, K. E., Ron, J., and Prakash, A. (2015). Who Survived? Ethiopia's Regulatory Crackdown on Foreign-funded NGOs. *Review of International Political Economy* 22(2), 419–456.

Favez, J.-C. (1999). *The Red Cross and the Holocaust*. Cambridge: Cambridge University Press.

Glasius, M. (2018). What Authoritarianism Is … and Is Not: A Practice Perspective. *International Affairs* 94(3), 515–533.

Gordon, S. and Donini, A. (2015). Romancing Principles and Human Rights: Are Humanitarian Principles Salvageable? *International Review of the Red Cross* 97(897–898), 77–109.

Grace, R. (2020). Humanitarian Negotiation with Parties to Armed Conflict. *Journal of International Humanitarian Legal Studies* 11(1), 1–29.

Hilhorst, D., Desportes, I., and de Milliano, C. W. J. (2019). Humanitarian Governance and Resilience Building: Ethiopia in Comparative Perspective. *Disasters* 43, S109–S131.

Hoge, W. (2004, April 10). The Saturday profile; Rescuing Victims Worldwide 'From the Depths of Hell'. *The New York Times*. https://www.nytimes.com/2004/07/10/world/the-saturday-profile-rescuing-victims-worldwide-from-the-depths-of-hell.html

ICG. (2010). *War Crimes in Sri Lanka: Vol. Asia Report 191*. International Crisis Group.

Jackson, R. H. (2000). *The Global Covenant: Human Conduct in a World of States*. Oxford: Oxford University Press.

Kahn, C. and Cunningham, A. (2013). Introduction to the Issue of State Sovereignty and Humanitarian Action. *Disasters* 37(s2), S139–S150.

Keen, D. (2008). *Complex Emergencies*. Cambridge: Polity Press.

Kool, L. D., Pospisil, J., and van Voorst, R. (2021). Managing the Humanitarian Micro-space: The Practices of Relief Access in Syria. *Third World Quarterly* 42(7), 1489–1506.

Korsgaard, C. M. (1997). The Normativity of Instrumental Reason. In: Cullity, G. and Gaut, B. (eds.). *Ethics and Practical Reason*. Oxford: Clarendon Press.

Krause, M. (2014). *The Good Project: Humanitarian Relief NGOs and the Fragmentation of Reason*. Chicago: University of Chicago Press.

Lepora, C. and Goodin, R. E. (2013). *Complicity and Compromise*. Oxford: Oxford University Press.

Lidén, K. (2019). The Protection of Civilians and Ethics of Humanitarian Governance: Beyond Intervention and Resilience. *Disasters* 43, S210–S229.,

Lidén, K., Wieland, C., Cervi, A., and Chiara-Gillard, E. (2023, January 16). *The ethics of humanitarian neutrality in Syria*. https://www.humanitarianstudies.no/events/the-ethics-of-humanitarian-neutrality-in-syria/

Magone, C., Neuman, M., and Weissman, F. (eds.) (2011). *Humanitarian Negotiations Revealed: The MSF experience*. London: Hurst.

Malkki, L. H. (2015). *The Need to Help: The Domestic Arts of International Humanitarianism* (p. dup;9780822375364/1). Durham, NC: Duke University Press.

Rieff, D. (2002). *A Bed for the Night: Humanitarianism in Crisis* (Nachdr.). New York: Vintage.

Roepstorff, K. (2013). *The Politics of Self-determination: Beyond the Decolonisation Process*. London: Routledge.

Roepstorff, K. (2020). A Call for Critical Reflection on the Localisation Agenda in Humanitarian Action. *Third World Quarterly* 41(2), 284–301.

Rubenstein, J. (2015). *Between Samaritans and States: The Political Ethics of Humanitarian INGOs*. Oxford: Oxford University Press.

Salomons, D. (2014). The Perils of Dunantism: The Need for a Rights-based Approach to Humanitarianism, 33–53. In: Zwitter, A., Lamont, C.K., Heintze, H.-J., and Herman, J. (eds.). *Humanitarian Action: Global, Regional and Domestic Legal Responses*. Cambridge: Cambridge University Press.

Slim, H. (1997). Doing the Right Thing: Relief Agencies, Moral Dilemmas and Moral Responsibility in Political Emergemcies and War. *Disasters* 21(3), 244–257.

Slim, H. (2015). *Humanitarian Ethics: A Guide to the Morality of Aid in War and Disaster*. Oxford: Oxford University Press.

Stroup, S. S. and Wong, W. H. (2017). *The Authority Trap: Strategic Choices of International NGOs*. Ithaca, NY: Cornell University Press.

Terry, F. (2002). *Condemned to Repeat?: The Paradox of Humanitarian Action* (Illustrated edition). Ithaca, NY: Cornell University Press.

The Syria Campaign. (2016). *Taking Sides: The United Nations' Loss of Impartiality, Independence and Neutrality in Syria*. http://takingsides.thesyriacampaign.org/

Walton, O. (2015). Dealing with Authoritarian Regimes. In: *The Routledge Companion to Humanitarian Action*. London: Routledge.

Wheeler, N. J. and Dunne, T. (1996). Hedley Bull's Pluralism of the Intellect and Solidarism of the Will. *International Affairs* 72(1), 91–107.

Whittall, J. (2021). Endless Siege: The Chain of Complicity in Syrian Suffering, 135–159. In: Whittall, J. (ed.). *Everybody's War*. Oxford: Oxford University Press.

Wieland, C. (2021). *Syria and the Neutrality Trap: Dilemmas of Delivering Humanitarian Aid through Violent Regimes*. London: I.B. Tauris.

Wolff, J. (2020). *An Introduction to Moral Philosophy* (2nd ed.). New York: W. W. Norton & Company, Independent Publishers Since 1923.

CONCLUSION

Theory and praxis – constructing the relationship between authoritarian practices and humanitarian negotiations

Andrew J Cunningham

Developing themes

The chapters in this book trace experiences in a variety of contexts and ana-lyse different political, social, and political environments, providing a mixture of perspectives on both authoritarian practices and humanitarian negotia-tions. A number of themes stand out. Most fundamentally, each chapter, in its own way, describes the friction of negotiations. If there are general rules of thumb underpinning the process of negotiations and generic humanitarian principles provide a reference point, in the real world practice is defined by tensions, dilemmas, and friction. Practice is context-specific, whether related to the humanitarian organisations involved, the nature of the context and humanitarian situation, or the type of government, as authoritarian practices are also variable. It is an often-stated truism in the aid world that everything is context-specific. On the political side, it is as much a truism that 'all poli-tics is local'.

Negotiations, whether at the level of individual aid workers, civil society organisations, or states, work within certain parameters. It is therefore im-portant to understand not only what is at stake but also what is possible. An individual's action will be guided by a moral compass, a community's by identity and a search for rights, and an organisation's programmes by prin-ciples, vision, and strategic objectives. A government's actions will be guided by a combination of economic, ideological, and security needs, whether do-mestically or regionally, or even at the level of the UN Security Council, as Bertamini describes in his chapter on access issues around humanitarian assistance to Syria. Ethical considerations are also in tension between hu-manitarian principles, politics, and organisational priorities, as examined by

DOI: 10.4324/9781003316541-19

Lidén and Roepstorff. These frictions are either played out on a public stage or silently, as elaborated upon by Garlin Politis concerning Venezuela. Humanitarian negotiations, as described by Nahikian and Tronc, take all of these aspects into consideration.

Given the above, three ways of building an analytical framework are offered. The first is to distinguish between the macro, meso, and micro. This framework helps us to home in on the particular nature of the various levels of engagement. Concerning authoritarian practices and humanitarian negotiations, the micro refers to the local level. In this book, the micro is developed by Schattner-Ornan in his discussion of the field-level negotiations in Ethiopia. The meso level deals with national issues, for example, Astarita (the Uyghurs in China), Munadi and Mena (aid in Afghanistan), Vladimirova (the Roma in Russia), and Garlin Politis (the aid assemblage in Venezuela). Bertamini's chapter on the Security Council's deliberations on Syria clearly deals with macro-level geopolitical themes. Another perspective on macro-level analysis is the chapters by Healy and Cunningham, Nahikian and Tronc, and Lidén and Roepstorff, which all develop transversal themes. Buth, who provides reflections on independence in association with Schattner-Ornan's work on Ethiopia and his concept of 'Grace' as applied to the document and the permit, is another macro-level contribution.

By focusing on different levels of analysis we can be more confident of obtaining a comprehensive view of how humanitarians negotiate access in authoritarian settings. But as the chapters in this book show, the meso-level is much better represented than the micro or macro. It is at the level of an individual state or humanitarian context that research most often occurs. Empirically, the very local (micro) or geo-political (macro) levels are less well researched. Operational humanitarian organisations certainly describe in their own grey literature project-level experiences with authoritarian practices, yet these are often not problematised and deeply studied. And as suggested by Dijkzeul's commentary, building better links between the disciplines of International Relations and International Law in the study of the geopolitics of humanitarian aid is indicated.

At a certain point, however, these analytical building blocks, however comprehensively articulated, must be stitched together into a coherent picture. Individual examples, at whatever level, and whether empirical or thematic, should be located within a general model of how civil society organisations negotiate with states that engage in authoritarian practices (Glasius, 2018). One method to accomplish this is to design a continuum of authoritarian practices allowing civil society organisations to adapt their negotiations to fit the dictates of any given political context. By plotting practices rather than regimes, such a continuum would assist organisations with attending to the practical constraints to access rather than diverting attention to reflections on regime type, with all of the subjective biases involved.

A continuum which plots the wide spectrum of authoritarian practice types, however, does not provide guidance on how civil society organisations should adapt their negotiations. This is the third step that needs much more attention. It is proposed that a set of heuristics be developed that could lead to organisational change on the macro (policy), meso (national government relations), and micro (local project management) levels. Once a good understanding of the nature of a certain context is reached, a set of heuristics embedded in an organisation's way of working would guide operational negotiations with that particular state.

At a higher level, beyond the dictates of negotiating access, another theme to examine more closely is the triangular relationship between civil society actors, authoritarian practices, and illiberal practices. It can be argued that illiberal practices are often the genesis of humanitarian or human rights crises which instigate civil society responses which are then constrained through authoritarian practices. For local actors working at the meso level, as discussed by Astarita, Vladimirova, and Garlin Politis, illiberal practices take on a different complexion as they are actors from the context negotiating with their own governments. For international organisations, illiberal practices may be a point of analysis related to the human rights or humanitarian crisis, but as organisations, they are not normally directly affected, although their staff may be citizens.

There are cases, however, where organisations are caught-up in illiberal practices, such as the dictates by the new Taliban regime in Afghanistan which increasingly prohibit the participation of women in society and as elaborated by Munadi and Mena and commented on by Bakr. Aid organisations of all types are in this way drawn into the implementation of decidedly illiberal policies as the price to work. Whether conceived of as complicity or collaboration, international organisations in such situations cannot escape making the sort of ethical choices elaborated upon by Lidén and Roepstorff.

There is therefore a great advantage to delineating between types of practices, adding nuance to the foundation work by Nahikian and Tronc. Any modelling of humanitarian negotiations, and by extension other forms of civil society negotiations with government, must take this potential into consideration. As many international aid organisations work in partnership with local actors, there is a need to be aware of how aid actors of all types react to and are affected by illiberal practices. Focusing solely on limitations to civic space is insufficient.

An additional link to be made to the research agenda as described above is with the work on politicisation and securitisation (Cunningham, 2018). What is the relationship between international aid actors, or the aid act itself, being politicised, or even securitised – where an aid actor is considered an existential threat to the state or the nation, and the constellation of authoritarian and illiberal practices? Initial reflections point to an incomplete overlap, with one set of processes focused on the identification of threats and one on actions. Certainly, all of the chapters and commentaries in this book in one way or another address the politicisation, and sometimes securitisation, or aid and aid actors. Astarita's work on China and the Uyghurs is a brilliant example. As well, commenting on Garlin Politis' discussion of aid assemblages, Mena highlights the importance of instrumentalisation and depoliticisation processes in analysing humanitarian contexts. Healy and Cunningham also describe multiple cases in their chapter from the MSF experience. The focus of this volume is on how these processes are actualised in practices which are authoritarian in nature or are locked into a triangle with illiberal practices. However, one cannot delink the two processes – practices do not come from the ether, and politicisation does have consequences. This line of enquiry needs more attention, as a framework which accounts for all forms of politicisation and practices should be developed.

Underpinning much of the above is the role played by discourse – as an action or as an analytical tool. Discourse can play a role in politicisation and securitisation (Cunningham, 2018). States define categories of actors and justify action through discourse. A narrative is formulated to prepare the public for anti-civil society action and the imposition of new laws, rules, or regulations to constrain the work of national or international NGOs. International NGOs can be associated with political controversies and labelled as undesirable political agents. In the most egregious cases, INGOs can be considered threats to the security of the regime, the state, or the nation (or at least to the dominant group). Discourse defines the way in which the state reacts to these circumstances. All chapters in this book discuss this phenomenon.

In certain cases, discourse will also be used to communicate with INGOs, as governments do not always communicate directly with international civil society actors but may choose to communicate indirectly. This can be accomplished via governmental statements, for example, or communication may be through actions such as spreading fear through manipulating security threats, targeting INGOs with harsh new laws or regulations that constrain action, or even by expelling organisations from certain regions or from the country as a whole (Cunningham, 2018).

In order to decipher discourse aid, actors can use the methodology of discourse analysis, as described in the chapter one commentary by de Kok and Cunningham. Paired with a solid analysis of the political context and the legal environment, as emphasised by Dijkzeul's commentary, discourse analysis can assist with negotiating access. As discussed in Nahikian and Tronc, the more each actor understands the other, the better the outcome. INGOs should be aware as well that states attend to their discourse; what INGOs say often goes unheeded. The interpretation of discourse analysis goes both ways.

In this book, several commentaries and chapters refer to discourse analysis, if not directly. Govender relates how symbolic imagery, information management, and reputation all played a role in negotiations; Bertamini speaks about the 'vocabulary of negotiations'; Astarita decodes narratives linked to slogans; Munadi relates how certain translations disappear in China; Schattner-Ornan examines the role paperwork plays in re-categorising IN-GOs as service providers rather than principled humanitarian actors; and intriguingly, Garlin Politis describes 'silence' as a form of discourse. In a very real way, the importance of proximity, as described by Cunningham in the commentary on Vladimirova's chapter, can be considered symbolic discourse.

What next?

This edited volume has brought together a number of cases and thematic discussions and has suggested a few theoretical frameworks, metaphors, and symbolic understandings in consideration of the theme of authoritarian practices and humanitarian negotiations. The analytical power of the concept of authoritarian practices rather than a focus on regime type has been demonstrated in these pages. The importance, as well, of linking the category of illiberal practices to humanitarian action has been clearly articulated in several of the chapters. The research gaps as outlined above, however, suggest that much more work is needed to build a coherent framework which not only takes into account authoritarian and illiberal practices but also ties these themes to the literature on the politicisation and securitisation of aid and aid actors. Methodologically, discourse analysis remains a rich opportunity for further exploration.

One further gap to address in the future relates to the robustness of our empirical understanding. Each context is different, and a volume such as this can only touch on a few case studies. There are many more areas of the world and types of contexts to research. In this collection of case studies, examples from the Global North are conspicuously missing, for example. And although this book is focused on humanitarian negotiations, case studies which examine the experiences of local civil society actors outside the humanitarian sector are very useful in providing insight into the practice of authoritarianism. Needless to say, these research efforts should be led by those closer to the contexts under consideration.

As much as this research agenda is of academic interest, humanitarian aid is in essence a practical endeavour, and aid workers and organisations are pragmatic actors. The ultimate objective is to provide guidance which allows humans to better help other humans in need. One aspect of this is how humanitarians (as well as other civil society actors) negotiate access with states, the most problematic of which being those which implement authoritarian practices to the detriment of aid provision.

References

Cunningham, A. J. (2018). *International Humanitarian NGOs and State Relations: Politics, Principles and Identity*. London: Routledge.

Glasius, M. (2018). What Authoritarianism Is … and Is Not: A Practical Perspective. *International Affairs* 94(3), 515–533.

INDEX

Note: **Bold** page numbers refer to tables.

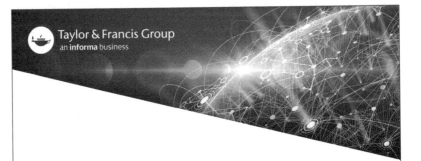

For Product Safety Concerns and Information please contact our
EU representative GPSR@taylorandfrancis.com Taylor & Francis
Verlag GmbH, Kaufingerstraße 24, 80331 München, Germany